AF606039

Approaches to Teaching Shakespeare's *The Taming of the Shrew*

Approaches to Teaching World Literature

For a complete listing of titles, see the last pages of this book.

Approaches to Teaching Shakespeare's *The Taming of the Shrew*

Edited by

Margaret Dupuis

and

Grace Tiffany

The Modern Language Association of America

New York 2013

Library of Congress Cataloging-in-Publication Data
Approaches to Teaching Shakespeare's The Taming of the Shrew /
edited by Margaret Dupuis and Grace Tiffany.
pages cm. — (Approaches to Teaching World Literature ; 123)
Includes bibliographical references and index.
ISBN 978-1-60329-118-7 (cloth : alk. paper)—
ISBN 978-1-60329-119-4 (pbk. : alk. paper)—
ISBN 978-1-60329-173-6 (EPUB)—
ISBN 978-1-60329-174-3 (Kindle)
1. Shakespeare, William, 1564–1616. Taming of the shrew. 2. Shakespeare, William, 1564–1616—Study and teaching. I. Dupuis, Margaret, 1950– editor of compilation. II. Tiffany, Grace, 1958– editor of compilation.
PR2832.A85 2013
822.3'2—dc23 2013027761

Approaches to Teaching World Literature 123
ISSN 1059-1133

Cover illustration of the paperback and electronic editions:
Lisa Dillon as Kate and David Caves as Petruchio in *The Taming of the Shrew*,
photographed by Sheila Burnett. © Royal Shakespeare Company.

Published by The Modern Language Association of America
26 Broadway, New York, NY 10004-1789
www.mla.org

This volume is dedicated to the many students, past and present, who have brought Shakespeare to life in our classrooms.

CONTENTS

Contexts

Teaching through and about Performance

PREFACE

This volume grew from our observation of a paradox. *The Taming of the Shrew* is the Shakespeare play most notorious for its apparently sexist representation of male-female—especially marital—relationships. Yet the play remains undyingly popular with students, instructors, directors, and film and theater audiences, not to mention Shakespeare scholars. How to explain the contradiction?

Our experience began to provide an answer. Teaching *Shrew* over twenty-odd years showed us that the play energizes students to do more than simply throw verbal bricks at the shrew tamer Petruccio, to do more than enjoy attacking his apparently retrograde domestic principles (though this can be fun). In fact, the play offers subtle, complicated, eloquent arguments on marriage and a host of other subjects—modes of early modern education, the uses of clever rhetoric, intergenerational politics, the power of theater as art and in life, class conflict and social mobility, sibling rivalry, and others. Our interviews with college instructors and our survey of historical and modern productions confirmed our view that successfully to teach and stage *The Taming of the Shrew* in North America requires more than raising the question of Kate's status at play's end—is she tamed or faking it?—however much that question still engages our interest. What was needed, our research showed, was a collection of essays fleshing out the wide variety of intelligent observations teachers (some of them directors) were making about this play. In other words, we wanted to build something we and others could use: a teaching volume that both philosophically and practically investigated *The Taming of the Shrew*, that not only analyzed its various parts but also illuminated how the play as a whole was being brought to life in college classrooms.

In response, we edited this volume, which features essays written by English and theater instructors who teach or have taught in a variety of academic settings and locations: universities; large public and smaller private institutions; theater programs and literature departments; and institutions in cities and in rural areas, including South Dakota, Texas, Georgia, New Mexico, New York, Southern and Northern California, Michigan, Kentucky, and eleven other states, as well as the District of Columbia. What unites these teachers is a love for bringing *The Taming of the Shrew* to students and a clear record of success at doing so. Herein, then, is their gallimaufry of topics and cogent teaching suggestions, including and involving early modern homilies, Hollywood versions of *Shrew*, Renaissance music lessons, and ribald student performances using hot dogs and turkey legs.

The idea for this book began in 2004 during a National Endowment for the Humanities Institute at the Blackfriars Playhouse in Staunton, Virginia. We would like to thank the faculty members who participated in that program as well as the talented actors of the American Shakespeare Center, whose brilliant performances of Kate and Petruccio prompted this investigation into how to help students more fully appreciate the witty complexities of *The Taming of the Shrew*. We are grateful for the unflagging and enthusiastic support of our husbands, Nic Witschi and Tom Lucking. (It was Nic who first said, "You should edit an Approaches volume on *Shrew* for the MLA"—an inspired suggestion.)

As we agreed when we started this project, *The Taming of the Shrew* isn't going away anytime soon. We hope this volume helps teachers confront the comedy's stubborn vitality and their students share in its pleasures.

MD and *GT*

Part One

MATERIALS

Editions

Complete Editions of Shakespeare

When preparing to teach a course on Shakespeare, an instructor must evaluate the many advantages of assigning a complete edition of Shakespeare's works and compare them with the cost and weight of such a large volume. As educators, we can see many reasons for asking students to invest in a complete edition of the works of Shakespeare. They will have all the plays and poems at their disposal, along with scholarly introductions and well-researched glosses. Most complete works also include useful illustrations, charts, and facsimiles of historical documents. Although students may not realize it until later in life, most of them will be happy to have such a reference book in their personal libraries and will consult the text for years to come. Students may complain about having to purchase the complete works if you assign only a small number of plays and poems, preferring to purchase individual editions. Increasingly, students opt to read the plays online, forgoing buying books altogether. If, however, you require your students to purchase a complete edition of Shakespeare's works, there are many excellent choices. The list below is meant not to be exhaustive but to suggest the range of options.

The *Norton Shakespeare*, edited by Walter Cohen, Stephen Greenblatt, Jean E. Howard, and Katharine Eisaman Maus, is based on *William Shakespeare: The Complete Works*, Gary Taylor and Stanley Wells, general editors, and is especially dependent on that work for textual notes and variants. The general introduction and those to the plays are, however, unique to the Norton edition. *The Norton Shakespeare* is also available in a two-volume set, *Early Plays and Poems* and *Later Plays*, as well as a shorter single volume, *Essential Plays / The Sonnets*. In the *Norton* is a lengthy contribution from Andrew Gurr, "The Shakespearean Stage," which contains an overview of early modern theatrical practices as well as etchings, photographs, and drawings. Greenblatt's general introduction presents a wealth of information on the social, legal, economic, religious, and political milieu of Shakespeare's plays and includes sections titled "The English Bible" and "Imports, Patents, and Monopolies." Unfortunately, the small print and the thin paper make the Norton edition difficult to read.

Jean Howard, the author of the introduction and explanatory notes for *The Taming of the Shrew*, emphasizes that this is one of Shakespeare's earliest comedies. She situates the play in the context of early modern methods for dealing with unruly women and includes a woodcut that illustrates a "husband dominator" (from a 1520 German playing card) and another depicting a cucking stool. Her introduction draws comparisons between the 1594 *The Taming of a Shrew* and Shakespeare's similarly named play and also contrasts the wife-taming technique of Shakespeare's Petruccio with the more brutal method employed by the husband in the 1550 ballad "A Merry Jest of a Shrewd and Curst Wife Lapped in Morel's Skin for Her Good Behavior." A brief selected bibliography of books and articles provides performance histories as well as enough contextual and critical material to give undergraduate students a starting point for research papers.

The second edition of *The Riverside Shakespeare*, edited by G. Blakemore Evans, is easier to read than *The Norton Shakespeare* because it has a higher paper quality and larger pages with double columns of type. The introduction to *The Taming of the Shrew* (and all other comedies) in *The Riverside Shakespeare*, second edition, is written by Anne Barton. While Howard's introduction in the *Norton* provides a new-historicist perspective on the play, Barton focuses on form and the comic tradition, situating the comedy among Shakespeare's more farcical plays and emphasizing the battle between the sexes. Although she also mentions "A Merry Jest," Barton finds in Shakespeare's play a radical alternative to the "mere vindictive savagery" of the earlier ballad (139). Barton does make extensive comparisons between *The Shrew* and *A Shrew*, especially when discussing the induction to Shakespeare's play. The most recent edition of the *Riverside* features an essay by Heather Dubrow on recent criticism and a production history by William Liston, as well as updated photographs from recent film and stage productions and two works recently attributed to Shakespeare. It retains from the 1997 edition an extensive general introduction; wonderful facsimile pages from the First Folio; and the very useful appendix, "Annals, 1552–1616," a timeline prepared by Evans; along with contemporary notices and criticism of the plays and poems and documents relating to the theater.

The Complete Pelican Shakespeare, edited by Stephen Orgel and A. R. Braunmuller, is printed in double columns in a type size that is large enough for easy reading. Along with theatrical and textual history, biographical material, and a discussion of the authorship question, the introduction to this volume contains a useful table illustrating how Shakespeare's writing changed over time. For each of the plays, it gives the number of lines; percentages of blank verse, rhyme, and prose; the number of scenes; proportion of men and women in the cast; the number of songs; and the longest roles (those over five hundred lines). An index of songs is also appended to the volume. The introduction to *The Taming of the Shrew* in the Pelican edition, written by Orgel, emphasizes the social and historical background of the play and provides an overview of the long history of performances of *The Taming of the Shrew* and its many variations from *Sauny the Scot* to *Kiss Me, Kate*. Orgel sees Katherine as unusual in that she is a shrew *before* marriage, an inversion of the traditional shrewish wife, who, like Bianca, is "all sweetness and good nature" before marriage but who becomes unmanageable after the wedding (145).

David Bevington is the editor of *The Complete Works of Shakespeare*, sixth edition. The general introduction focuses on recent Shakespeare scholarship and contains a number of illustrations providing historical and cultural background to Shakespeare's work. This edition contains a full-color, sixteen-page insert including photos from recent films and stage performances. Appendixes include timelines of the plays and poems, source material, a genealogy of English royalty, maps, and a section on Shakespeare in performance (written with Lois Potter). A smaller collection of Shakespeare's works, *The Necessary Shakespeare*, also edited by Bevington, is analogous to Norton's *Essential Plays / The Sonnets*. In his introduction to *The Taming of the Shrew*, Bevington describes in some detail the traditions, sources, and stock characters that Shakespeare borrowed and adapted to create a uniquely English comedy. Bevington emphasizes the theme of illusion that permeates the play, most notably in the induction, where Sly's naïveté mirrors that of a credulous audience, "calling attention to art's ability to confound reality" (2).

The Arden Shakespeare Complete Works, edited by Richard Proudfoot, Ann Thompson, and David Scott Kastan, includes extensive introductory material featuring several photos from stage and film and illustrations from early texts. The appendixes include an extensive bibliography, as well as indexes of the first lines of the sonnets and songs from the plays. The introduction to *The Taming of the Shrew* is written by Brian Morris, who edited the Arden Shakespeare, Second Series edition of the play.

Single Editions

With low cost and light weight in their favor, single editions of Shakespeare's plays are becoming the norm in many classrooms. As more instructors incorporate performance into their pedagogy, they are moving away from complete editions to single editions of the plays, which are easier to handle and are usually printed in paperback editions. Of these, the Signet edition (ed. Heilman) is well liked in part because it is one of the least expensive. It includes comprehensive explanatory notes, introductory material, modernized spelling and punctuation, bibliographies, and performance histories, as well as an interpretive essay on film adaptations of the play and an extensive filmography. Signet, an imprint of Penguin, also publishes a collection titled *Four Great Comedies*, comprising *The Taming of the Shrew*, *A Midsummer Night's Dream*, *Twelfth Night*, and *The Tempest*. Individual Signet titles are available in a number of formats, including e-book, graphic novel, compact disc, and MP3.

The Folger edition, edited by Barbara A. Mowat and Paul Werstine, prints the text on the recto pages with notes on the verso pages. In 2004, the editors greatly expanded its supplementary materials by two hundred pages to include contextual reading such as excerpts from *The Taming of a Shrew*, the full text of "A Homily of the State of Matrimony" and "A Merry Jest of a Shrewd and Curst Wife Lapped in Morel's Skin for Her Good Behavior," and documents from the *querelles des femmes*. The Folger edition is useful because of its convenient size and low price and because of the wide array of accompanying material it contains, which makes it competitive with the contextualized versions of *Shrew* published by Bedford and Norton.

The Arden is one of the most trusted single editions of *The Taming of the Shrew*. Barbara Hodgdon, editor of the third edition (published in 2010) has written an extensive 130-page introduction that addresses issues of genre, editorial history, the induction and sources, as well as performance and critical histories. The Arden edition pays particular attention to the relation between Shakespeare's play and *The Taming of a Shrew* and so includes the full text of that play in an appendix. The appendixes also contain a lengthy section on textual analysis and a discussion of editorial principles.

In 2008, Barnes and Noble published a paperback edition, edited by Nicholas F. Radel, which features an introduction by David Scott Kastan. This edition of *The Taming of the Shrew*, one in a series of new editions of Shakespeare's plays, is intended for beginning readers of Shakespeare. As with other inexpensive single editions, this one provides cursory introductions to Shakespeare and his language. After the text of the play, the editors give a brief performance history as well as information on the anonymous *The Taming of a Shrew*.

Frances Dolan's *The Taming of the Shrew*, published in 1996 by Bedford in the series Texts and Contexts, offers nearly forty pages of introductory material. This edition uses the text of Bevington's *Complete Works of Shakespeare* and includes more than thirty primary sources from the early modern period. These are arranged in four sections: "Alternative Endings" (which includes excerpts from *A Shrew*), "Marriage," "The Household: Authority and Violence," and "Shrews, Taming, and Untamed Shrews." The inclusion of so many contextual pieces makes this text especially useful in upper-division undergraduate and graduate courses, where students are expected to do more research than are those at lower levels. Students have access to a wide range of sources within one book.

In 2009, Norton published an edition of *The Taming of the Shrew*, edited by Dympna Callaghan, in its Norton Critical Editions series. In addition to a brief introduction and the text of the play, the Norton includes a section titled "Sources and Contexts," comprising excerpts from Ovid's *Metamorphoses*, several scenes from George Gascoigne's 1566 play *Supposes*, and a portion of "A Merry Jest of a Shrewd and Curst Wife Lapped in Morel's Skin for Her Good Behavior," followed by fifteen critical essays. The final section of the book is called "Rewritings and Appropriations" and includes excerpts from *A Shrew*; *The Tamer Tamed*, by John Fletcher; John Lacy's *Sauny the Scot*; and Cole Porter's *Kiss Me, Kate*, among others.

In 2010, Hackett published a very useful volume, *Three Shrew Plays* (Gaines and Maurer), which sandwiches Shakespeare's *The Taming of the Shrew* between the anonymous 1594 *The Taming of a Shrew* and John Fletcher's *The Woman's Prize; or, The Tamer Tamed*. This volume is edited, with introduction and notes, by Barry Gaines and Margaret Maurer. By collecting these three plays in one volume, Gaines and Maurer provide a convenient tool for teachers who want to focus on variants of the shrew-taming story, especially those contemporaneous with Shakespeare's play. The editors have chosen to offer minimal glosses to the texts of all three plays. These are located in the right margin of each page, making them accessible to readers.

Single editions of Shakespeare's plays are regularly reprinted, and instructors should check with publishers' representatives to be informed of the latest publications.

Teaching Resources

Sources

The Taming of the Shrew belongs to a long tradition of wife-taming stories dating back to the oral tradition, as Jan Harold Brunvand documents in his article "The Folktale Origin of *The Taming of the Shrew*." These stories continue in printed form, most notably in the particularly brutal depiction of abuse in the ballad "A Merry Jest of a Shrewd and Curst Wife Lapped in Morel's Skin for Her Good Behavior," published anonymously in 1550. The French fabliaux supply background context for the age-old battle for supremacy in marriage. A collection of English translations by John Duval of these humorous works can be found in *Fabliaux, Fair and Foul*. The essay by Joseph Ricke in this present volume provides numerous examples of shrewish women from biblical, medieval, and early modern sources. Another useful essay by David Bergeron, "The Wife of Bath and Shakespeare's *Taming of the Shrew*," draws the lineage of shrewish women from Chaucer to Shakespeare.

Teachers of Shakespeare's *The Taming of the Shrew* can make useful comparisons between his text and the anonymous *A Pleasant Conceited History, Called the Taming of a Shrew*, printed in quarto in 1594. Shakespeare's *The Taming of the Shrew* shares several characters with *A Shrew*, and the similarities in their plots lead scholars to debate whether *A Pleasant Conceited History* was written by Shakespeare. Today critics generally believe that the play, known as *A Shrew*, is a response to Shakespeare's play or that both plays refer to an earlier ur-*Shrew*. Brian Morris, in his introduction to the Arden edition of *The Taming of the Shrew*, thoroughly investigates the relation between *The Shrew* and *A Shrew*. A full text of *A Shrew*, edited by Stephen Roy Miller, is available from Cambridge and in Gaines and Maurer's edition published by Hackett, which pairs *A Shrew* with the texts of Shakespeare's *Shrew* and Fletcher's *The Tamer Tamed*. For the material in the subplot involving Bianca and her suitors, Shakespeare appears to have drawn heavily from Gascoigne's *Supposes*, a translation of Ariosto's *I Suppositi* (1509). See chapter 6 of Lorna Hutson's *The Usurer's Daughter: Male Friendship and Fictions of Women in Sixteenth-Century England* for a discussion of how Shakespeare was able successfully to translate this material into popular comic drama.

Some particularly useful overviews of Shakespeare's sources include Geoffrey Bullough's *Narrative and Dramatic Sources of Shakespeare*, Stuart Gillespie's

Shakespeare's Books: A Dictionary of Shakespeare's Sources, and Kenneth Muir's *The Sources of Shakespeare's Plays*.

Background Material

Teachers of Shakespeare are often eager to contextualize the plays within the cultural milieu of sixteenth- and seventeenth-century daily life. For those teaching *The Taming of the Shrew*, much of the relevant contextual material has to do with gender relations, specifically marriage. Dolan, in her 1996 edition of the play, has collected an array of early modern documents that gives teachers and students a sense of the prevailing beliefs and expectations for women and men in Shakespeare's time. Many of these are religious in origin, since even in post-Reformation England marriage was first and foremost a sacrament of the church. Two contributors to this volume chose to write about "A Homily of the State of Matrimony," published by the Anglican Church as part of an official compilation of sermons that were to be read by parsons to their congregations on a regular basis. This sermon, along with the "Solemnization of Holy Marriage" from The Book of Common Prayer, makes plain the church's expectations that husbands and wives should love and honor each other and that wives should obey their husbands, tenets of what has come to be known as companionate marriage, an ideal of Protestantism. Nonliturgical writings about marriage, however, sometimes emphasized other expectations for the married state, especially the duties of wives. One such text included by Dolan is Robert Snawsell's *A Looking Glass for Married Folks*, a translation and adaptation of a dialogue on marriage by Erasmus, in which a pious woman instructs two shrewish women on their wifely duties. Another source of marital instruction was William Whately's A *Bride-Bush; or, A Direction for Married Persons.* The segment included in Dolan's text deals with a man's authority and whether a husband has the right to beat his wife. Another piece that addresses husbands' authority over their wives is *Of Domestical Duties: Eight Treatises*, by William Gouge.

Because shrewish women could not easily be controlled, they were often accused of witchcraft or of being possessed by demons. Most American students have heard of the Salem witch trials and so are aware of the hysteria about women who were perceived to be in league with the devil. Nevertheless, it may be useful to have them read early modern sources that outline what signs indicated that someone was a witch. Two seventeenth-century texts on how to discover whether a woman is a witch are *The Discovery of Witches*, by Matthew Hopkins, and John Stearne's *A Confirmation and Discovery of Witchcraft*.

Petruccio uses falconry as a metaphor for taming Katherine. Some treatises on falconry contemporary to the play that may prove interesting to students include *The Book of Falconry or Hawking*, by George Turberville, and *Latham's Falconry*, by Simon Latham.

References and Guides

Teachers of Shakespeare's works can readily draw on a wide variety of general reference guides, beginning with the First Folio, whether in print form (*First Folio*, published by Norton) or online (*Shakespeare's First Folio*, available on *Project Gutenberg*).

Companions to Shakespeare are useful for providing a quick overview and are thus especially helpful to teachers who do not regularly teach Shakespeare or who are incorporating a single Shakespeare play into a syllabus containing a wide variety of texts. *The Bedford Companion to Shakespeare: An Introduction with Documents*, by Russ McDonald, offers a brief biography; discussions of early modern English, the theater, sources, texts, and political, religious, and social history; and a brief performance history of Shakespeare's plays. *The Bedford Companion* is particularly useful in introductory Shakespeare survey classes to give students a broad contextual overview. The large-format *Oxford Companion to Shakespeare*, edited by Michael Dobson and Stanley Wells, is in encyclopedia format, with alphabetical entries on everything from Aaron to Zuccaro. Each of Shakespeare's plays (listed alphabetically amid other entries) receives special attention, and textual information, a synopsis of the plot, and critical, stage, and film histories are included in the volume. Several black-and-white photos enhance the text and make it accessible for browsing. David Scott Kastan has edited *A Companion to Shakespeare*, a volume in the Blackwell Companions to Literature and Culture series. Each of the twenty-eight essays creates a portrait of one aspect of the theatrical, political, social, literary, and intellectual worlds influencing Shakespeare's writing and each is followed by an extensive bibliography. *The New Cambridge Companion to Shakespeare*, edited by Margreta de Grazia and Stanley Wells, contains twenty-one essays addressing various topics in Shakespeare scholarship, ranging from the playwright's early life and reading materials to Shakespeare and popular culture. Instructors will find Marjorie Garber's *Shakespeare after All* a great asset when preparing to teach. The essays, based on her lectures at Harvard, cover all thirty-eight plays in chronological order. Without using jargon, Garber draws on gender, postcolonial, and performance studies to provide insightful close readings.

Samuel Schoenbaum's texts remain the gold standard for biographical information on Shakespeare, particularly the first two sections of *Shakespeare's Lives* and *William Shakespeare: A Documentary Life*, which includes facsimiles of documents related to the life of Shakespeare. An older and very thorough source is *William Shakespeare: A Study of Facts and Problems*, by E. K. Chambers. Russell Fraser's *Young Shakespeare* looks at Shakespeare's first thirty years and how his life influenced his writing. *William Shakspere's Small Latine and Lesse Greeke*, by T. W. Baldwin, details the grammar school education that Shakespeare was likely to have received and challenges critics who argue that Shakespeare was not educated enough to have been the author of these plays.

Many teachers rely on David Cressy's *Education in Tudor and Stuart England*, which features collections of documents that illustrate early modern curriculum and the management of education. Cressy's *Birth, Marriage, and Death: Ritual, Religion, and the Life-Cycle in Tudor and Stuart England* offers a wealth of information on daily life in the time of Shakespeare.

The works of Andrew Gurr offer authoritative information on early modern London theaters and the actors and playgoers who frequented them. His 1970 book *The Shakespearean Stage, 1574–1642* (now in its fourth edition) provides a wealth of information on the acting companies and actors who performed Shakespeare's plays and the playhouses where they were staged. *Playgoing in Shakespeare's London* focuses on the lives and habits of the audiences who attended Shakespeare's plays, while *Staging in Shakespeare's Theatres*, which Gurr wrote with Mariko Ichikawa, reconstructs original staging practices. For an examination of commercial relations among the theater companies during Shakespeare's lifetime, Roslyn Lander Knutson's *Playing Companies and Commerce in Shakespeare's Time* is useful, since it supplies evidence that the theaters of sixteenth- and seventeenth-century London worked cooperatively, following the economic model of the guild. Instructors and students who want to delve into the particulars of theater operation can consult a facsimile, edited by R. A. Foakes, of the diary of Philip Henslowe, owner of the Rose Theatre during the 1590s. Alan C. Dessen and Leslie Thomson have compiled *A Dictionary of Stage Directions in English Drama, 1580–1642*, which can provide suggestions for classroom performances or merely help us in understanding how terms were used in Shakespeare's time.

Because Shakespeare's language can present a barrier for some students, teachers will want to consult a number of language resources. Two informative glossaries can be valuable references: *A Shakespeare Glossary*, by C. T. Onions, and *Shakespeare's Words: A Glossary and Language Companion*, by David Crystal and Ben Crystal. The *Oxford English Dictionary*, now available online, gives a sense of the changing meanings of words over time as well as the range of possible meanings for any given word. When students are confused about sexual references or double entendres, Eric Partridge's *Shakespeare's Bawdy: A Literary and Psychological Essay and a Comprehensive Glossary* can offer insight. Jonathan Hope's *Shakespeare's Grammar* and the Arden's *Reading Shakespeare's Dramatic Language*, edited by Sylvia Adamson and others, are also very useful resources. Miriam Joseph's *Rhetoric in Shakespeare's Time* is a classic that offers a valuable discussion of Elizabethan rhetorical theory that can help students see the importance of specialized language "tricks" in the plays. For those interested in music in Shakespeare's plays, *Shakespeare's Songbook*, edited by Ross W. Duffin (foreword by Orgel), provides musical notation, words to songs, and a brief history for nearly two hundred songs associated with Shakespeare's plays. An accompanying compact disc features eighty-one of the songs from the songbook.

Performance History

Those interested in a comprehensive history of the staging of *The Taming of the Shrew* should consult Elizabeth Schafer's edition in Cambridge's Shakespeare in Production series. Introductory material includes a table of productions from 1594 to 2001, as well as the accounts of playgoers, contemporary criticism, promptbook marginalia, drawings and photos, and directors' notes and interpretations. Footnotes to Ann Thompson's New Cambridge Shakespeare text of the play indicate how actors and directors interpreted the lines in various productions. The epilogue (scene 15) and the Sly interludes from *A Shrew* are appended, followed by a list of spin-offs and adaptations of the play. *Shakespeare: An Illustrated Stage History*, edited by Jonathan Bate and Russell Jackson, includes twelve chapters describing the history of Shakespeare's plays on the stage, with topics ranging from archaeological discoveries of early modern London theaters to stories of well-known and obscure directors and companies to personal accounts from actors like Judi Dench, who discusses her career playing Shakespeare on stage. The volume is abundantly illustrated with photos and drawings, making it suitable for browsing as well as careful perusal. John O'Connor and Katharine Goodland have edited *A Directory of Shakespeare in Performance*, a thoroughly researched book that includes detailed listings of all the major Shakespeare plays on the stage and screen. Another useful guide to the play's stage history is Tori Haring-Smith's *From Farce to Metadrama: A Stage History of* The Taming of the Shrew, *1594–1983*. The first chapter provides an overview of performances up to 1800, and the remainder of the book examines nineteenth- and twentieth-century portrayals and reception of the play. Theater historians will find the "Chronological Handlists of Performances in England and North America" a useful reference tool.

Many characters in *The Taming of the Shrew* resemble the stock characters from the Italian commedia dell'arte tradition. For example, Gremio is a classic *pantalone* and Bianca and Lucentio can be played as *innamorati*. The well-known 1976 production by the American Conservatory Theater of San Francisco with Fredi Olster as Kate and Marc Singer as Petruccio was staged in the style of commedia dell'arte. For an extensive history of this influence, see *The Commedia dell'Arte: A Documentary History*, by Kenneth Richards and Laura Richards.

Performance Pedagogy

As evidenced by the essays in this volume, teachers are increasingly using performance in their classrooms, which gives voice and motion to the characters on the page and thus deepens students' understanding of Shakespeare's plays. *Teaching Shakespeare through Performance*, edited by Milla Cozart Riggio, provides effective approaches for instructors to incorporate performance into their pedagogy. The book is divided into five parts: "Theory and History"; "Teaching Strategies"; "Exemplary Courses"; "Films and Electronic Resources"; and "Annotated Guides." It offers guidance from nearly thirty instructors who have extensive experience with using performance in their Shakespeare pedagogy. Similarly, Edward Rocklin's *Performance Approaches to Teaching Shakespeare* includes a chapter on teaching *The Taming of the Shrew.* Rocklin incorporates several suggestions for performing scenes from the play to obtain teaching objectives. For teachers and students who want to explore the commedia dell'arte aspects of the play, *Commedia dell'Arte: An Actor's Handbook*, by John Rudlin, can be a useful tool.

Shakespeare: Script, Stage, Screen, edited by David Bevington, Anne Marie Welsh, and Michael L. Greenwald, is an anthology of fourteen of Shakespeare's most filmed plays, including *The Taming of the Shrew*. It is a thorough treatment of stage and film productions, and the section following the text of *Shrew* offers an extensive review of stage productions from the Elizabethan era to the present. The section "*The Taming of the Shrew* on Film and Video" is equally informative and features a "close-up" look at director Franco Zeffirelli. Michael Flachmann's *Shakespeare from Page to Stage: An Anthology of the Most Popular Plays and Sonnets* also includes the text of *The Taming of the Shrew*, followed by a list of research and discussion topics, a filmography, and an annotated bibliography, all of which make this volume a useful pedagogical tool. *Shakespeare into Film*, by James Welsh, Richard Vela, and John C. Tibbetts, includes a discussion of the Douglas Fairbanks–Mary Pickford 1929 film version of the play. Lynda Boose and Richard Burt have coedited two volumes on popular culture interpretations of Shakespeare: *Shakespeare, the Movie: Popularizing the Plays on Film, TV, and Video* and *Shakespeare, the Movie II: Popularizing the Plays on Film, TV, Video, and DVD*. Both volumes include essays by Diana E. Henderson that review film adaptations of *The Taming of the Shrew* (the second an updated version of the earlier essay).

Critical Texts

A valuable resource for locating Shakespeare scholarship is the *World Shakespeare Bibliography Online*, edited by James Harner and published for *Shakespeare Quarterly*. This database provides annotated entries for all important scholarly and popular materials related to Shakespeare from 1960 to the present and is updated quarterly. The *MLA International Bibliography* and the *Annual Bibliography of English Language and Literature* (Modern Humanities Research Association) are effective tools for identifying and tracking down relevant scholarship. Other important sources include *Shakespeare, a Bibliographical Guide*, edited by Stanley Wells, and *Shakespeare, a Selective Bibliography of Modern Criticism*, edited by Linda Woodbridge.

Increasingly, teachers of Shakespeare's plays are returning to textual study and challenging many of the editorial interpolations that have accrued over the past four centuries. Now that quarto and folio versions of the plays are available on the Internet, teachers are using these resources in their classrooms and are encouraging students to consult documents that were previously inaccessible to them. Leah Marcus, in her 1996 book *Unediting the Renaissance*, contends that the range of interpretations and productions of Shakespeare that we experience today have been narrowed over time by editorial practice. In her chapter "The Editor as Tamer: *A Shrew* and *The Shrew*" she argues that the 1623 folio version of *The Shrew* and the 1594 quarto *A Shrew* are variants of the same play and that by limiting ourselves to the 1623 folio version of *The Shrew*, we also limit our interpretive possibilities.

Most scholarship on *The Taming of the Shrew* focuses on gender, marriage, and the relation between the sexes. As a consequence, many instructors consult books that provide an overview of the social status of women in the early modern period and sometimes also assign excerpts for students to read. Commonly used texts include *Half Humankind: Contexts and Texts of the Controversy about Women in England, 1540–1640*, edited by Katherine Henderson and Barbara McManus; *Chaste, Silent, and Obedient: English Books for Women, 1475–1640*, by Suzanne Hull; and *Women in Early Modern England, 1550–1720*, by Sara Mendelson and Patricia Crawford. Lisa Jardine's *Still Harping on Daughters: Women and Drama in the Age of Shakespeare* looks at strong female figures in early modern drama. *Rewriting the Renaissance: The Discourses of Sexual Difference in Early Modern Europe*, edited by Margaret Ferguson, Maureen Quilligan, and Nancy Vickers, is a collection of essays on patriarchy and its effects. A more recent volume by Phyllis Rackin, *Shakespeare and Women*, challenges the scholarly emphasis on patriarchy by arguing that the way critics approach Shakespeare's plays is determined by their own points of view. Marjorie Garber's *Coming of Age in Shakespeare* draws on the work of psychologists, anthropologists, and sociologists to investigate situations in Shakespeare's plays where characters undergo crises that bring about personal growth. *Shakespeare, Law, and Marriage*, by B. J. Sokol and Mary Sokol, combines legal, historical, and literary documents that provide insight into the practice and theory of marriage in Shakespeare's time.

Lynda Boose's "Scolding Brides and Bridling Scolds: Taming the Woman's Unruly Member" highlights the linguistic and cultural associations between using bridles to tame horses and the taming of brides by controlling their tongues. This essay is anthologized in Dolan's The Taming of the Shrew: *Texts and Contexts*, in Callaghan's edition of the play (2009), and in Dana Aspinall's The Taming of the Shrew: *Critical Essays*, among other texts, and is therefore widely available to students. Another essay by Boose, "*The Taming of the Shrew*, Good Husbandry, and Enclosure," is a particularly valuable teaching resource.

A useful essay for examining the dynamics of marriage, "*The Taming of the Shrew*: Shakespeare's Mirror of Marriage," by Coppélia Kahn, maintains that while the success of Petruccio's hypermasculinity and his desire for control mirror the ethic that approves the place of men over women in the social and domestic hierarchy, the ethic itself calls men's power into question, since Petruccio's success depends on a myth of female weakness, as well as on his having a woman to dominate. Along the same lines, Karen Newman's "Renaissance Family Politics and Shakespeare's *The Taming of the Shrew*" argues that the women in the play are publicly subjugated to display men's control, just as unruly women in early modern times were punished by being exhibited. Yet she contends that because Shakespeare's women were played by boy actors, the containment of women's subversive energies is not wholly successful. Laurie Maguire, in "The Naming of the Shrew," explores the complex linguistic significance of the double names of Katherine/Kate and how this onomastic doubling reflects other theatrical, mutually self-canceling twinnings that ultimately lead to anonymity. Natasha Korda looks at the economics of marriage in "Household Kates: Domesticating Commodities in *The Taming of the Shrew*," arguing not only that Kate is a commodity for exchange between men but also that, by taming her, Petruccio is training her to be a wise consumer of commodities.

For a more positive view of the marriage between Katherine and Petruccio, instructors might consult "Patriarchy and Play in *The Taming of the Shrew*," by Marianne Novy, who finds that Shakespeare joins patriarchy with cooperation in that the marriage, despite its confines, allows the couple room to play. Likewise, John C. Bean, in "Comic Structure and the Humanizing of Kate in *The Taming of the Shrew*," sees Kate's final speech as a "humanized vision" of the ideal companionate marriage, although it is delivered in circumstances that are dehumanizing to Kate (71). A chapter in Camille Wells Slights's *Shakespeare's Comic Commonwealths*, "The Raw and the Cooked in *The Taming of the Shrew*," provides one of the more hopeful judgments of the play's marriages, arguing that its mockery of social conventions is simultaneously a didactic and progressive suggestion that human beings can make those conventions acceptably flexible.

Sean Benson's "'If I Do Prove Her Haggard': Shakespeare's Application of Hawking Tropes to Marriage" includes a careful discussion of Petruccio's use of the language of hawking to describe Kate's taming, focusing on the particular significance of Petruccio's terms as well as on Shakespeare's special interest in this metaphor for marriage. Helga Ramsey-Kurz frames the relationship between Petruccio as falconer and Katherine as falcon in a more positive light in her article, "Rising above the Bait: Kate's Transformation from Bear to Falcon." In "The Taming of the Scold: The Enforcement of Patriarchal Authority in Early Modern England," David Underdown attributes concern about shrewish women to a more widespread fear of societal breakdown, which was manifested in a desire to preserve the hierarchy of patriarchy.

Among the helpful discussions of the play's metatheater is Amy L. Smith's "Performing Marriage with a Difference: Wooing, Wedding, and Bedding in *The Taming of the Shrew*." Drawing on Judith Butler's theory that reiteration of "ritual social dramas" provides opportunities to question and alter such rituals, Smith considers the interpretations of marriage roles in *The Taming of the Shrew*, suggesting that the play shows that weddings, as reiterated performances, demonstrated marriage's susceptibility to changing interpretations of the behavioral codes the ceremony prescribed (Butler qtd. in Smith 290).

By pairing the shrew in Shakespeare with unruly women in the works of the Wakefield Master, Valerie Wayne suggests that both writers used these representations of women to raise questions about marriage without endorsing the mistreatment of women. In "Refashioning the Shrew," she points out that although the notion of the shrew arises out of patriarchy, shrewish women were instrumental in criticizing the misuse of power by husbands and others in positions of authority. Pamela Allen Brown's *Better a Shrew Than a Sheep* looks at depictions of women in early modern English jest literature and determines that being a shrew was probably women's best defense. These shrewish women are not afraid to pursue their desires, and they gain agency by refusing to accept male domination.

Although most criticism on *The Taming of the Shrew* focuses on the tumultuous marriage of Katherine and Petruccio, instructors may wish to focus on approaches that examine cultural influences not directly related to issues of gender. Published work in this vein includes Martha Carlin's amusing "'What Say You to a Piece of Beef and Mustard?': The Evolution of Public Dining in Medieval and Tudor London," which contextualizes Petruccio's taming methods and demonstrates that his tantalizing offer of food to the famished Kate was scripted in imitation of London eating houses' advertising of "specials" by proprietors to their high-toned clientele. The cultural influence of fashion on the play is discussed in Kelly N. O'Connor's "Fine Array and Mean Habiliments: Costuming the Shrew," an instructive source for information on costumes. This essay uses photos to show the clothing of famous Kates and Biancas, which can provide a catalyst for discussing how these characters should be portrayed.

Teachers who want to take a cynical approach to the negative implications of the play can assign W. Thomas MacCary's chapter on *The Taming of the Shrew* in his *Friends and Lovers: The Phenomenology of Desire in Shakespearean Comedy*. Attending closely to the play's dream imagery, MacCary interprets the comedy as a misogynistic male fantasy. Implicitly agreeing that the play is misogynistic, Penny Gay, in a chapter on *The Taming of the Shrew* in her *As She Likes It: Shakespeare's Unruly Women*, provides an entertaining account of the dramatic strategies by which twentieth-century productions have evaded serious considerations of this play's domestic politics.

Many scholars will argue that the induction has become central to their understanding of the play, and, increasingly, more teachers are asking students to think and write about the implications of including Sly in the story. Jay Halio's essay, "The Induction as Clue in *The Taming of the Shrew*" provides a close reading of the play that fully incorporates the induction. Power dynamics in the play are explored by Dale G. Priest in "Induction, Theatricality, and Power in

The Taming of the Shrew," and Frank Ardolino explores Thomas Kyd's play *The Spanish Tragedy* as a possible source in "The Induction of Sly: The Influence of *The Spanish Tragedy* on the Two Shrews." Barry Weller draws connections between transformations in *Shrew* and Ovid's *Metamorphoses* in "Induction and Inference: Theater, Transformation, and the Construction of Identity in *The Taming of the Shrew*."

Shrew *on Film*

Despite the play's many anachronistic attitudes about marriage and the relationship between men and women, *The Taming of the Shrew* is one of the most popular of Shakespeare's comedies; there are well over a hundred film versions and adaptations. Its popularity often puzzles scholars, who view *Shrew* as an inferior comedy, typical of Shakespeare in his early period, when he was still learning his craft. Nevertheless, this play seems particularly well suited for translation to film, a fact that would probably not surprise folklorists, who trace its story lines back at least two millennia, a testament to the story's enduring attraction.

Teaching *The Taming of the Shrew* to students who are offended by the very idea of a man taming a woman can present a serious problem, which is why teachers often concentrate on other aspects of the play or deal with the misogyny by looking at performances of the play to see how directors and actors have come to terms with these challenges. Often, the most engaging and difficult aspects of the play are one and the same—Kate's prickly behavior and Petruccio's callousness, for example. Examining how various productions have addressed these challenges can also help students who try to avoid the misogynistic elements and insist on "seeing the taming as good fun rather than abuse." For many, the hardest part of the play to deal with is Katherine's final speech, and films find a variety of ways to treat it.

The first film version of *The Taming of the Shrew* dates to 1908, when D. W. Griffith used the story line as a vehicle for a farcical romp. However, the first "blockbuster" Hollywood film of Shakespeare's play was Sam Taylor's 1929 rendition starring Douglas Fairbanks and Mary Pickford. At only sixty-eight minutes, this is clearly the "condensed version" of the story. Pickford's Katherine character, called Kate, is a strong-willed woman fighting to survive in a man's world, who is finally won over by Petruccio's charms. In an essay in this volume, James Welsh compares this early version of the play with the extravagant 1967 production directed by Franco Zeffirelli and starring Richard Burton and Elizabeth Taylor. Zeffirelli makes use of his background as an opera director to create a lush and carefully detailed rendering of Renaissance Italy but unfortunately sacrifices much of the play's witty dialogue to stunning visuals.

One film version popular with both teachers and students is the video of the 1976 commedia dell'arte interpretation by the American Conservatory Theater (ACT) of San Francisco (*William Shakespeare's* The Taming of the Shrew).

By highlighting the farcical elements of commedia through stylized costumes, broad physical gestures, and sound effects, this production avoids controversy by making light of the taming.

The British Broadcasting Corporation (BBC) produced films of *The Taming of the Shrew* in 1980 and in 2005. The earlier version, a videotape of a stage production directed by Jonathan Miller, starred John Cleese as Petruccio and Sarah Badel as Katherine and seems almost a reaction against the Zeffirelli version, choosing to downplay the visual element and highlight dialogue. The 2005 BBC production, directed by Sally Wainwright, is a four-part television miniseries starring Shirley Henderson as thirty-eight-year-old Katherine, a highly successful politician, and Rufus Sewell as the dashing young Petruccio, whose challenge it is to soften the hard-driving Katherine. This version is set in contemporary London and is replete with tabloid stories about Bianca's latest suitors.

One of the most appealing (yet difficult to find) films is the video of the 1981 Stratford (Ontario) Shakespeare Festival's production directed by Peter Dews and starring Len Cariou and Sharry Flett. By incorporating audience response, this film constantly reminds viewers that it is a stage production. The wooing scene highlights a genuine attraction between Petruccio and Katherine, and, unlike in the ACT staging of this scene featuring a wrestling match, Cariou and Flett rarely even touch. Of all the films of *Shrew*, this is the only one that includes the induction scenes.

In 1953 George Sidney directed *Kiss Me Kate*, a Hollywood film production of Cole Porter's 1948 musical adaptation of *The Taming of the Shrew*. The film stars Howard Keel as Fred Graham, who sings "I Have Come to Wive It Wealthily in Padua," and Kathryn Grayson as Lili Vanessi, who sings "I Hate Men." Ultimately, the two kiss and make up, leaving Kate's final speech a foregone conclusion.

An adaptation that students find appealingly familiar is Gil Junger's *Ten Things I Hate about You*. Heath Ledger and Julia Stiles star as Patrick Verona and Kat Stratford, two twentieth-century high school students in Seattle. This version is only loosely based on Shakespeare's play, preserving the basic story and only a couple of lines from Shakespeare's text. Nevertheless, it makes some of the central issues in the play more accessible to students.

Online Sources

In wired classrooms, particularly those with projection capability, some teachers access college or university library film collections while teaching. One resource that has now been purchased by many libraries is "Theatre in Video," which makes viewable the 1976 ACT commedia dell'arte filmed stage production of *The Taming of the Shrew*, as well as the Royal Shakespeare Company Workshop: *Speaking Shakespearean Verse* (recorded in 1979). A more casual and haphazard online resource is *YouTube*, an ever-expanding collection that offers scenes from various films and some random stage productions of *Shrew*. (*YouTube* is a double-edged sword, however, since just as frequently it turns up parodies of the play that students will invariably want to see instead of the real thing, such as *Taming of the Shrew Robot Chicken.*) Finally, Web sites of the BBC (www.bbc.co.uk/drama/shakespeare/), the Royal Shakespeare Company (www.rsc.org.uk/home/default.aspx), and the Folger Shakespeare Library (www.folger.edu/), as well as the Web site *Shakespeare's Globe* (www.bardweb.net/globe.html), can provide useful information about the play in performance and the critical and cultural traditions that help illuminate *The Taming of the Shrew* for readers.

Part Two

APPROACHES

Introduction

Grace Tiffany

Contending in a wrestling match is a good analogy for teaching *The Taming of the Shrew.* We signal our aggression when we place it on the syllabus—indeed, as the first play on the syllabus, as many instructors do. Our confrontational stance is assumed. Some students expect that stance and, with us, go on guard. We voluntarily engage our partner and opponent, the play, for the pleasure of the sport it provides but stay wary, knowing this encounter both exposes us to attack and demands that we fight back. We come with a variety of strategically planned moves, but we rely as well on our capacity to improvise, to regain our footing when temporarily thrown by the play's dangerous sexual and domestic politics. More than any other Shakespeare work, this comedy—which dramatizes the subduing of a sharp-tongued bride by a wild "swearing Jack" of a groom (2.1.280)—casts its readers, watchers, and teachers in the roles not only of playfellows but also of combatants.[1] Unlike *The Comedy of Errors* or *Twelfth Night*, *Shrew* does not require us to suspend our disbelief in stark unlikelihoods: to "entertain the offered fallacy" (*Err.* 2.2.186) or "[l]et fancy still [our] sense" (*TN* 4.1.58). Rather, it challenges us to a mental and verbal contest ("He that knows better how to tame a shrew, / Now let him speak!" [*Shr.* 4.1.191–92]). Struggling with this play is a prerequisite for enjoying it.

Indeed, of the one hundred eight college and university instructors who wrote to us with questions and suggestions about teaching this play, including the twenty-seven whose contributions are included in this volume, most described the teaching exercise in terms of its pleasurable contentiousness. Words like "argument," "debate," "biting," "clashing," "battlefield," "violent," and "one-upmanship" abound in these responses.[2] Students and even some teachers love to hate *Shrew.* However, the stimulating conflicts represented and those engendered by the play lead to pedagogical puzzles. Those who wrote to us posed numerous questions, including, What strategies can be used to manage students' often spirited disagreement about the patriarchal ethos that seems to underlie this play's plot? How can a female instructor foil students who see her as a natural ally of shrew-Kate, or a male instructor foil those who see him as a secret friend to Kate's tamer, Petruccio—especially when students tailor their comments to support "what the teacher thinks"?

These and other questions tended to be embedded in three larger ones, now reflected in this volume's main subdivisions. The first and most complicated question concerns language: how can students best be taught to discern thematic patterns woven by the play's reiterated verbal images and—to invoke a late, great scholar's excellent phrase—"symbolism" (Altick 339)? How can an instructor engage students, especially Shakespeare neophytes, who are, for example, baffled by Grumio's obscure statement "he'll rail in his rope-tricks"

(1.2.107) or alarmed by Petruccio's calling Kate a "slow-winged turtle" (2.1.205)? How, as well, can one enliven the textual study that reveals important discrepancies between modern editions of the play and Shakespeare's First Folio—and that instantiates the fundamentally contested nature of many of Shakespeare's play texts? The second question concerns contexts: where and what are the cultural materials that would aptly historicize, for instructors as well as their students, the play's conflicts and its sometimes competing moral messages? The last question pertains to performance: how can instructors show students that performance choices radically influence the meaning of *Shrew*'s dialogue, making possible a startling variety of Biancas, Lucentios, Petruccios, and Kates—and some very different sorts of marriages?

Readers of this volume will find, of course, that these questions of language, context, and performance overlap at many points. They will see that some teachers use performance to illuminate linguistic obscurities, that others' lessons about Elizabethan culture include the study of early modern textual production or Renaissance stagecraft, and that still others allude to Renaissance social and political contexts to illuminate *The Taming of the Shrew*'s language. (For example, in the first section, "Language and Texts," Laurie Ellinghausen's essay describes how its author prefaces her unit on bossy feminine speech in Shakespeare's play with references to powerful female speakers in Shakespeare's England—most notably Queen Elizabeth I.) In these essays, readers will also find a resounding affirmative answer to another commonly asked question: Are there conflicts to explore besides those of gender in this play? In *Shrew* and in our classrooms, who should wrestle whom, and how?

To move from questions to answers, here proposed and described are a range of pedagogical approaches whose worth in the classroom instructors have demonstrated over time, among many kinds of students, from generalists to theater or English majors (and even merchant marines). Among other things, the essays herein demonstrate that *Shrew*'s dueling adversaries are many and exist inside and outside the play.

The Taming of the Shrew centers, of course, on the struggle between Katherine, or Kate, and Petruccio, whose pairing Kate's father aptly calls "a match" (2.1.311): a competition as much as a betrothal. Confronting the play, teachers aggressively engage not only Shakespeare's work but also students of both sexes who find its "wife-taming" theme retrograde. On the other hand, students who find value in the play's suggestions about wifely submission and husbandly dominance (or even leadership) may argue vociferously with classmates who oppose those things or may simply clam up, challenging instructors by their silence. Students who talk, like critics, may disagree over interpretations of the play's key scenes, particularly its last one. Can Kate really *mean* her final speech championing a woman's subservience to her husband, her "lord" and "king" (5.2.142)? Is the play worse or better if she does? Are the broad winks to camera and audience given by the screen heroine Mary Pickford or the stage actress Fredi Olster at that speech's conclusion preferable to Elizabeth Taylor's robust sincerity as she kneels before her real-life Petruccio, Richard Burton? The scene invites endless debate, which instructors tend to see as a good thing. (Indeed, one essay in this book describes an in-class performance-exercise in which a female student playing Kate was antagonized by a male student-director, who—according to the instructor's plan—argued with her over how her last speech was to be interpreted. He provoked a spirited counterargument, which delighted the watchers.)

Nor indeed are the arguments the play sparks confined to its central, eponymous subject, the battle between the sexes. One contributor to this volume, James Hirsh, offers a "taxonomy" of "pervasive contentiousness in *The Taming of the Shrew*," finding in the play's induction and five acts "conflicts between members of the same household," class conflicts, "rivalries among gentlemen," and disputes among gentlewomen, quarrels between tradespeople and customers, and arguments between players and their audiences. He adds to these quarrels the implicit disputes between Shakespeare and his readers, among the play's critics, among students, and between teachers and students (the last of which subjects the play also explores). Hirsh concludes that "the contention between Petruccio and Kate is only one example of the discord that is . . . a pervasive ingredient in human relations." Contention is more than exercise and entertainment, Hirsh's students are led to see. It is the stuff of learning, love, and life.

Teachers choose this play, then, not to avoid but to prompt arguments, often leading with it on their syllabi to inspire enthusiastic student engagement with difficult texts, a response they hope will become habitual for students over a term and persist during their lifetimes. Having chosen *Shrew*, they are supported by a wealth of instructional materials made available because of film and theater directors' and audiences' similar affinity for the play. Arranging opportunities for students to see *The Taming of the Shrew* in live performance is often possible, since it continues to be one of the most frequently staged of Shakespeare's comedies and is routinely produced for mainstream audiences in urban or festival locations. But even if a trip to the live theater is impossible for an instructor, his or her students can see a variety of filmed versions of *Shrew* in class. The "Materials" section of this volume describes the many video, DVD, *YouTube*, or library-database versions available, and "Approaches" includes two essays providing detailed evaluations of cinematic and otherwise filmed productions of the play. James M. Welsh's "Scenes from a Renaissance Marriage: *The Taming of the Shrew* on Film" compares Mary Pickford and Douglas Fairbanks's 1929 movie version with Elizabeth Taylor and Richard Burton's 1967 film, showing how these two blockbuster productions showcased the celebrities who starred in them and received box-office impetus from those stars' respective reputations as sweetheart and swashbuckler (Pickford and Fairbanks) and battling spouses (Burton and Taylor). Welsh discusses how, counterintuitively, "sweet" Pickford played her submission speech ironically (she was first with the famous wink), while nearly forty years later contentious Taylor chose to play Kate's capitulation straight. Sheila T. Cavanagh also goes to the movies, as well as to the television set, in "Whose Play Is It, Anyway? Viewing *The Taming of the Shrew* Pedagogically." She examines fourteen filmed productions and adaptations of *The Taming of the Shrew*, which range from the relatively straightforward 1980 BBC version (dir. Miller) to the "Atomic Shakespeare" episode of the ABC series *Moonlighting* in 1986 and the 1999 Gil Junger teen film *Ten Things I Hate about You*. Both Welsh and Cavanagh discuss how history has inflected productions and acting styles and demonstrate, for example, how the "grand gestures" of the nineteenth-century stage and vaudeville saw early cinematic reflections: the grandness of Douglas Fairbanks's heroic-gallant Petruccio, the vaudeville humor of his comic interplay with Pickford's Katherine.

Other essays allude to the usefulness of various video or DVD versions of the play for teaching. Bruce E. Brandt's "The Harlequin *The Taming of the Shrew*" focuses on the value of the American Conservatory Theater (ACT) of San Francisco's "energetic and acrobatic" *The Taming of the Shrew* (1976), demonstrating how the film of that performance helps students understand the commedia dell'arte and farce traditions that influenced Shakespeare in his earliest period (to which this play belongs). Brandt's essay speaks to instructors interested in theater history, as well as those who want to consider features of the play besides the man-woman conflict. Still, his essay doesn't exclude the play's matrimonial themes. Brandt also uses the enjoyable ACT film to prompt class discussion about how comedy and theater more generally neutralize violence and misogyny. In a similar vein, Silver Damsen's "Dominating Humor in *The Taming of the Shrew*" offers a strategy for using two made-for-television films of the play, Jonathan Miller's 1980 BBC production and Peter Dews's 1986 CBC (Canadian Broadcasting Company) film of the live Stratford (Ontario) production. While centering on the Kate-Petruccio combat, Damsen's essay, like Brandt's, shows how film can be used to draw students' attention to other elements of *The Taming of the Shrew*. Damsen—who successfully used this strategy in the classroom of one of this volume's editors—focuses students' attention on scenes that enact "domination and subordination" of various types: between sexes, certainly, but also between older and younger men and between gentry and servants. What in the way these interactions are staged, Damsen asks, makes such subordinations "funny"?

Few indeed are the teachers of *Shrew* who don't use at least some of these widely available films in the classroom. Instructors often invite students to compare scenes from different productions, allowing classes to see the power directors and actors have to influence audiences' responses to the play's dialogue, and even to affect that dialogue's meaning. While using productions comparatively fulfills that purpose and facilitates the understanding of Shakespeare's language for any of his plays, teachers of *Shrew* use film for an additional purpose. They find it helps show students that while shrew taming might seem distasteful on the page, its comic enactments, particularly by handsome and funny Petruccios, make it go down with alarming ease. The example I use to prove this point to my classes is *Kiss Me, Petruchio*, the 1981 made-for-television film of the 1978 production of *Shrew* put on by the New York Shakespeare Festival (also known as the Public Theater), which starred Meryl Streep and Raúl Juliá. However, an Internet search and years of inquiry have convinced me that I own the only copy. (And no, you can't borrow it.)

The abundance of provocative *Taming of the Shrew* films makes the play particularly fun to teach because of these films' widely varied ways of bringing Shakespeare's script to life. Students are happy to discuss the differences among performances. However, many instructors also strive to expose their classes to some early modern cultural textual materials to help students contextualize what they are reading on the page, seeing on a screen, or speaking in performance exercises. In "*The Taming of the Shrew* as Introduction to a Shakespeare Course," Peter H. Greenfield describes how a combination of "close reading" exercises, "exploring options for performance," and the teaching of secondary texts that reveal "the values and practices of Shakespeare's culture" help his students understand Shakespeare better over the course of a term. Both Peter C. Herman and Robert Matz ask their students to read, alongside the play, Elizabethan sermons and prayers concerning matrimony. In " 'The Woman Is a Weak Creature': The Homily of Matrimony and *The Taming of the Shrew*," Herman proposes asking classes a set of questions about a widely read, anonymously written sixteenth-century marriage sermon. The inquiry prompts students to notice the surprising sympathy the tract extends to women, who experience "grief and pain" at the loss of their liberties in marriage. Herman invites students to see that Shakespeare's play registers similar sympathy for Kate. However, Herman also notes moral contradictions in the "Homily of the State of Matrimony." So does Matz, who, in " 'To Serve, Love, and Obey': *The Taming of the Shrew* and Early Modern Marriage," finds a tension between the values of husbandly "authority and . . . forbearance" that are championed by the homiletic text. Matz argues that the tract's condemnation of husbands' hitting unruly wives is weakened by its author's emphasis on male authority, which carries the shadowy implication that men sometimes—however regrettably—*have* to smack their women. While in *Shrew* only Kate actually slugs anyone, the torments served up by Petruccio (he denies Kate sleep and food) may well have drawn approval from Elizabethan playgoers who knew the "Homily of the State of Matrimony."

Some instructors who prize students' knowledge of early modern contexts assign an assortment of materials, including not only the homiletic but the literary and dramatic. Todd M. Lidh, for example, exposes students to the wider early modern theatrical context, showing classes that debates on marriage were fueled by other Renaissance "marriage plays." Lidh looks mainly at *The Woman's Prize; or, The Tamer Tamed*, the sequel to *The Taming of the Shrew* penned by Shakespeare's sometime collaborator John Fletcher. In Fletcher's play, the tables are turned on Petruccio. Lidh's essay, " 'To Teach Both Sexes Due Equality,' " notes that Fletcher's sequel initiated a long history of responses to Shakespeare's play onstage. Focusing on the first of these "comebacks," Lidh chronicles how allowing his students to perform scenes from both *The Tamer Tamed* and *The Taming of the Shrew* helped them more deeply appreciate the variety of arguments about marriage that obtained among early modern people. This, in turn, helped them see affinities between ideas in Shakespeare's time and in ensuing centuries, including our own.

Lidh's points are well taken, since, as several instructors have noted, stage "interrogations" of Shakespeare's play have continued since its inception. After Fletcher's first response came his second, *Swetnam the Woman-Hater* (1618). Then came John Lacy's *Sauny the Scot; or, The Taming of the Shrew: A Comedy* (1667); James Worsdale's *A Cure for a Scold* (1735); and David Garrick's *Catherine and Petruchio* (1756), which surpassed Shakespeare's play in popularity in the second half of the eighteenth century. In the nineteenth century, *The Taming of the Shrew*, which accommodated Victorian ideals of virtuous wifehood, regained primacy on the stage, much to the dismay of George Bernard Shaw, who found Shakespeare's last scene "altogether disgusting" ("Chin"). No doubt Shaw would have preferred Cole Porter's well-loved 1948 adaptation of Shakespeare, *Kiss Me, Kate*, wherein an actress playing Shakespeare's Kate gets fed up with her role and walks out on the production. Or perhaps Shaw *did* prefer *Kiss Me, Kate* (and would have approved the 2010 decision of the Stratford Shakespeare Festival, in Ontario, to stage Porter's play rather than Shakespeare's). Shaw lived until 1950, long enough to see or at least to have heard of the musical. Atomic Shakespeare, indeed: he departed an age already gone nuclear and missed by little more than a decade an explosion of feminist reinterpretations of Kate's final speech in both English and American film and theatrical productions. These—which continue apace—included a 1990 Central Park staging in which Kate (Tracey Ullman) ended by pulling the chair out from under her husband (Morgan Freeman) and sending him sprawling, and the Chicago Shakespeare Theatre's addition in 2010 of a frame play, scripted by Neil LaBute, in which the actress playing Kate refuses to say her final speech. Shaw would have loved both.

Of course, the Elizabethan *Taming of the Shrew* had a past as well as a future. That past was largely medieval. In a journal essay, Jonathan Gil Harris has written that when the original Petruccio warned Kate and their wedding guests to "look not big, nor stamp, nor stare" he was relying on his audience's knowledge of cycle plays' Herod actors and of those actors' sixteenth-century avatars, like the famously hammy Edward Alleyn of the Admiral's Men theater company. "I stampe! I stare! I looke all abowtt!" says hysterical Herod in the Coventry Cycle play, foreshadowing Alleyn's performances in Marlowe's plays at the Rose (qtd. in Harris 369, 368). Like Herod, "Katherine . . . may very well look big, stamp, and stare as she delivers the lines preceding Petruchio's," Harris writes. Petruccio's ensuing rebuke is thus both a criticism of unseemly behavior and a wry critique of over-the-top late medieval and early sixteenth-century performing habits (367).[3] Like Harris, one contributor to our volume looks at *Shrew*'s medieval antecedents, delineating connections not between *The Taming of the Shrew* and later plays but betwen Shakespeare's play and its predecessor "shrew" plays, as well as among other Shakespeare plays that dramatize "shrews." Joseph Ricke's "Kate, the Commonplace: The Framing of the *Shrew*" describes a syllabus that includes English religious plays that contain "saintly shrew[s]," or virgin martyrs; *The Second Shepherds' Play* (with its vociferous wife Gill); and *Much Ado about Nothing*'s Beatrice and *The Winter's Tale*'s Paulina. Introducing students to these "ubiquitous shrew[s]" helps sharpen their sense of Shakespeare's participation in the shrew debate. On the other hand, requiring attention to outspoken, virtuous, and even life-saving Shakespearean women from other comedies shows students that Shakespeare didn't always agree with himself about loudmouthed women. Ricke also discusses two negative stereotypes of men in early English "shrew" plays: if they aren't dominant, they're namby-pamby.

As noted above, many instructors point out that *The Taming of the Shrew* is not just about the marital hierarchy. For these teachers, the task is often to disabuse students of the idea that they know what Shakespeare's play is about because they've read its title and, furthermore, have seen *Ten Things I Hate about You*. Thus, in "Music, Ovid, and the Renaissance Classroom in *The Taming of the Shrew*," Joseph M. Ortiz explains how he orients his class toward the study of music and education. Ortiz plays his own clarinet in the classroom to demonstrate facts about the "gamut," or scale, alluded to in the play's music-lesson scene, when Hortensio (disguised as Licio) introduces Kate's sister, Bianca, to the lute. Ortiz discusses the place Elizabethan educational theorists accorded musical training in pedagogical programs and invites his students to give one another brief lessons in things like sign language and guitar playing, so they can experience the physical dimension of learning. This dimension is crucial to the play, wherein Bianca refuses to bend her fingers to the lute and Kate learns much through (enforced) bodily suffering. Margaret Dupuis explores another facet of Elizabethan education in "'Practise Rhetoric in Your Common Talk': *The Taming of the Shrew* as an Exercise in Rhetorical Strategy." Unlike Matz, who finds in the play a "brutal" wife-training program indirectly sanctioned by "A Homily of the State of Matrimony," Dupuis points to Shakespeare's displacement of violence by rhetorical debate, whereby strategies described in Thomas Wilson's *Rhetorique* are dramatized. Dupuis demonstrates that Shakespeare showcases his knowledge of rhetorical devices by having Petruccio tame Kate through "rope-tricks" (rhetorics). These include the ploy of automatic agreement and (when Petruccio deals with the Tailor) a technique known as "shrinking."

Many of the pedagogical methods described above—that is, the methods used by modern college instructors to teach *The Taming of the Shrew*—involve students in some sort of performance exercise. The use of performance is particularly helpful for teaching this play, which is concerned with social and domestic performances and heavily invested in metatheater. It is not surprising to find brief dramatic exercises an almost ubiquitous feature of teaching this play in college classrooms, or to discover that some pedagogical programs put student performance at the center of instruction. In "What Does the Induction Do? Introducing Concepts of Action," Edward L. Rocklin proposes beginning study of *The Taming of the Shrew* by having students enact the two induction scenes, wherein Christopher Sly, a drunken tinker, is "pranked" into thinking himself a lord and the play proper is performed for his entertainment. Through performance of the induction, his students find that its scenes raise issues of transformation through game playing that the inner play of Kate, Petruccio, Lucentio, and Bianca will continue to explore. In "The Teaching of *A Shrew*: Exploring Textual Differences through Classroom Performance," Michael McClintock describes his assignment of twin performance exercises: the first, of scenes from *The Taming of the Shrew*, the second, of analogous scenes from *The Taming of a Shrew*, the play of anonymous authorship that closely resembles Shakespeare's and was printed in quarto around the time Shakespeare's *Shrew* first appeared. Avoiding questions of authorship and chronology, McClintock simply requires that his students discover, through acting, the differences between *A Shrew*'s and *The Shrew*'s main characters' motivations and draw conclusions about the meanings of each play's "taming." In "Students Stage *Shrew*! The Theater as Classroom," Cynthia Lewis recounts a semester-long Shakespeare seminar devoted to staging *The Taming of the Shrew* for an outside audience. Though Lewis is an English professor teaching an English (rather than a theater) class, she led her students through a rigorous rehearsal process. They learned that "to play a character involve[d] suspending judgment about that character" and required an actor to deliver (for example) Kate's or Petruccio's lines "wholeheartedly," whatever his or her moral reservations regarding the speech.

Teachers like Lewis often find that, even in play, male students have trouble assuming among female classmates and friends the superior attitude implied by Petruccio's falcon-taming speech (4.1), which represents Kate as a bird in training and Petruccio as her master. Two instructors risked increasing that discomfort in a theatrical exercise that required the male director of the play's last scene to share Petruccio's arrogant demeanor. In "Fifteen Women and Nick Sly, the Astrophysicist: Staging Critical Engagements with *The Taming of the Shrew*," Alice Dailey, an English professor, and Shawn Kairschner, a theater professor, describe teaching a class in which "text, criticism, and performance" were "reconstellated" to suggest "not only how the work of literary scholarship can animate dramatic production but also how acts of interpretation become dramatic content." The end event of their seminar was a performance of several scenes, enacted by women but continually interrupted by the male (student) director. Repeatedly commenting on the women's portrayal of Bianca and Kate's argument in 2.1 and Kate's final speech in 5.2, the director engaged the women of the class in a critical dispute about what was actually happening in these scenes, using dialogue borrowed "directly from the specific language of the scholarly debate." This exercise was a novel pedagogical attempt to merge techniques of performance and literary criticism while simultaneously showing how gender can condition ways of talking about this play.

Teachers of Shakespeare classes often place *The Taming of the Shrew* first on their syllabi for several reasons. First, the play is a fine instance of Shakespeare's early comedy for a Shakespeare class that presents Shakespeare's work chronologically, as many do. Second, in a course on comedy, this play introduces students to important conventions and terms, like commedia dell'arte characters and situations, farce traditions, stichomythia, romantic-comic plot devices, and an Elizabethan playwright's typical habit of adapting sources to his or her present purpose. (For *Taming*, for example, Shakespeare borrowed shamelessly from Ariosto's *I Suppositi*—mediated by its translation, George Gascoigne's 1566 *Supposes*—and possibly also from *The Taming of a Shrew.*) A third reason instructors begin with *Shrew* is that the play guarantees lively debate, which they hope will set a precedent for later discussions.

Of course, using *The Taming of the Shrew* as an early or "test" work means that—particularly in general education or introductory Shakespeare classes—students not yet used to Shakespeare will struggle with the play's language. Aware of that hurdle, several of our contributing instructors offer suggestions to inculcate close reading strategies that, when well practiced, facilitate students' encounters with Shakespeare thenceforth. In her essay for this volume, Laura Grace Godwin invites her "millennial students"—accustomed, as she says, to "variant narratives" from their experiences of "computer gaming"—to compare editions of *The Taming of the Shrew.* They look, for example, at the First Folio, wherein a stage direction tells Petruccio to exit alone in the final scene, and then at the modern Norton edition, where Petruccio is directed to leave "[*with* KATHERINE]." Inevitably, her class's close analysis of these differing texts invigorates students' discussion of editors' interpretive authority. Margaret Maurer also has students compare the First Folio version of the play to a "modern revision" (the Norton), paying particular attention to the Bianca scenes, as she explains in "Reading Bianca." Teaching a combination of close reading, historical context, and performance, Maurer leads her classes to various conclusions regarding how the differently edited scenes contribute to the play's overall theme of the "socially disruptive possibility of gentling, a process whereby a man acquires a social status higher than his father's. Gentling is seen in the Lord's experiment with Sly, and the masquerade that Lucentio undertakes to woo Bianca, with its premise that [his servant] Tranio could impersonate Lucentio, also entertains the possibility of counterfeit gentling."

Also concerned with close reading, Douglas Bruster, in "Teaching Form in *The Taming of the Shrew*," describes his use of the play to show that "meaning springs from numerous choices about style and structure." He encourages students to note how *Shrew*'s metatheatrical concern with its genre is registered in its induction—a part of the play usually omitted in performance—when "Christopher Sly presses for a definition of *comedy*." ("Is not a comonty / A Christmas gambol, or a tumbling trick?" [sc. 2, lines 132–33].) Bruster asks his classes to attend both to large questions of form, such as the question raised by the Sly induction, and to smaller inquiries. What, for example, are the differences in meaning between the titles *The Taming of a Shrew* and *The Taming of the Shrew*? What varying levels of intimacy are invoked by characters' uses of "thou" and "you" in the play? Like Bruster, and like Rocklin in his performance exercises, Jay L. Halio also focuses on the induction—a device rarely used by Shakespeare. Halio examines the duped tinker Christopher Sly's language, which grows loftier in response to his being told he's noble, just as Kate's speech grows gentler after gamesome Petruccio tells her she is gentle. Such is the power of suggestion. Of course, sharp speech is also fun for classes to examine. In "Teaching Wit: Attention to Barbed Dialogue in *The Taming of the Shrew*," Laurie Ellinghausen recounts her experience teaching students to insult one another and, eventually, reach agreements using terms drawn from Shakespeare's play. "Slow-winged turtle," "buzzard," and various amazingly dirty jokes are explicated in the process. The approach works well at Ellinghausen's institution, which enrolls many older undergraduates who "work full-time and care for children or older relatives" and who—pressed for study time—are quick to ask, "Why is this important to know?" In response, she argues the importance of a principle crucial to and enacted in this play, namely, that "language is a way to create, explore, and maintain relationships."

Comparing shrews on film, comparing play texts, initiating classroom performances, teaching about teaching, providing information about cultural and historical contexts, involving students in close reading exercises—these are the rough "gamut" of pedagogical strategies described in this book. Unlike Bianca, most undergraduates cannot claim to be "past [this] gamut long ago" (3.1.69). Our classes are often their introduction to such activities. While virtually all this volume's contributors propose strategies to make the encounter productive as well as fun, we also include a section of brief essays, "Short Takes," that focuses narrowly on in-class exercises and assignments that particular teachers have found useful. These "takes" include lists of provocative questions that probe students' opinions about domination and subordination in the play and in life (Damsen); accounts of work with food props (including dog bones and Slim Jims) in the "starvation scene" in 4.1 (Gossage); strategies to encourage textual analysis and performance of 2.1, when Kate hauls her sister onstage with a rope (Aune); suggestions for guiding students to create performance DVDs (Kisting); and a description of how information about Elizabethan scolding rituals can help contextualize four scenes in the play (Pearson). Two "Short Takes" authors comment on how instructors' or students' sex can complicate teaching and offer suggestions for addressing such complications. Grace Tiffany's essay, "What's in a Word? Teaching *Play* with the *OED*," shows that using the *Oxford English Dictionary*'s definitions of *play* to describe Kate and Petruccio's battles helps students escape conscious or unconscious gender constraints. Specifically, awareness of the play's ludic context helps men and women in Tiffany's classes shed the sense that they had better champion the play's women—since, after all, their teacher is female. Another kind of gender liberation is described in Laury Magnus's "Cross-Dressing, Comic Power Inversions, and 'Supposes':

Performing the Beginning and the End of *The Taming of the Shrew*." In Magnus's class at the United States Merchant Marine Academy, marines in training play Kate, Bianca, and Hortensio's widow with women's costumes "layered over their uniforms."

Clearly, *The Taming of the Shrew* offers a host of opportunities for spirited, often hilarious bouts between students, between instructors and students, and between all of us and the script. We engage this comedy on a range of fronts, and it always battles back. In the end, like the wrestler Orlando in *As You Like It*, the play "overthrow[s] / More than [its] enemies" (1.2.220–21). It triumphs through inspiring our interest and, usually, our affections. Looking forward to a rematch, we let it win. "'Tis a wonder, by your leave, [that we] will be tamed so" (5.2.193).

NOTES

[1] In this volume, all citations of Shakespeare plays come from *The Norton Shakespeare* (2008) unless otherwise indicated. The name of Katherine's husband is spelled Petruccio in this edition, and Hortensio's assumed persona's name is spelled Licio, so we use these spellings. Exceptions occur where the characters' names in particular productions or editions that are the subject of a contributor's pedagogical inquiry are spelled Petruchio and Litio.

[2] Unless otherwise indicated, all quotations are drawn from contributors' essays in this volume.

[3] The play, cited in Harris, is *Pageant of the Shearmen and Taylors*.

LANGUAGE AND TEXTS

Teaching Form in *The Taming of the Shrew*

Douglas Bruster

Form offers one of the most practical and rewarding ways into a literary text. Form shows us that the *what* of a literary work comes largely through its *how*, that meaning springs from numerous choices about style and structure. Each of these choices could have been made differently, producing a different text. Accordingly, there is not a single approach to form in *The Taming of the Shrew* but many. After briefly discussing an issue that complicates the play's structure, this essay describes various strategies for teaching *Shrew* through an emphasis on literary form. Most of these strategies assume a student reader who has access to an annotated copy of the play. The essay closes with a coda mentioning some useful external resources.

The Framing of The Taming of the Shrew

One of the first things readers notice about *The Taming of the Shrew* is that it begins not in Padua, with Katherine and Petruccio, but in England, with Christopher Sly and the Hostess. The play's first two scenes make up its induction. On the Elizabethan stage, inductions were a dramatic form that often used extended stage action in the here and now to ease an audience into a play's fiction. If beginning readers are baffled by the opening, they may also be puzzled when they finish the play. For the odd thing about the induction of *The Taming of the Shrew* is that its characters do not return at the end. After a practical joke is set up—a sleeping Sly is dressed as an aristocrat and persuaded he is actually a lord—the play within the play arranged for Sly's enjoyment becomes *the* play that we generally identify as *The Taming of the Shrew*. Sly and the rest of his plot are forgotten.

A related formal complication involves another play, the somewhat mysterious *Taming of a Shrew*. Published in 1594, *A Shrew* presents essentially the same plot as *The Shrew*, although with different speeches and character names. Seen by some as a source of Shakespeare's play and by others as an imitation of it, *A Shrew* is significant because it not only opens with an induction but closes by returning to these frame characters. With the practical joke over, this play's Sly is carried onstage asleep and in his own clothing. Waking, he mentions his "dream," and declares "I know now how to tame a shrew" (Miller 15.12, 16 [Oxford ed.). In this way *A Shrew* finishes more conventionally than Shakespeare's play—which ends, again, without returning to its induction characters. *A Shrew*'s frame ending can be reproduced or simply summarized for students, in part to introduce questions of closure: Why does Shakespeare's story "forget" Sly? Is this a conscious choice of the author, or should we imagine that a concluding scene has been lost? What difference would it make if *The Taming of the Shrew* returned to Sly at its end? What would be likely to happen in such a conclusion? How would the play be different?

What Does the Title Mean?

We have seen that the title of *The Taming of the Shrew*'s companion play differs in only a single word: "a" rather than "the." Because titles introduce us to literary and dramatic works, it is worth asking how they do so. After drawing students' attention to the title, a teacher could point out that it is unlike the titles of Shakespeare's other plays in that it gives us a gerund: "taming." What effect does this have? What if the play were retitled—as it later was, in one of its many adaptations—*Catharine and Petruchio*? Or *Kiss Me Kate*? *Ten Things I Hate about You*? How does each of these titles change one's expectations? Issues of gender are built into this play's battle of the sexes. Depending on the students' level of sophistication, it may be worth pointing out that, grammatically, the closest Shakespearean title to *The Taming of the Shrew* is *The Rape of Lucrece*. This poem was written only a few years after *Shrew* and tells the tragic story of a sexual assault on a legendary Roman woman and her subsequent suicide. What might the structural similarity between these two titles suggest about the roles of men and women in Shakespeare's fictional worlds? or audience members' and readers' imaginations? That is, why might Shakespeare, his acting company, or publishers have used these titles to market these works? For purposes of comparison, similar subtitles from the period include *The Spoiling of Lady Verity* (from *Somebody, Avarice, and Minister* [*c.* 1550]) and *The Untrussing of the Humorous Poet* (the subtitle of Dekker's *Satiro-mastix* [1602]).

The meaning of the word *shrew* in the title seems almost self-evident, but students are usually intrigued to know that it did not always refer to women.

Before and during Shakespeare's career, in fact, it was used also for men. Could we think of Sly—the quarrelsome commoner who begins the play by threatening the Hostess over glasses he has broken—as "the" shrew in the comedy? one of several shrews? The play's shrews might include Sly, Katherine, and Petruccio (all three of whom are loud and boisterous). In this way, the Lord's trick could be seen as no less a taming than Petruccio's taming of Kate—and, as many see it, Kate's taming of Petruccio. Students interested in following up the textual dialogue that *The Taming of the Shrew* started may consult not only *A Shrew* but also John Fletcher's *The Woman's Prize; or, The Tamer Tamed*, a comedy first staged around 1611 that continues Shakespeare's story with a difference.

A "Pleasant Comedy"

In *The Taming of the Shrew*'s induction, and as a prelude to the play within the play, Christopher Sly presses for a definition of *comedy*. "Is not a comonty / A Christmas gambol, or a tumbling trick?" he asks, or "household stuff?" (sc. 2, lines 132–33, 134). His mispronunciation of *comedy* signals his lack of sophistication, of course, and anticipates a vein of linguistic comedy that Shakespeare would work throughout his career. But the answer Sly is given—"It is a kind of history" (135)—is so general that we may be grateful to the tinker for the specifics of his guess. Comedy in the early modern era, as now, is too "big" a genre to be defined very precisely. Approaches to comedies like *Shrew* are thus usually more successful going from the text toward an idea of genre, rather than vice versa.

How does *The Taming of the Shrew* define comedy? A class session might start by gathering responses to this question and seeking out patterns. If all drama is built on conflict, what are the conflicts that motivate this play? What kinds of things happen repeatedly in *Shrew*? What kinds of things are said, and by what kinds of characters? What are the ideas they invoke, and how are these ideas contested? Students might offer that *Shrew* is interested in education (though not only, or primarily, formal education), sexual attraction, city life, money, physical and linguistic sparring, and identity. Disguise is central to its plot and serves to complicate the theme of identity as well. Like many Shakespearean comedies, there is a movement toward reconciliation (of characters who were once strangers, of male and female, and of old and young), symbolized in Lucentio's "our jarring notes agree" and Petruccio's "Nothing but sit, and sit, and eat, and eat" before the concluding banquet (5.2.1, 12). Like many Shakespearean comedies, this reconciliation is not without its own "jarring notes," for, however it functioned or may have been meant to function originally, Katherine's final speech has proved problematic over time and at the very least highlights the differences that remain in the marriages of Bianca and Lucentio, on the one hand, and the Widow and Hortensio, on the other.

Comedy has long centered on the pursuit of happiness. But how that happiness is pursued and attained differs from play to play. An approach to the issue of comedy in *Shrew* might ask students to identify what each character seems to want, whether she or he gets it, and under what conditions any desires are (or are not) fulfilled. In this way Sly's original query about what comedy *is* becomes one of the most consequential questions in the play.

Working with the materials in *The Taming of the Shrew* itself eventually leads readers to the play's dependence on a kind of theater called commedia dell'arte. This Italian phrase translates as "comedy of art" or, more loosely, "practical comedy." It describes a largely improvisational form of theater featuring such stock characters as the young lovers, the braggart captain, and old men who stand in the way of love. One of these older characters is Pantaloon (the Italian Pantalone), a miserly busybody who typically lusts after, and pursues, the attractive young female love interest. Gremio is described as "*a pantaloon*" in the stage direction that accompanies his first entrance (1.1.47sd), which shows us that Shakespeare had some knowledge of the commedia dell'arte. This genre of sexy, practical comedy—it is almost invariably contrasted with the Italian commedia erudita, or learned, "university" comedy—appears to have had a strong influence on Shakespeare's *Shrew*.

Language: Verse and Prose, "You" and "Thou"

The language of Shakespeare's plays divides into verse and prose. There is a further distinction between rhymed verse and blank verse ("blank" because unrhymed), and most plays feature shorter excerpts of verse and prose in various forms. In *Shrew* this includes the quoted Latin of Lucentio/Cambio's school lesson (3.1.28–56), Hortensio/Licio's musical poem (3.1.71–76), Petruccio's ballads (4.1.121–22, 126–27), and the Tailor's "note of the fashion" for Katherine's gown (4.3.127–40).

Although Shakespeare's language can be introduced technically in the classroom, with dry schematics of syllables, feet, stresses, and pauses, perhaps a more engaging way into the topic is to start with the basic *bilingual* structure of his dramas. Like his fellow playwrights in Elizabethan England, Shakespeare tended to "hear" the lower orders of society speaking prose, and those from the middle and upper levels of society speaking verse. Because many students come from households that are multilingual, they tend to grasp the idea of verse and prose representing different languages that are appropriate to and valued differently in various situations. Stimulating discussion usually arises when students are canvassed for personal accounts of how multiple languages work in their families—when and by whom particular languages are used, for instance, and what conditions lead speakers to switch from language to language.

Verse and prose worked like different languages for Shakespeare. He adapted this bilingual system from other playwrights and used it throughout his career. Verse speakers can and do "cross over" into prose in certain situations, but verse remains their dominant language. Prose speakers sometimes speak or sing verse, but usually not verse as elegant as the aristocrats. If we could imagine

Shakespeare following a list of "rules" for his speakers—a set of conditions, that is, that he probably did not have to stop and think twice about—we might represent them as follows. Verse is spoken by characters of higher rank and educated characters in matters that are serious, formal, ceremonial, that have to do with sentiment. It is typically used for speech that has or is connected to proper English, decorum, sobriety, and sanity. Verse typically brings a useful tension to the drama and is the controlling language of tragedy. Prose, in contrast, is spoken by characters of middle and lower rank in matters that are playful, informal, commercial. It is the sphere of slang and nonstandard English and is used for satire, criticism, and overt sexual joking, as well as by characters that are drunk or insane. Prose is the language of relaxation (in contrast to verse's tension) and is the major language of comedy.

This general dichotomy should not obscure the fact that Shakespeare can and does say almost anything in either verse or prose, as he chooses. The template drawn here is meant only to suggest *tendencies*. For instance, if a scene is to feature servants, Shakespeare is likely to write prose for it: thus when 4.1 opens at Petruccio's house, Grumio speaks in prose to Curtis (and receives prose in return). But when Petruccio enters speaking verse at line 101, Grumio immediately switches "languages," uttering the verse line "Here, sir, as foolish as I was before" (109).

Blank verse, as in the preceding line, was unrhymed iambic pentameter. Blank verse lines tended to have five "feet" of two syllables each (for a total of ten syllables) and alternated unstressed and stressed syllables. Shakespeare has his Lord engage in the kind of regular, sweet blank verse that Christopher Marlowe had brought to London's stages when the Lord says to an astonished Sly: "Thy hounds shall make the welkin answer them / And fetch shrill echoes from the hollow earth" (induction, sc. 2, lines 43–44). Sly, who has spoken only prose to this point, is eventually persuaded that he is indeed a lord himself. We can appreciate Shakespeare's sly joke when he has his tinker launch into blank verse that (like his question about "comonty") shows that he is not a natural resident of this sphere:

> Am I a lord, and have I such a lady?
> Or do I dream? Or have I dreamed till now?
> I do not sleep. I see, I hear, I speak.
> I smell sweet savours, and I feel soft things.
> Upon my life, I am a lord indeed,
> And not a tinker, nor Christopher Sly.
> (induction, sc. 2, lines 66–71)

Like an infant taking its first steps, or a student of a foreign language constructing short and manageable utterances in a difficult tongue, Sly gives us blank verse that is much less smooth than the Lord's: "I do not sleep. I see, I hear, I speak. / I smell sweet savours, and I feel soft things." In its halting monosyllables, this blank verse is almost prose and thus helps confirm a point of the Lord's practical joke: a beggar taken off the street remains a beggar even when clothed as a lord and speaking the tongue of the aristocracy.

This formal division between "higher" and "lower" in *The Taming of the Shrew* can also be seen in Shakespeare's use of "you" and "thou." Like many European languages, early modern English used pronouns differently depending on the social status and emotions of its speakers. "You" is the more polite, plural form, and is generally used by characters toward those above them. "Thou" is the more informal, familiar form, and is generally used by characters toward those below them, or with whom they are intimate. What sounds simple in this description is of course anything but simple in the fictional worlds Shakespeare creates, since a host of factors (including family status and emotional states like anger and love) can influence whether his characters "choose" to say "you" or "thou" in particular situations. Following the French pronouns *tu* and *vous*, linguists tend to use the letters *t* and *v* to represent the "thou" (including "thou," "thee," "thy," "thine" and "pri*thee*") and "you" ("you," "your," "yours," "ye") system. Rewarding time can be spent tracking these pronouns as characters use them in *The Taming of the Shrew*. Particularly interesting, in this respect, is Petruccio and Katherine's initial encounter (2.1.180–324). In her study of the *you-thou* (*t/v*) system in Shakespeare's plays, Penelope Freedman devotes substantial attention to this scene and sheds light on "the changing tactics in Petruccio's campaign" for Katherine (42; see also 41–52). A useful teaching exercise is to map the uses of "you" and "thou" in this scene. This can be extended to constructing a diagram of the *you-thou* (*t/v*) system in the play; my class uses boxes to represent the various characters and lines and arrows to represent where "you" and "thou" are addressed to and received from others. Students may notice that the resulting map is both social and emotional in nature and that these relations change over the course of the play.

Roles in Shrew

The Taming of the Shrew features many disguises. Some of these are literal, such as those assumed by Sly, Bartholomew, Lucentio, Hortensio, Tranio, and the Pedant. Others are more figurative and leave us guessing: Is Petruccio really the bully he plays? Is Katherine actually "tamed" and subservient at the end of the play? Or might she be performing the picture of the obedient wife, just as she placates Petruccio by calling the sun the moon and old Vincentio a "Young budding virgin, fair, and fresh, and sweet" on their return to Padua (4.6.1–42)?

Shakespeare was fond of performing performance—that is, of showing life's theatrical textures within his pieces for the theater. One of the energizing forces behind his imagination was the *theatrum mundi* metaphor. Drawn from the Latin for "theater of the world," this idea was a two-way street for Shakespeare: theaters like the Globe playhouse represented the world, and the world they represented was itself deeply theatrical. Life is a kind of play, with all of us acting our parts.

In Shakespeare's theater, actors were given roles *as* roles—that is, as pasted-together strips of paper containing mainly their lines plus a few cue words from the speeches immediately preceding their own. Our word *role*, in fact, comes from the French *rôle*, which referred to these actors' parts. We are used to getting Shakespeare's plays whole: when not in a collected-works edition, in single-play volumes that contain all the speeches in order. None of Shakespeare's fellow actors would have had this luxury. Before their first rehearsal, they would have learned their parts from their individual paper roles. They would have seen how their characters fit together with others largely during their first rehearsal.

How does *The Taming of the Shrew* look when studied through its individual roles? The play's basis in commedia dell'arte makes its presentation of "typed" characters particularly interesting. Students can be challenged to select particular parts—picking from among male and female, servants and masters, important and functionary characters—to study *as* roles. This can be done as a group activity or as an outside assignment. *The Taming of the Shrew* can be accessed as an electronic text online and the relevant role saved as a separate file. (If desired, three or four "cue" words preceding each speech can be made part of this role.) Given only the words on this page, what can be determined about the character who speaks them? Does she or he use particular kinds of sentences (e.g., questions, statements, interjections) more than others? Does the character speak long speeches or short ones? What kinds of nouns, verbs, adjectives, and adverbs does she or he tend to use? Are there any particular metaphors or images that recur in this character's speech? Do any of these things change noticeably at any time during the play? If so, what might account for those changes? Instructors should note that although the roles of Katherine and Petruccio seem most rewarding in relation to such an exercise, they are also comparatively long: 584 and 219 lines, respectively (Spevack 1: 957–1014). Some of the shorter roles—such as Bianca (70), Baptista (174), Sly (65), Grumio (183), and Gremio (169)—are complex and more manageable.

Further Reading

This essay has stressed reading form in *The Taming of the Shrew* from inside out, rather than reading form that begins with templates that might constrict students' attention to what is in the play itself. Yet in many situations students as well as instructors will benefit from outside resources. Scholarship on the question of form in Shakespearean drama is overwhelming, and only a few of the many valuable resources can be mentioned here. A useful handbook is David Crystal and Ben Crystal, *Shakespeare's Words: A Glossary and Language Companion*. The major issues involved in the bilingual system of verse and prose are set out in Douglas Bruster. For a good introduction to the workings of genre during this period, see Stephen Orgel, "Shakespeare and the Kinds of Drama." On the commedia dell'arte, see Kenneth Richards and Laura Richards. On language games in early modern comedy, readers may consult Keir Elam. The *you-thou* distinction is explored in Freedman's *Power and Passion in Shakespeare's Pronouns*. For roles, see Simon Palfrey and Tiffany Stern's *Shakespeare in Parts*. The best modern edition of *The Taming of a Shrew* (the companion play to Shakespeare's) is Miller's The Taming of a Shrew*: The 1594 Quarto*; the best edition of Fletcher's *The Tamer Tamed; or, The Woman's Prize* is that of Celia R. Daileader and Gary Taylor. Each of these editions features an introduction and detailed notes.

A Puzzle for Students: Is Shakespeare's Shrew Tamed or Unmasked?

Jay L. Halio

A good question to put to students of Shakespeare's *The Taming of the Shrew* asks whether Katherine really is a shrew or not: at the end of the play, does she become tamed under Petruccio's discipline or does she reveal her true self? Although Shakespeare's title proclaims that she is tamed, what evidence can you find in the play as it has come down to us that she is not? In this age, the view that she is tamed at the end is highly problematic, and students tend to be divided—not only along gender lines—over the question of whether Shakespeare is, after all, a patriarchal male chauvinist or something else. Solving this puzzle requires close scrutiny of the text, which can provide clues to whether Katherine is feigning what she has come to believe herself or whether she is truly the tamed woman Petruccio claims she is, his hyperboles notwithstanding.

The first clue lies in the induction, which, unfortunately, many recent productions omit. It highlights role playing and thus indicates what the main action of Shakespeare's play is really all about. In it, Christopher Sly is made to believe that he is not the sot he appears to be but is, rather, the lord of a manor, complete with a loving wife, servants, rings on his fingers, beautiful clothes, and everything else pertaining to higher status in society. This trick is played on him by a real lord, whose servants are ordered to persuade Sly that he has been lunatic, that his real self is what it now seems, not what he thought it was.

The Lord's servants and the Lord's page, impersonating Sly's wife, convince Sly exactly as the lord wished.[1] When Sly awakens and sees what has happened to him, he at first thinks he is mad, but eventually he comes to believe that what the others around him are saying is true. The Lord says: "Thou art a lord, and nothing but a lord. / Thou hast a lady far more beautiful / Than any woman in this waning age" (induction, sc. 2, lines 59–61). Sly's response indicates his initial doubt: "Am I a lord, and have I such a lady? / Or do I dream? Or have I dreamed till now?" (66–67). Which view is reality, and which a dream or illusion? This conflict between reality and appearance (as often in Shakespeare) poses the central issue in the play that follows. Is it to foreground this conflict that the skit is presented before Sly by the players who arrive at the Lord's mansion and are enlisted to entertain Sly and the rest?[2] Compare Graham Holderness's comment: "The Induction in the Folio text alone establishes a theatrical perspective in which the action of the play is illuminated, by stimulating in the audience an invigorated skeptical consciousness" (*Shakespeare* 7). Students should ponder this "invigorated skeptical consciousness" as something essential to a clearer understanding of what Shakespeare does in *The Taming of the Shrew*.

A related approach is to ask students to consider a well-known psychological phenomenon that they may have experienced or witnessed themselves: when people are told over and over again they are such and such, they eventually come to believe it. Katherine is repeatedly told by everyone around her, including her father, that she is a shrew.[3] She is introduced in exactly that way. Hortensio and others proclaim that she is "too rough" (1.1.55), a "devil" (66), "stark mad and wonderful froward" (69), a "fiend of hell" (88), and her actions and language immediately demonstrate that she seems indeed to be just what they say.

Petruccio is not put off by Kate's rough behavior. When he meets Kate he shows that he is up to the worst that she can throw at him and will not only survive but also overcome. The question is, What does he overcome? Is it perhaps not a question of overcoming but of revealing what lies behind her seeming?

Before going further let us digress briefly to recall the aspects of deception and illusion first presented in the induction and then developed in less elaborate fashion in act 1, scene 1. No sooner does Lucentio catch a glimpse of Bianca than he falls head over heels in love with her. But how does Lucentio go about winning Bianca? To gain surreptitious access to her, he decides to trade places with his servant Tranio. They change clothes so that Tranio appears to be the son of old Vincentio, and Lucentio appears as his servant. Through this deception Lucentio becomes Bianca's tutor, thus enabling him eventually to have private conference with her. Hortensio meanwhile also engages in deception for the same purpose, disguising himself as Bianca's music teacher. In these ways Shakespeare introduces another play within the play.

Now to Petruccio's first confrontation with Katherine. Is his initial tactic reverse psychology? While everyone refers to Katherine as a shrew, Petruccio calls her by different names. He announces his strategy in his soliloquy at 2.1.166–79 and then addresses Katherine as Kate. When she corrects him, he insists:

> You lie, in faith, for you are called plain Kate,
> And bonny Kate, and sometimes Kate the curst,
> But Kate, the prettiest Kate in Christendom,
> Kate of Kate Hall, my super-dainty Kate—
> For dainties are all cates, and therefore "Kate". . .
> Myself am moved to woo thee for my wife. (183–92)

Kate is not nearly as "moved" as Petruccio claims he is. She is not moved at all, in fact. Or so it seems. What follows is rapid stichomythia in which they trade witticisms, ending with Petruccio's bawdy pun—"What with my tongue in your tail?" (214)—and Katherine striking him.[4] By no means put off by the blow, Petruccio warns her that if she strikes him again, he'll cuff her, and the witty stichomythia resumes, until Katherine apparently tires of it all and tries to leave. But Petruccio refuses to let her go, saying, "I find you passing gentle. / 'Twas told me you were rough, and coy, and sullen, / And now I find report a very liar . . ." (235–37).

Is Petruccio kidding? Is he trying to motivate an alternative behavior by describing it? Or does he perceive a gentle Kate beneath the enacted shrew?

After a few more lines of dialogue, Petruccio tells Katherine that her father has consented to their union: “And will you, nill you, I will marry you” (263). As Baptista and others enter, he continues: “For I am he am born to tame you, Kate, / And bring you from a wild Kate to a Kate / Conformable as other household Kates” (268–70).[5] Katherine’s reaction to all this is predictable. She tells her father that Petruccio is “half-lunatic” and “[a] madcap ruffian” (279, 280). But again, Petruccio is not put off by what she says. On the contrary, he persists in his strategy, even now before Baptista:

> Father, ’tis thus: yourself and all the world
> That talked of her have talked amiss of her.
> If she be curst, it is for policy,
> For she’s not froward, but modest as the dove.
> She is not hot, but temperate as the morn.
> For patience she will prove a second Grissel,
> And Roman Lucrece for her chastity.
> And to conclude, we have ’greed so well together
> That upon Sunday is the wedding day. (282–90)

How much does Petruccio exaggerate? A lot, it appears. Or perhaps he detects something about Katherine’s behavior that may be true, at least in part: that is, her “curst” behavior is but “for policy.” In a way, they actually have gotten on well together, not in the usual sense, but their witty repartee suggests that after a certain fashion they are compatible. Are they two birds of a feather, performing rough behavior for reasons of their own?

Petruccio continues:

> Be patient, gentlemen. I choose her for myself.
> If she and I be pleased, what’s that to you?
> ’Tis bargained ’twixt us twain, being alone,
> That she shall still be curst in company.
> I tell you, ’tis incredible to believe
> How much she loves me. O, the kindest Kate!
> She hung about my neck, and kiss on kiss
> She vied so fast, protesting oath on oath,
> That in a twink she won me to her love. (294–302)

To all this, what does Katherine say? Nothing. Just how significant is her silence here? Before Petruccio leaves, he tells Katherine to kiss him, promising that they will be married “o’ Sunday” (316). Again, what does Katherine say? Does she kiss him? Does she take Petruccio’s hand as he asks her? The original stage directions do not tell us. Whatever modern editors interpolate, the Folio text simply states “*Exit Petruchio and Katherine.*”

When act 3, scene 2 opens, Katherine, in the company of her father and sister and others, awaits the arrival of Petruccio on the day of their marriage. When Petruccio finally does show up, his appearance astonishes everyone. Outlandish as he appears, his behavior is even worse and marks the next phase of his "taming" of Katherine. He rejects the pleas of Baptista and Tranio to change into more presentable clothes—"To me she's married, not unto my clothes," he cries (3.2.110). Shortly afterward, Gremio enters and describes what happened at the church where Petruccio and Katherine have been married.[6] Gremio calls Petruccio "a devil, a devil, a very fiend" (3.3.28), to which Tranio responds, "Why, she's a devil, a devil, the devil's dam." But Gremio rejects that and says: "Tut, she's a lamb, a dove, a fool to him" (30). Is this the first explicit indication by someone other than Petruccio that Katherine may not be all that she has seemed?

Petruccio's outrageous performance in this scene surpasses Kate's own. He has knocked the priest down, caroused heavily with wine, and delivered Kate a kiss "with such a clamorous smack / That at the parting all the church did echo" (51–52). As if that were not bad enough, when the bride and bridegroom enter with the wedding guests, Petruccio refuses to stay for the banquet. When Katherine pleads, "Now if you love me, stay," Petruccio ignores her and orders Grumio to fetch his horse. Katherine then reverts to her shrewish persona, but to no avail. Petruccio carries her off with Grumio—forcibly or otherwise, the Folio stage directions do not indicate. Baptista concludes the scene by asking Lucentio (actually Tranio still in disguise) to take the bridegroom's place at the wedding feast; and, perhaps more significantly as things turn out, he tells Bianca to take her sister's place (120–21).

Time passes. Petruccio, Kate, and Grumio wend their tortured way to Petruccio's country house, some distance from Padua. Act 4 opens with Grumio's complaint about the difficult trip, the cold, and "all mad masters" (4.1.1). When Curtis, one of Petruccio's household servants, asks if his master is coming with his wife and if she is "so hot a shrew as she's reported" (17), Grumio replies: "She was, good Curtis, before this frost; but thou know'st, winter tames man, woman, and beast, for it hath tamed my old master, and my new mistress, and myself, too, fellow Curtis" (18–21). But if winter's "taming" is temporary, what about the struggles Katherine has endured on the trip? Are they just a harbinger of what she will endure when she and Petruccio finally arrive at the house? Curtis comments sharply on what Katherine and Grumio have already suffered at Petruccio's hands: "By this reckoning he is more shrew than she" (70).

Curtis is right. But doesn't the insight he articulates here sound like something new to him, as it will be to the rest of the household staff? By behaving more shrewishly than Katherine, not only to her but to all his servants, is Petruccio holding a mirror up to his wife, showing her how bad her behavior has been? In fact, he outdoes her both in language and action, scolding and beating Grumio and ordering the others about rudely. When supper is served at last, he severely criticizes the cooking, does not let Katherine eat it, and apparently throws everything off the table.[7] Whenever Katherine tries to intercede on the servants' behalf and calm him down, Petruccio lashes out all the more violently and takes her, hungry, up to bed. As Peter comments, "He kills her in her own humour" (160).

From Curtis we next learn that Petruccio has been

> Making a sermon of continency to her,
> And rails, and swears, and rates, that she, poor soul,
> Knows not which way to stand, to look, to speak,
> *And sits as one new risen from a dream.* (163–66; emphasis added)

Like Christopher Sly in the induction, Katherine is no longer sure what is reality and what is a dream. Does Petruccio's exaggerated reflection of her shrewishness awaken her to an awareness of her real self? If so, the awareness is fresh, and Katherine still has to reckon with it before she can entirely shed her former persona.

Less subtle instances of role-play characterize the action back in Padua, where Tranio (as Lucentio) and Hortensio (as Licio, the musician) observe Lucentio (as Cambio) courting Bianca. Tranio pretends to be disgusted by Bianca's supposed fickleness. So is Hortensio, who then is moved to reveal his true identity—the first of several unmaskings that occur in the last two acts of the play. Tranio pretends to follow his lead, likewise forswearing his love for Bianca, but he does not yet reveal his true identity. Actually, after Hortensio leaves, declaring he will wed a wealthy widow, Tranio and Lucentio contrive a further deception they feel is necessary before Bianca may be won. Acting on Biondello's discovery, they persuade a merchant traveler to assume the role of Lucentio's father in order to persuade Baptista that it is all right for Lucentio and Bianca to marry (4.2.60–122).

Petruccio continues his harsh treatment of Katherine, who complains to Grumio, "The more my wrong, the more his spite appears" (4.3.2). Kate shows some spirit in the dialogue with the Haberdasher, but when the Tailor shows the gown he has made for her and Petruccio and Grumio disparage it roughly, she remains mostly silent. At the end of the scene, in the most polite terms she can muster, she corrects Petruccio's assertion that it is nearly seven o'clock but again reverts to silence when Petruccio reminds her how dangerous it is to cross him (185–89). Has Katherine begun to mend her ways, as she ultimately does on the road back to Padua? Why else does she declare that the sun is the moon and vice versa and declare that whatever Petruccio says it is "[a]nd so it shall be still for Katherine" (4.6.23)?

Is Katherine by this time onto Petruccio's game, having learned how to play it along with him? Note how she reacts when they encounter the true Vincentio, and compare C. C. Seronsy's statement:

> The field is now won for Petruchio. . . . It may not be altogether fanciful to see an allusion to Katharina's gradually-won perception of things, her

> buoyant self-discovery, in the line "That everything I look on seemeth green." In this final encounter, she enjoys more than a half-share of the honors as the two of them enter into full partnership. (23)

Consider also the way that the rest of the play is taken up with further revelations and their thematic implications. Vincentio encounters his impersonator and unmasks him, though not without some difficulty. Lucentio appears as himself, secretly wed to Bianca, and receives his father's blessing as well as Baptista's. Petruccio asks Katherine to kiss him in the street, and, after a brief demurrer, she does, calling him "love" and apparently meaning it (5.1.123–28). But the greatest example is, of course, her famous long speech in the last scene. There, before all the assembled company at the banquet, where Bianca and Hortensio's widow show *their* true selves, she lectures them on the wifely virtues. The lecture may be a game, as some believe, played to help Petruccio win his bet, but recall that Katherine is unaware of the wager. Or is it more likely that the lecture is delivered to show everyone that she has learned what is necessary for a happy marriage and conforms accordingly? Though at the end of her speech she offers to place her hands beneath her husband's foot as a sign of duty, Petruccio does not demand that show of submission. Instead, he says, "Why, there's a wench! Come on, and kiss me, Kate" (5.2.184). She does, this time without a moment's hesitation. They are truly and safely married.

As Petruccio and Katherine depart for bed, Hortensio comments: "Now go thy ways, thou hast tamed a curst shrew," and Lucentio adds: " 'Tis a wonder, by your leave, she will be tamed so" (192–93). But is she "tamed" or "unmasked"? Or, to place all the foregoing in a different perspective, has Katherine at the end simply assumed a new persona? Whatever the case, Petruccio seems pleased with his newly won Kate, and so, it seems, is everyone else—on the stage, though perhaps not in the audience.

NOTES

[1] As Seronsy says, the Lord's technique is essentially Petruccio's, as shown later in the play proper (26).

[2] For a fuller discussion of the importance of the induction, see Seronsy 25–28; compare with Halio.

[3] The actress Fiona Shaw has said, "After a while, when people are calling you a shrew, you start living the name. . . . So by the time we meet [Kate] she is somebody whose identity is linked to her behavior" (qtd. in Rutter [1989] 8).

[4] This stage direction is in the Folio text.

[5] Seronsy says: "Petruchio's method is to suppose (and he is correct) or assume qualities in Katharina that no one else, possibly even the shrew herself, ever suspects. What he assumes as apparently false turns out to be startlingly true. His 'treatment' is a steady unfolding of her really fine qualities: patience, practical good sense, a capacity for humor, and finally obedience, all of which she comes gradually to manifest in a spirit chastened but not subdued" (19). Although Seronsy and I basically agree, including about the

importance of the induction, our arguments, like the details of evidence we cite and analyze, differ in a number of respects.

6 Although the scene that Gremio describes is sometimes enacted in modern productions, as in Zeffirelli's film, none of the holy sacraments were permitted to be presented on Shakespeare's stage.

7 This is the way it is usually enacted, following the stage directions inserted by modern editors, and because of the implications of Petruccio's statement at line 145.

Teaching Wit: Attention to Barbed Dialogue in *The Taming of the Shrew*

Laurie Ellinghausen

> 'Tis not the trial of a woman's war,
> The bitter clamour of two eager tongues,
> Can arbitrate this cause betwixt us twain.

In this passage from *Richard II* (1.1.48–50), the aggrieved Lord Thomas Mowbray prepares to duel with his adversary, Henry Bolingbroke, in order to resolve a cycle of mutual defamation. Mowbray disdains the exchange of harsh words between "two eager tongues" as a "woman's" way of fighting, implying that only action can "arbitrate this cause" in a manner befitting men. Words created the dispute in the first place, and, with King Richard's encouragement, Mowbray and Bolingbroke will spend the rest of the scene and the first hundred lines of the actual duel in 1.3 doing exactly what Mowbray deems beneath them: trading insults, taunts, and accusations. More ironically still, no duel actually comes to pass because, at the last minute, Richard banishes both men from England. Despite the expressed contempt for words as a "woman's" way to fight, words begin the conflict among men, intensify it, and bring it to a close through Richard's pronouncement of exile. Here and throughout Shakespeare's plays, words play a major role in the creation and transformation of human relationships. Moreover, they measure and affect an individual subject's relation to larger communities. If the primacy of words is evident in the masculine military context of the history plays, it becomes even more so in the feminized spheres of household and marriage, where women exert agency through their power of speech. Verbal sparring is of particular interest in Shakespearean comedy in the relations between the sexes.

In Shakespearean drama, words *do* things as well as *mean* things. This fact presents a major challenge to modern students. Students spend so much time struggling to extract basic meaning from unfamiliar diction that many cannot begin to fathom the nuances of the words. I bring this challenge out into the open on the first day of my Shakespeare survey class, when I ask my students to reflect on this question: Why is Shakespeare generally considered a "great" or "important" writer? Inevitably, students will answer, "the language." Yet they also will acknowledge that this same language makes Shakespeare's works extremely daunting. Their frustration is compounded by a tendency—not always discouraged by teachers of literature—to approach texts as abstruse puzzles reducible to a single "meaning" that requires a PhD to access with certainty. To counter students' feelings of intimidation, I structure the course in a way that encourages them to see language not as a repository of some singular, elusive "answer" but as a theatrical form of play that has the potential to engage audiences beyond Elizabethan England. This method calls for a shift from viewing the text as closed artifact to viewing it as a flexible, responsive piece of art. The text's language becomes a blueprint for creative interpretation, not only for the play's audience of readers but also for the characters, who find themselves negotiating social rules. *The Taming of the Shrew* is an ideal play for showing students that language is a way to create, explore, and maintain relationships—in this case, a marriage between two headstrong individuals. Here I will detail how *Shrew* can be used to increase students' comfort with Shakespeare's language by helping students see the things words can do between people as well as the things words can "mean" to the individual reader.[1]

A few details about my institution and the course I teach will support my rationale for this approach. The University of Missouri, Kansas City, serves students from a range of ethnic, regional, and socioeconomic backgrounds, most of whom commute from off campus. The average undergraduate student's age is twenty-eight. Many of them work full-time and care for children or older relatives. These students make my teaching particularly rewarding because they expect value for their investment, in terms of both their expectations of faculty members and their expectations of themselves. Students commonly ask, Why is this important to know? or, What will I get out of this assignment? I answer by asking them to reflect on the centrality of language and performance in their lives, particularly with respect to personal and professional communication, and to watch for how Shakespeare illuminates the role of words in negotiating relationships. In teaching the exercises described below, I remain conscious of the need to clearly articulate the rewards of studying Shakespeare, both in terms of its intellectual payoff and in terms of students' career and life goals.

The course covers all four dramatic genres and is required of all English, English secondary-education, and theater majors. The diversity of majors in a typical classroom requires me to teach in a way that does not take Shakespeare's "greatness" for granted—in fact, some students put off taking the course for as long as possible, expecting a belletristic exercise in someone else's idea of "greatness." Yet while I know it is important to examine the plays' literary value, I also strive to present the works in a way that illuminates their appeal for future actors, teachers, creative writers, and literature majors, as well as general readers whose main interests reside in other disciplines. This broad approach also takes into account the students' wide range of previous Shakespeare experience. Some have taken courses with me already, others have transferred from different institutions, and some have managed to avoid Shakespeare even in high school.

While recognizing the distinct limits of a "one size fits all" approach, I identify *The Taming of the Shrew* as a play that can grab students' interest early in the course. Students can easily relate this play to cultural texts familiar to them, namely romantic comedies, where fractious battles of wit between heroes and heroines evolve into explicit mutual attraction. In this genre, what is superficially *unexpected*—two avowed enemies gradually discovering feelings for each other—creates the comedy, where surprises happen within the bounds of generic convention. Barbed dialogue between the hero and heroine intensifies the contrast between their initial relationship and its ultimate outcome—a figural and sometimes literal marriage of souls. To borrow a set of terms from Stephen Greenblatt, the initial "friction" between the two lovers creates the "fiction" of their desire ("Fiction").

Furthermore, the witty sparring between Shakespearean lovers puts pressure on early modern gender hierarchies by casting the woman as an equal player in the verbal game. During the exchange of insult and innuendo, we see early modern women—routinely advised by conduct literature to be "chaste, silent, and obedient"—discover a degree of power and agency that allows them to craft their relationships with men. Throughout the semester, students notice that Shakespeare's comedies tend to display intelligent, strong, multidimensional women. The comic heroines' facility with witty dialogue makes their complex personalities a source of delight for audiences.

I typically approach a three-day session on *The Taming of the Shrew* by focusing on the following components: the theatrical potency of language, women and marriage in historical context, and a close reading of Katherine and Petruccio's initial meeting. I always allow for the possibility that any one of these topics may arise organically from the others. Before examining the play, however, I spend at least one session (usually our second class day) introducing students to the idea of language as play for the *sake* of play. I assign a selection of Shakespeare's sonnets that will allow us to explore this notion through small, fourteen-line compositions. When we analyze sonnet 20, for example, students typically are divided evenly on whether the speaker's "master-mistress" (line 2) is a man or a woman. While Walter Cohen's introduction to the sonnets treats the addressee as a male "youth" (1919), in class we treat the addressee's gender only as a possibility and, through our own discussion, arrive at the conclusion that the sonnet's only real "intention" is cleverly to unsettle the reader's preconceptions about gender and desire. Through such riddling, Shakespeare teases readers by drawing on the compelling ambiguity of the addressee's beauty while also invoking the distinct conventions of the female "beloved" of the traditional sonnet and the practice of using male actors to portray women onstage. In a similar vein, sonnet 135 demonstrates the delight achieved by punning, where Shakespeare, in apparent allusions to himself, uses the word "will" and its variants fourteen times in as many lines. When we acknowledge a multiplicity of meanings—both early modern and contemporary—for this word, we see that the sonnet generates different meanings with its various uses of this one word and that this is, indeed, the "point" of it.

After working with the sonnets, we turn to *The Taming of the Shrew*. I start by eliciting students' general reactions to the play through a five-minute freewriting exercise and a brief ensuing discussion. Their responses tend to replicate the play's controversial production history, during which directors have offered wholly "tamed" and persistently "untamed" Kates. Some students express revulsion at the palpable misogyny of the male characters, while others see the play's potential for a sympathetic, perhaps even transgressive, exploration of Katherine's dilemma. At this point, students are eager to learn more about early modern ideologies of gender as they related to girls and women. Drawing on the work of Sara Mendelson and Patricia Crawford, I offer a model of a typical woman's "life stages" in three parts: childhood (a girl bound to her father), service (a young woman bound to a master, mistress, or well-connected relatives), and marriage (a woman bound to her husband) (75–148). As one would expect, the patriarchal "chaste, silent, and obedient" dictum sounds repressive to most modern students, but I do not let them rest with the idea that women were "powerless" in the period, at least not in the terms that modern readers recognize. Rather, I stress that women could and did exert power. This is not only true in the obvious case of Queen Elizabeth I. Across social classes women exerted agency in the domains of household, relationships, and community. In these spheres, women relied heavily on the power of conversation, gossip, or persuasion—in other words, their power of effective speech. A play like *The Merry Wives of Windsor* makes women's capacity for agency particularly visible, as Mistresses Ford and Page combine clever verbal persuasion with their intimate knowledge of the local community to give the lusty Falstaff his comeuppance and prove that "[w]ives may be merry, and yet honest, too" (4.2.89).[2] The primacy of women's words in Shakespearean comedy becomes a basis for understanding the importance of artful talk in the negotiation of relationships between characters.

A consideration of the play's Elizabethan theatrical context further builds students' sense of the importance of verbal exchange. I ask students to consider a world without digital imaging, recorded sound, camera close-ups, and elaborate machinery. What is left to create the pleasurable forms of illusion on which entertainment relies? The answer, of course, is the auditory effects of words, particularly when we take into account the large numbers of players and audience members who could not read and write. I offer further support for the primacy of spoken words by describing the period as one heavily invested in magic, spells, and witchcraft, where words were commonly imagined to affect material reality. Many students come to the course already familiar with *Macbeth*, a play rife with magical utterances that exert far-reaching effects on the characters. Moreover, as anyone who has spent time on a playground knows, words can hurt at least as much as "sticks and stones"—witness their impact in *Much Ado about Nothing*, where Hero worries that her cousin Beatrice will "mock me into air . . . laugh me / Out of myself, press me to death with wit" (3.1.75–76). A sharp wit like Beatrice can not only sting her victim in the moment but also bring the victim "out of [her]self," shaking the very foundations of her self-knowledge.

These observations become more meaningful to students through practical application. The Folger Shakespeare Library's excellent *Shakespeare Set Free: Teaching* A Midsummer Night's Dream, Romeo and Juliet, *and* Macbeth

(O'Brian) contains an exercise that helps students test how the language of insult can escalate friction between characters (123–25). The lesson asks students to examine the "Shakespeare Insult Kit," which features three columns of nouns and adjectives from the plays and invites readers to construct their own three-pronged insults (with "thou" placed in front for emphasis) like "thou craven hell-hated lewdster" and "thou vain onion-eyed lout."[3] Then the lesson directs instructors to divide the students into two feuding groups ("Capulets" and "Montagues"), who shout their newly created insults at each other, demonstrating the way verbal volleying builds tension between rival factions.[4] If I am concerned about the impact of noise on neighboring classrooms, I will modify this approach by simply asking select students to share their insults. These invitations naturally lend themselves to a game of one-upmanship, where each insult is funnier than the last. The lesson suggests letting students look up their words in the *Oxford English Dictionary* (*OED*). However, I prefer to let students ponder what makes an insult merely "sound funny." Just as one can still, on some level, follow a Shakespearean performance without knowing every single word, these insults do not need to be defined explicitly to do much of their rhetorical work. Alliterative insults seem to provoke the most laughter—for example, "thou currish crook-pated clack-dish" or "thou fawning flap-mouthed foot-licker." The anonymous snark on today's gossip blogs sounds remarkably uninventive by comparison.

By the time we start a close reading of the play, the "insult kit" exercise has given students a new perspective from which to examine the wordplay between Katherine and Petruccio. Of particular interest is the rapid-fire stichomythia of the lovers' first meeting. Insults build on insults through the use of clever punning, as Petruccio becomes more determined to achieve his "twenty thousand crowns" (2.1.120) and Katherine becomes more incensed (while, paradoxically, more fascinated) by his impertinence. Petruccio may, in the words of one student, "completely ignore Kate's wishes," but he does not ignore her words, nor does she ignore his. The exchange of insults, for all its combativeness, represents an early attempt to craft the terms of their relationship. Through the clever use of bawdy puns, each acknowledges the other's previous statement in a way that both unbalances the hearer and invites him or her to answer:

PETRUCCIO. Alas! good Kate, I will not burden thee,
For knowing thee to be but young and light.
KATHERINE. Too light for such a swain as you to catch,
And yet as heavy as my weight should be.
PETRUCCIO. Should be?—should buzz.
KATHERINE. Well ta'en, and like a buzzard.
PETRUCCIO. O slow-winged turtle, shall a buzzard take thee?
KATHERINE. Ay, for a turtle, as he takes a buzzard.
PETRUCCIO. Come, come, you wasp, i' faith you are too angry.
KATHERINE. If I be waspish, best beware my sting.

PETRUCCIO. My remedy is then to pluck it out.
KATHERINE. Ay, if the fool could find it where it lies.
PETRUCCIO. Who knows not where a wasp does wear his sting?
In his tail.
KATHERINE. In his tongue.
PETRUCCIO. Whose tongue?
KATHERINE. Yours, if you talk of tales, and so farewell.
PETRUCCIO. What, with my tongue in your tail? Nay, come again . . .

(2.1.200–13)

Students enjoy hearing this passage read aloud, relishing not just the bawdy language but its heady pace. In order to evoke the audience's laughter, the volley of insults requires an acute responsiveness between the actors who portray the couple. Because we typically encounter this passage soon after my introductory lesson on iambic pentameter, a puzzled student will sometimes ask, "Why are the lines so short?" The scene shows that iambic pentameter is not intended as a stylistic straightjacket but as a guiding principle for rhythmic language that allows plenty of room for creative divergences. The legendary Royal Shakespeare Company director John Barton notes that lines of iambic pentameter divided between two characters (such as 2.1.204) usually prompt actors to pick up immediately the cue and respond quickly—the dialogue simply falls flat if delivered otherwise (35–38).

As we examine the language further, I ask the class to comment on the passage's most prominent images. The punning sexual innuendo strikes students most immediately, as when Petruccio attempts to scandalize Katherine: "knowing thee to be but young and light" and "my tongue in your tail." Students also notice the passage's abundant animal imagery, particularly in relation to body parts: "tongue," "tail," "wasp," and "buzzard." Of course, readers familiar with the entire play will testify to the use of animal imagery throughout, particularly in reference to the taming of Katherine. Brian Morris's Arden edition notes that the play applies the word "shrew" to Katherine fifteen times (123). This information alerts students to the word's importance as a defining term for Katherine. A search of the online *OED*, which we routinely perform in class when a word repeats itself, links the figure of the unruly woman to "any of the small insectivorous animals . . . much resembling mice but having a long sharp snout." Adjective forms of "shrew" associate it with persistent, niggling irritation: "shrew-bitten," "shrew-afflicted," and "shrew-run." As a creature endowed with "energy, irascibility and (above all) noise" (B. Morris 124), the "shrewish" woman is characterized by her loud, boisterous speech. The would-be tamer thus finds himself in a "flyting match," where the contestants vie in one-upmanship. Noise is Katherine's primary weapon and an index of her freedom not only in speaking but also in negotiating her relationship with Petruccio. (When as a class we watch Franco Zeffirelli's film version in which Richard

Burton and Elizabeth Taylor court one another through barbed, witty insults, noise quickly emerges as a key component of this joyful, rambunctious scene.)

Our classroom work with the potency of words serves as practice for the first major essay assignment: a five-page paper in which students choose a significant word from a play or a set of sonnets, research its various definitions in the *OED*, brainstorm contemporary meanings, and bring these associations together to argue for how a particular word functions in the text. The assignment requires students not only to account for the word's cognitive meaning but also to speculate on its auditory impact. Is the word repeated throughout the text? If so, how often and by whom? Is it set in iambic pentameter, in another type of meter, or in prose? Where exactly does it occur in the line—in other words, where does the stress fall? Does it happen during a soliloquy, a philosophical discussion between or among friends, or within a sharp dialogue between or among adversaries? Does the passage use punning or any other literary effects? How does the word fit the intention of the passage—that is to say, why is it there? At first, many students resist this assignment because it plunges them into ambiguity, asking them to engage questions and possibilities instead of easy answers. I want them to consider the word with attention to both sound and sense, assessing its dramatic impact for past and present audiences. Students sometimes comment later that, once they started the *OED* research, they found themselves generating much more material than they had expected. I hope that, even if they struggle initially with the assignment, they complete it with at least a beginning sense of language as creative function, not simply as the vehicle for single, stable meanings.

The biggest overall challenge to teaching Shakespeare's language, I believe, is getting today's students to be comfortable with play, ambiguity, and the possibility of "overcorrectness." As I hope I have demonstrated here, strict adherence to established interpretive certainties confounds students' attempts to understand language's creative potential. When teachers permit students to think more expansively, students become more confident in their own impressions about how Shakespeare's language engages readers. These impressions form the basis of the kinds of original insight that make "our" Shakespeare truly and authentically *theirs*—conferring a kind of ownership that honors the role of students' creative and critical thinking in the pursuit of their education.

NOTES

[1] Occasionally, a student enrolled in Introduction to Linguistics or Introduction to Literary Criticism will recognize this approach as a form of "speech act theory." Indeed, my thinking about the banter between Shakespeare's comic couples owes much to John L. Austin's notion of "performative utterances" in *How to Do Things with Words*.

[2] For book-length examinations of women's verbal and social agency, see Gowing; Capp.

[3] O'Brian's *Shakespeare Set Free* provides an insult sheet to photocopy, but I prefer to put an online version on the overhead projector. The version I use can be located at www.pangloss.com/seidel/shake_rule.html.

[4] This lesson appears in a series of exercises on *Romeo and Juliet*. However, I find it useful for many other Shakespearean contexts as well.

Pervasive Contentiousness in *The Taming of the Shrew*

James Hirsh

Long before students read Shakespeare's *Taming of the Shrew*, they know that it is a depiction of "the battle of the sexes" because that is how the play is generally described in popular culture. This preconception about the play is misleading, however, because it obscures the fact that that particular battle is only one of many dramatized in the play. When I open a classroom discussion of the play by asking students to describe conflicts or rivalries in the play other than the discord between Petruccio and Kate, they have no trouble recalling numerous examples. After this process has generated a large and varied list, I ask students to categorize these conflicts. The play depicts not only many particular conflicts but also many different kinds of conflicts. With occasional prompting on my part, students eventually construct a taxonomy that includes hostilities or rivalries within households, within social groups, between members of different social groups, between individuals and social conditions, and between city-states. Rather than a narrow examination of a single example of gender conflict, the play is an exploration of the nearly universal combativeness of human beings.

Our classroom procedure is rigorously inductive. During the first stage of this process, I write on the board, in the random order in which students mention particular conflicts, the names of the antagonists ("Kate vs. Bianca," "Gremio vs. Hortensio," etc.). I ask students to locate at least one scene in which each conflict is depicted or described, and I put these scene numbers on the board next to the names. After reading a sample passage dramatizing or describing each conflict, we discuss its causes and consequences, the motivations of the adversaries, the manner in which characters express antagonism, and so on. Since some of these conflicts are intertwined, in the process of analyzing a passage illustrating one conflict, we often stumble upon another to add to our growing catalog. When students can recall no further disputes or rivalries, I point out ones they have not mentioned. In the occasional instances when students cannot quickly locate a scene in which a particular discord occurs, I help out. When we move to the second stage of the process and I invite students to categorize the conflicts amassed in the first stage, I put these categories on the board and list under each category one or more of the individual conflicts that fall into that category. Some of these categories can be grouped into larger categories, and the result is a complex system of classification.

Conflicts between Members of the Same Household

Fathers and children Baptista's attempts to exert patriarchal control over his daughter Kate meet with vigorous resistance, as vividly dramatized in 2.1. The superficially dutiful daughter Bianca marries a man behind her father's back. Lucentio's efforts to circumvent his father's authority cause Vincentio public embarrassment in 5.1 when he is arrested and his identity is questioned.

Siblings Sibling resentment is illustrated by Kate's verbal and physical attack on her younger sister, Bianca, in 2.1.

Spouses In addition to episodes that depict quarrels between Petruccio and Kate after their wedding, the play dramatizes other instances of discord between spouses. In the final scene, Bianca and the Widow refuse to obey their new husbands' peremptory commands to appear. After they eventually do arrive onstage, spousal bickering ensues.

Masters and servants The play contains numerous examples of quarrels between masters and their servants. In 1.2 Petruccio gives his servant Grumio a simple command to "knock" (5) when they arrive at the house of Hortensio. Grumio pretends to believe that Petruccio wants him to strike an imaginary person. When Petruccio uses the word "me" as an indirect object in the phrase "knock me" (8), as in "bake me a cake," Grumio pretends to believe that Petruccio wants to be struck himself (as if the word "me" were a direct object). In response to Grumio's willful misunderstanding, Petruccio "wrings him by the ears" (17sd). Grumio presumably knows that his pretense of misunderstanding his master's command will result in his own corporal punishment, but he engages in the pretense anyway. Grumio's behavior illustrates the notion that contentiousness is such a powerful element of human psychology that a person might not be able to suppress it even when its expression goes against the person's practical self-interest. Other instances of strife between masters and their servants are conspicuously dramatized in later episodes. In 4.1 Petruccio brutalizes his entire household staff. Although Kate intercedes in an attempt to protect the servants of the household of which she has become the nominal mistress, Grumio fails to reciprocate her compassionate behavior. Presumably on his master's orders, he tantalizes Kate with the prospect of a meal but then refuses to give her any food (4.3). Biondello denies that his master Vincentio is Vincentio and receives a beating (5.1). In disguise as Lucentio, Tranio also denies his master's identity, and as a result Vincentio is arrested for impersonating Vincentio.

Servants Antagonism between masters and servants does not necessarily lead to comradeship among servants. Unable to retaliate against his master, who wrung his ears for misunderstanding a command involving the word "knock," Grumio takes out his frustration and resentment on his fellow servant Curtis by boxing his ear. Shakespeare connects the two episodes by a verbal echo. Grumio explains to his fellow servant, "this cuff was but to knock at your ear"

(4.1.54–55). The linkage between the episodes makes the point that one conflict can lead to other conflicts in a kind of chain reaction.

Conflicts between Members of the Same Social Class[1]

Gentlemen A major focus of the action is the depiction of rivalries among gentlemen. Within the course of 1.1 an initial rivalry for the hand of Bianca between Gremio and Hortensio becomes a three-way competition when (unbeknownst to those suitors) Lucentio falls in love with her at first sight. The situation becomes even more complex when, in disguise as Lucentio, Tranio enters the competition in 1.2 as a stalking horse for his master. Further developments in this plotline occur in 2.1, 3.1, 4.2, and 5.1. The rivalry among suitors of Bianca, introduced in the opening scene set in Padua, is balanced in the final scene by the rivalry among the new husbands Petruccio, Lucentio, and Hortensio, who hold a contest to determine whose wife is the most obedient. The play depicts other conflicts between gentlemen as well. In the opening scene the two initial suitors of Bianca are at odds not only with one another but with her father Baptista, who refuses to allow them to court Bianca until her sister, Kate, is married. In 5.1 Petruccio insults a stranger of his own class when he describes Vincentio as a girl. The Pedant participates in a plot to deceive Baptista by posing as Vincentio and heaps verbal abuse on the real Vincentio in 5.1. Duped into believing that Vincentio is a madman or an imposter, Baptista insults him and calls for his arrest.

Gentlewomen In the final scene, a conflict arises among gentlewomen. Bianca and the Widow are outraged at Kate's apparent submissiveness to her husband.

Upper-class members of opposite sexes The quarrels between Kate and Petruccio and the squabbles between spouses in the final scene are by no means the only contentions involving upper-class members of opposite sexes. In 2.1 Hortensio reports an offstage incident in which Kate broke a lute over his head. In a soliloquy at the end of 3.1 he expresses resentment toward Bianca after he witnesses a display of mutual affection between her and "Cambio" (Lucentio in disguse). Kate joins Petruccio in insulting Vincentio in 4.6. The Widow and Bianca engage in raillery with Petruccio, Gremio, and Vincentio in the final scene.

Members of the working class Members of the working class can be turned against one another by those with power over them. The page Bartholomew and other servants obey the command of their lord to carry out an elaborate deception of Sly, a member of their own class.

Conflicts between Members of Different Social Groups

Tradespersons and customers In the opening lines of the play, the Hostess, who runs the tavern, quarrels with her customer Sly. In 4.3 Petruccio insultingly dismisses the Haberdasher and the Tailor.

The laity and the clergy According to Gremio's account in 3.2, Petruccio disrupts his own wedding by insulting and physically assaulting the priest.

The aristocracy and lower classes Even though a member of the aristocracy does not appear in the main plot of the play, Shakespeare nevertheless planted in the play the seed of discord between an aristocrat and a member of a lower class. In the induction the Lord sets up a practical joke on Sly, a lowly tinker.

Gentlemen or tradesmen and members of the working class Quarrels between masters and their own servants are not the only disputes that arise between gentlemen or tradesmen and members of the working class. In his disguise as Lucentio, the servant Tranio engages in an overt rivalry with the gentlemen Hortensio and Gremio for the love of Bianca and covertly conspires against them in aiding the real Lucentio's courtship. Although Tranio aims to help his master, he clearly enjoys the opportunity to dupe members of a higher social class. This situation, in which a lower-class person dupes members of the gentry, balances the induction, in which an upper-class person devises an elaborate scheme to dupe a lower-class person. In the final scene, after Tranio has resumed his status as a servant, he openly mocks Petruccio. At his wedding, Petruccio mistreats not only the priest but the sexton, into whose face he throws the sops of a wine glass. In 4.3 Grumio follows his master's lead by insulting the Tailor. In 5.1 an officer is enlisted to arrest Vincentio, his social superior, for identity theft.

Conflicts between Individuals and Social Conditions

Baptista is not dramatized as an exceptionally cruel patriarch, so Kate's rebelliousness is a reaction not merely against his efforts to dominate her but against the patriarchal system that sanctions such efforts. Similarly, Petruccio is at war not just with Kate, but with elements of the social system. He ignores or parodies conventional courtship rituals. He demolishes the solemnity of the wedding ceremony and thereby undermines the conventional respect accorded to the institutions of marriage and religion. The superficial motive for Petruccio's madcap behavior is to tame Kate, to get her to refrain from shrewishness by giving her a dose of her own medicine. But his behavior is out of proportion to that single, simple motive. That he gratuitously attacks other characters besides Kate; that his violations of norms of social behavior are so extreme, numerous, and varied; and that he engages in them with such gusto all imply that taming Kate provides Petruccio with an excuse and an opportunity to unleash anarchic attacks on social convention in general. Playgoers who resent social pressure to conform but who are tamed by the threat of public humiliation or ostracism can experience a vicarious pleasure when they encounter a character in a play who confidently and flagrantly defies convention.

Conflicts between Communities

Tranio convinces the unnamed Pedant from Mantua to impersonate Vincentio by telling the Pedant that Padua and Mantua are now at war and that, if his identity as a Mantuan becomes known, he will be executed (4.2). Even though the supposed war is presumably a fiction invented by Tranio, the episode nevertheless paradoxically dramatizes the actual prevalence of hostility among Italian city-states. The Pedant is easily convinced that a conflict has erupted between Mantua and Padua while he was en route from one to the other because conflicts between Italian city-states were commonplace in the period and sometimes erupted without warning. Accounts of these conflicts by Machiavelli and other writers were disseminated widely. No area of Europe was immune from the threat of war; England itself had been threatened by the Spanish Armada only a few years before the first performance of the play. The ease with which the Pedant is convinced that a state of war has arisen out of the blue is both comic and sad.

Metadramatic Conflicts

Performers and playgoers The same play that depicts a series of quarrels between tradespeople and their customers also acknowledges the potential for an adversarial relationship between performers and playgoers. The main action of the play begins as a play within the play. The onstage performers participate in the duping of Sly by going along with the deception that he is a lord. The onstage playgoer Sly begins to nod off and responds to the efforts of the players in the play within the play with disparagement: "Would 'twere done" (1.1.246–47). By depicting an onstage playgoer as gullible, inattentive, obtuse, and unappreciative, the actual performers poke fun at actual playgoers on the sly (so to speak).

Playgoers and readers Shakespeare also cleverly set the stage for contentions among playgoers and readers. A number of elements in the play are open to a wide range of strikingly different interpretations and have as a result become the subjects of debates among playgoers and readers, including professional critics. One very prominent example is Katherine's long speech in the final scene. Some critics have taken this speech as evidence that Kate has been successfully indoctrinated by Petruccio. These critics fall into radically opposed subgroups. Some readers and playgoers have found it reassuring that even an inveterate shrew can be made to recognize that men and women have been intelligently designed for different roles. Others have been horrified at the depiction of successful brainwashing. A large group of critics have disagreed with the fundamental premise of the first group, that the speech is a sincere expression of Kate's viewpoint. Within this large group, critics disagree about Kate's primary motive for expressing opinions with which she does not agree. Some argue that the speech is an intentional parody constructed by Kate to expose the foolishness of the ideal of womanly behavior promoted by patriarchal ideology. Commentators who regard the play as simply a rollicking farce, on the other hand, assume that Kate is merely being facetious and deny that she has a political agenda. Still others regard Kate's speech as the result of collusion with Petruccio. Some of these critics imagine that the motive is simple one-upmanship (to win the bet and to discomfit the other couples). Others have found in the supposed collusion evidence that Kate and Petruccio have achieved a relationship based on mutual affection, equality, and cooperation. If, by refusing to supply an unequivocal answer to a major question raised at the very end of the play, Shakespeare sought to arouse contention among playgoers, he succeeded magnificently. Four centuries after its first performance, the play is still provoking disputes among playgoers, readers, and critics.

Complicating Factors

The classification system outlined above is not the only possible one. Other categories cut across those already mentioned. A different taxonomy, one based primarily on gender, would highlight the startling fact that, although famous for its depiction of a battle *between* the sexes, *The Taming of the Shrew* actually devotes more stage time to rivalries or disputes between members of the *same* sex. (Petruccio and Kate are onstage at the same time for only about 740 of the nearly 2,600 lines of the play.) The mistreatment of Vincentio and the Pedant by younger characters to whom they are unrelated suggests the existence of a generation gap beyond that between parents and children. Most of the conflicts cataloged above are overt, but some are covert at least for a while. Lucentio is at first an undercover rival of Gremio and Hortensio for the hand of Bianca. The practical joke by the Lord involves an initial stage in which Sly is deceived into believing he is a lord. Most of the conflicts are depicted, but some are merely reported. Most of the conflicts are genuine, but a few are pretences (such as the supposed war between Padua and Mantua and the supposed competition between Tranio as Lucentio and the overt suitors for the hand of Bianca, Gremio and Hortensio). Some interactions are mock conflicts (in which both parties are facetious). From 4.5 onward, quarrels between Petruccio and

Kate seem merely facetious and thus different in kind from earlier quarrels in which Kate exhibited genuine anger and outrage. Some conflicts are resolved, but some (such as the practical joke perpetrated by the Lord against Sly) are left unresolved. Several characters have more than one dispute going on at the same time. Characters sometimes form alliances, but some of these are formed merely to wage war against a common opponent. Most of the conflicts are explicit, but some (such as the debate provoked among playgoers and readers by Kate's final speech) are implicit.

What to Make of the Pervasive Conflicts

Students and I eventually turn our full attention to the conflict between Petruccio and Kate, but the prior lengthy exploration of the many other conflicts in the play defamiliarizes the conflict for which the play is famous. Our investigation reveals that, instead of being an isolated instance of hostility, the contention between Petruccio and Kate is only one example of the discord that is dramatized as a pervasive ingredient in human relations. Contentiousness is the general rule, not the exception. The most conspicuous difference between the interactions of Kate and Petruccio and the interactions of other characters is not that those two quarrel while the rest get along with one another but that Kate and Petruccio quarrel with more verve and imagination than the others. (Other essays in this volume will discuss the relationship between Petruccio and Kate in detail, so I will not do so here.) A startling and disturbing conclusion arises from our inductive analysis of conflicts in the play. If a shrew is a combative person, then this play implies that just about everyone, including just about every playgoer and reader, is a shrew waiting to happen.

Our discussions of the diverse causes of the various conflicts in the play highlight the disturbing corollary that almost any spark can ignite a conflict: desire, jealousy, envy, competitiveness, resentment, simple orneriness, the restrictiveness of social conventions, an impulse to play pranks, and so on. Total strangers encountered by chance can quickly be at odds. But familiarity and commonality can also be breeding grounds for conflict. The play suggests that members of a group (based on biological gender, social class, age, locality of origin, or another factor) are as apt to quarrel with other members of the same group as members of different groups are to quarrel with one another. Some conflicts involve family members or lifelong acquaintances. The play disturbingly implies that combativeness is a nearly irresistible impulse in nearly every human being, ready to be activated by the slightest provocation. Another disturbing implication is that individual conflicts are not easily contained. One conflict often leads to others. Petruccio engages in indirect conflict with Kate by stirring up conflicts with many other characters. By the end of our discussion, students are able to view the conflict between Petruccio and Kate in the context of a dense web of contentions in the play and understand better some of the causes and consequences of contentiousness.

The play also dramatizes the ludic element in many conflicts. Games and sports provide an outlet for the inherent combativeness of human beings, and some games have more serious (significant) consequences than some serious (solemn) conflicts. Indeed, it can be hard to draw the line between games and conflicts. The supposedly friendly wager in the last scene of the play to establish whose wife is most obedient opens up or reveals genuine rifts between spouses. As noted above, some of the conflicts depicted in the play, such as the disputes between Petruccio and Kate in later scenes, are mock conflicts in which both combatants are facetious. The dispute between Petruccio and Grumio about the direct object of "knock" is a language game that the servant is punished for winning. Characters frequently employ gaming or sporting terminology to refer to contentious situations. The Lord describes his elaborate practical joke, which is designed to lead eventually to the painful disillusionment and public humiliation of Sly, as a "sport" (induction, sc. 1, line 87). Early in the play Petruccio pretends to believe that reports of Kate's shrewishness are false and that she is merely "gamesome" (2.1.238). Bianca's suitors (even Lucentio at times) seem driven less by a heartfelt commitment to the lady than by the desire to win a competition. Bianca's father explicitly describes their rivalry as a contest: " 'Tis deeds must win the prize" (2.1.334). Gremio addresses his apparent rival "Lucentio" (Tranio in disguise) as "young gamester" (2.1.392). In an apostrophe addressed to the just-departed Gremio, Tranio implicitly acknowledges the validity of Gremio's characterization when he compares his own trickery in his conflict with Gremio to a maneuver in a card game: "A vengeance on your crafty withered hide! / Yet I have faced it with a card of ten" (2.1.396–97). Line 397 can be paraphrased as follows, "Yet I have bluffed and won a hand with a card of low value." Contention can be a form of entertainment for bystanders. This disturbing truth about human beings is illustrated by our own amusement at the depiction of conflicts in the play. The human proclivity to be entertained by contention is not limited to fictional contentions. After witnessing a disagreement between Baptista and the would-be suitors of Bianca and then a quarrel between Baptista and Kate, Tranio says to Lucentio in an aside, "Husht, master, here's some good pastime toward" (1.1.68). From Tranio's perspective, the combatants are real people, not characters in a play. Tranio's response is dramatized not as the result of some idiosyncratic quirk of personality but as a commonplace human reaction. When Katherine and the Widow quarrel in the final scene, the dispute is treated as a sporting event by their husbands:

> PETRUCCIO. To her, Kate!
> HORTENSIO. To her, widow!
> PETRUCCIO. A hundred marks my Kate does put her down.
> (5.2.34–36)

Even the metaphor of taming, which Petruccio uses to describe the contentious methods he adopts to change Kate's behavior, is derived from the sport of falconry: "My falcon now is sharp and passing empty" (4.1.170). According to

Petruccio, success in this sport requires an innate ability that he himself possesses: "For I am he am born to tame you, Kate" (2.1.268). At another point he describes his victory in his struggle with Kate in terms derived from the game of bowls: "Thus the bowl should run, / And not unluckily against the bias" (4.6.25–26).

Though our classroom discussions explore some genuinely disturbing issues, those discussions are nevertheless comic rather than grim. Students are amused that Shakespeare managed to cram so many different kinds of conflict into a single play, that a play so famous for its battle between the sexes depicts examples of so many other kinds of conflicts, and that the farcical, frenetic, chaotic set of hostilities depicted in the play can be organized into an orderly taxonomy of human contentiousness.

The manic exuberance of the antagonisms in the play is, however faintly, reenacted by the enthusiasm of students in cataloging types of antagonism. Students compete with one another in locating contentions in the play, and sooner or later a student says something that is explicitly or implicitly at odds with a statement made by another student or myself. Contention, it seems, can erupt even in the classroom! After I point this out, students and I explore two seriocomic paradoxes that this shocking revelation illustrates. One is that people can disagree without being disagreeable. The second and more important is that intellectual disputation—the process by which scientists, scholars, and others engaged in the pursuit of knowledge rigorously question, test, and refine one another's hypotheses—far from being a deplorable side effect, is a necessary element in the advancement of genuine understanding. In most cases a valid new idea conflicts directly or indirectly with preexisting conventional wisdom. *The Taming of the Shrew* illustrates this positive side of shrewishness. It exposes some of the injustices and irrationalities of patriarchal authority, social conformity, the class structure, and other features of the status quo and thereby suggests that a person who takes a stand against these social conditions, someone who behaves shrewishly, may have just cause.

This approach to teaching *The Taming of the Shrew* provides more than an in-depth exploration of a major theme of the play. Along the way, students and I analyze the motives of most of the characters and the dynamics of many particular episodes. This approach also gives students practice in locating, analyzing, and organizing evidence and in drawing tenable conclusions from the evidence collected. Instead of taking the form of a lecture, the enterprise is cooperative. Most of the evidence and a good deal of the analysis are supplied by students in response to questions. After this unit, students are better equipped to explore other issues on their own with both imagination and rigor.

NOTE

[1] In the sixteenth century sumptuary laws and social convention dictated that individuals wear clothes deemed appropriate to their social class. Unless a character is in

disguise or is dramatized as intentionally flouting these dictates, the costume worn by the character would have indicated the character's social class. Certain occupations even had distinctive wardrobes. Hence, in the Renaissance theater, playgoers would have in most cases instantaneously recognized the social class of a character even before he or she spoke. A character's social class would have been confirmed by details of the character's situation and relationships with other characters as these were specified in the dialogue or implied.

Reading Bianca

Margaret Maurer

Reading, in the sense of interpretation, involves balancing two complementary impulses: respect for the literal sense of a passage and alertness to innuendo, subtexts, and secondary meanings. All Shakespeare's plays are good pretexts for reflecting on this tension, but *The Taming of the Shrew* is a particularly apt choice because discussion of that play always comes down to the debate over how to read the shrew's final speech of submission. Must we assume that Katherine means what she says by it? Can we explain it as her change of heart? Is she manipulating Petruccio? Or is she in collusion with him to win the wager? Uncertainty about how to read this speech foregrounds the hazard that attends interpretation generally. The meaning we derive from the words and gestures that convey a situation can be affected by the assumptions and desires we bring to it. In other words, we are liable to make things mean what we need or want them to mean.

The action that unfolds around Katherine's sister, Bianca, presents particularly subtle instances of this aspect of the interpretive experience. Because Bianca says less than Katherine, the ways others in the play impose their meanings on her are less noticeable. Her character may thus be understood variously by the play's readers, who also have a number of ways to understand how she functions as a foil to her sister. By comparing the standard modern text to the earliest version of the Bianca scenes in 3.1 and 4.2, advanced students may even be brought to consider how canonical Shakespeare—that is, the generally accepted text of a Shakespeare play—has been affected by the preconceptions or desires of earlier readers.

To foreground the issue of reading in the play and the students' own reading practices, I begin my teaching of this play by distributing pages photocopied from a facsimile of the First Folio printing of Shakespeare's plays, the only early text of the play we have.[1] The first time I did this, I used the entire play, and the exercise inspired one of my students to undertake the project I describe below. In fact, however, students do not need exposure to the entire First Folio text in order to have the experience that is my goal for this assignment; even as few as two pages of the early text will suffice when paired with the modern text of the induction and act 1.

I ask students to read the Folio version of the play side-by-side with the play in their textbooks (usually the Riverside or Pelican complete works) and write an essay about any difficulties they have or discoveries they make. I urge them to read aloud, maybe in pairs or small groups. I let them collaborate on the essay if they collaborate on the reading. I tell them it is reasonable for them to prefer their modern text, but I secretly hope that at least some will come to appreciate that editorial assistance, while necessary and valuable, should not utterly prevent or disqualify their own efforts.

Once they have completed the assignment, I use their observations to highlight places in the text where the meanings they assign to words in order to follow the story may not allow them to appreciate what is happening at a given moment. I encourage students to listen to words as well as look at them, and then I ask students to register their difficulties and double takes. Confusing factors that loom large in their write-ups are, of course, the long *s*, nonstandard spellings (which, some note, make puns more apparent), and unclear and varying speech headings.

But students make other points as well. They report to their dismay that they must read more slowly and go back and reconsider—habits I want to foster. A frequent comment is that the Folio text, with its few stage directions and no marked asides, requires them to work harder to understand who hears what. When, in the best of circumstances, a student reports that he or she mistook a word in its modern meaning and needed the correction of an editor's footnote to understand the speech (I lavishly praise the courage of admitting to this), it is an opportunity for me to make the point that both meanings may be in play in the passage. In my institution, students have easy access to the online *Oxford English Dictionary*. Once shown how to use it, some students resort to it routinely to supplement the notes in their books.

In a term when I assigned the whole Folio text, a student noticed that the placement of some speech headings in 3.1 and 4.2 differs from the modern text: lines that the modern text indicates are spoken by one character are spoken by a different character in the Folio. This student was particularly intrigued by the coincidence that these differences occur in the two scenes in the play when Bianca is alone with her suitors. In an independent study the following term, this student then traced how the modern text of both of these scenes evolved. I myself became interested in the fact that both moments in the play revolve around reading and that in one of the scenes (3.1) a canonical text—four lines of the Latin poet Ovid's *Heroides*, poem 1 (Penelope to Ulysses), that are an encapsulated account of the Trojan War—is misconstrued. The mistake, seemingly inadvertent in the modern text, is pointed in F1, where Bianca is the one who makes it and the effect of her "mistake" is that she mocks one of her suitors.

The Taming of the Shrew has never been the same for me since. By acting out 3.1 with two of his friends, that student concluded that the Folio version is not only more coherent but more interesting than its modern revision. Taking on the part of Lucentio himself, he got his girlfriend to play Bianca and reported how much less sure he, or rather, Lucentio, was of her in the Folio version of the scene. A few years later, four other students demonstrated the intricacy of the Bianca intrigue in the Folio text by acting out all the versions of 3.1 and 4.2 through to their present state in the modern text. (All modern texts are essentially the same in these scenes.)

Thanks to these students, I began to see the value of stressing that *The Taming of the Shrew* is a play concerned partly but by no means entirely with shrew taming. I began to move away from total preoccupation with the Katherine-Petruccio "household stuff" (induction, sc. 2, line 135) and began suggesting that students consider that shrew taming is a version (and a tame one, at that) of what was in Shakespeare's time the more profoundly socially disruptive possibility of gentling, a process whereby a man acquires a social status higher than his father's. Gentling is seen in the Lord's experiment with Sly, and the masquerade that Lucentio undertakes to woo Bianca, with its premise that Tranio could impersonate Lucentio, also entertains the possibility of counterfeit gentling. Now, when students ask if Sly ever recovers from the Lord's trick or whether Katherine fakes submission, I ask them to specify what makes them uncertain about those points and disclose my perplexity: if Lucentio's father had not come unexpectedly to Padua, who would be Bianca's husband? Or rather, since the answer to that would be obvious in word if not in deed (Lucentio), who would be the father of a gentleman son born to Bianca?

Students may need encouragement to read attentively the crucial parts of the play pertaining to this question and to think through the implications of Lucentio's situation. A good place to begin is the moment when Tranio explains to the besotted-at-first-sight Lucentio that no one can have access to Bianca until her sister is wed. The dialogue involves few lexical or syntactical difficulties but is nevertheless provocatively tricky.

We take it speech by speech, articulating what, in each comment, inspires the response. Tranio begins,

> Thus it stands:
> Her elder sister is so curst and shrewd
> That till the father rid his hands of her,
> Master, your love must live a maid at home,
> And therefore has he closely mewed her up,
> Because she will not be annoyed with suitors. (1.1.173–78)

If they do not do so on their own, I make students pause over that word, *annoyed*. I support the ones who interpret it as Tranio's suggestion that Bianca is not eager to be married. Why might Tranio think that? The question directs attention to Bianca's only speech in the scene:

> Sister, content you in my discontent.
> [*To* BAPTISTA] Sir, to your pleasure humbly I subscribe.
> My books and instruments shall be my company,
> On them to look and practice by myself. (1.1.80–83)

Lucentio hears this and compares Bianca at this point to the crafty virgin warrior-goddess Minerva; but later he seems to have forgotten her expressed desire for solitude, recalling only that he "saw her coral lips to move, / And with her breath she did perfume the air" (1.1.168–69).

Consequently, Lucentio does not pick up on Tranio's suggestion about Bianca's wish for solitude. Instead, he focuses on her father:

> Ah, Tranio, what a cruel father's he!
> But art thou not advis'd, he took some care
> To get her cunning schoolmasters to instruct her?
> (1.1.179–81)

At this, Tranio and Lucentio seem simultaneously inspired:

> TRANIO. Ay, marry am I, sir; and now 'tis plotted.
> LUCENTIO. I have it, Tranio. (1.1.182–83)

Tranio deferentially concedes to Lucentio:

> Master, for my hand,
> Both our inventions meet and jump in one. (1.1.183–84)

Lucentio's next line—"Tell me thine first" (1.1.185)—is a good one for students to ponder. It will lead them to wonder whose idea it is for Lucentio to conceal his status and pose as a tutor, Tranio's or Lucentio's?

Once Lucentio's schoolmaster disguise is plotted, Tranio unambiguously leads Lucentio to suggest that he must assume Lucentio's identity while Lucentio lowers himself to be "some other . . . , some Florentine, / Some Neapolitan, or meaner man of Pisa" (1.1.198–99)—which is advantageous to Tranio, as Biondello is quick to register at 1.2.231. Then, forty lines later, after Biondello has arrived and been "charmed" to keep up the ruse of changed identities, Lucentio, unprompted, adds another flourish to their device:

> Tranio, let's go.
> One thing more rests, that thyself execute—
> To make one among these wooers. If thou ask me why,
> Sufficeth my reasons are both good and weighty. (1.1.238–41)

This speech prompts us to ask, what *are* those "good and weighty" reasons? Why *does* Lucentio want Tranio-turned-Lucentio to woo Bianca? This question is underscored by the last notice that the Folio takes of "the presenters above" (sd before 1.1.242). A servingman urges the ennobled Sly to "mind the play" (1.1.242), and a stage direction specifies, "They sit and mark" (1.1.247sd).

The problem Lucentio attempts to address with this additional instruction is that Bianca is being wooed by other suitors, and if one succeeds and secures her father's consent, she will be married to that man. This problem is substantially worsened by the speed with which Petruccio, about to make his entrance, will win the hand of Katherine, making Bianca available to her other suitors. Lucentio needs to prevent a paternally sanctioned marriage between Bianca and any suitor but himself. Tranio as Lucentio "mak[ing] one among these wooers" can secure Baptista's consent to Bianca's marrying Lucentio and be the acknowledged bridegroom in the official ceremony. Presumably, the masquerade could continue indefinitely, with Bianca married publicly to one Lucentio and privately to another. But the danger Lucentio neutralizes by having Tranio bid for Bianca's hand under his own (Lucentio's) name places Lucentio in an ambiguous situation. With or without his father Vincentio's eventual arrival in Padua, Lucentio's household would include Bianca's husband and a man with whom (it is her father's suggestion, but these are Tranio's words) she has "practice[d] how to bride it" (3.3.122).

Having students articulate the jeopardy Lucentio is in as a result of the scheme he employs requires students to read passages of the text where the injunction to "mind the play" is crucial. They must read inferentially but also with due regard for what the characters literally say. Thus investigating Lucentio's problem leads quickly to questions about how to read, that is, how to understand, Bianca's character. Katherine's question of 2.1 is all the more pertinent: which suitor does she truly prefer, if any? And is she deceiving others as to her preference? I do not discourage such inquiries. Instead I ask, What evidence is there in the play of her affection for any of her suitors? Even the modern edition's version of 3.1 admits some uncertainty on this point. This discussion is fruitful regarding parts of the play before Bianca and Lucentio's entrance together in 4.2, when her preference for Lucentio seems established.

The Folio version of 3.1, in which Bianca and the disguised Lucentio are reading and construing (that is, interpreting) *Heroides* 1.33–36, offers the ground for a careful examination of Bianca's character and provides a good example of a text being read in different ways by different people.[2] In this scene, Bianca and Lucentio exchange interpretations of the passage while a disguised Hortensio tries to overhear them. In poem 1 of *Heroides*, Ovid imagines a letter Penelope might have written to reproach Ulysses for his two-decades-long absence. In the scene in *Shrew*, Bianca and her tutor have come to the first distich of a four-line summary of something Penelope says she has heard all too often from travelers about the Trojan War:

> *Hic ibat Simois, hic est Sigeia tellus,*
> *Hic steterat Priami regia celsa senis.* (3.1.28–29)

Literally, the lines convey meaning far afield of what Lucentio will impose on them. They describe geographic features of the theater of the war ("Here was the river Simois, here the Sigeian land, / here stood the lofty palace of old Priam"; my trans.), but Lucentio makes them another occasion ("As I told you before" [31]) to declare his identity as "son unto Vincentio of Pisa . . . disguised thus to get your love" and to insist "that Lucentio who comes a-wooing . . . is my man Tranio" (3.1.32–34). Bianca parries Lucentio's advance with a misconstruction of her own, using the same lines to say that she does not know or trust him but that she is willing to entertain his secret suit, as long as he will "presume not" and "despair not" (3.1.42–43).

Notes typically stop short of underscoring the significance of the indirect allusion to Penelope in the scene. Notoriously wooed by many men in the absence of her husband, her strategy was to keep alive the hopes of all the men but give herself to none of them. Penelope is thus the paradigmatic case of Bianca's situation in 3.1, which, especially in the Folio version, presents a Bianca who is encouraging and frustrating both of her suitors equally.

Hortensio interrupts Lucentio and Bianca, and he and Lucentio exchange insults until one of them, Hortensio in the modern text and Lucentio in the Folio (see my appendix), says,

> How fiery and forward our pedant is!
> Now for my life, the knave doth court my love.
> *Pedascule*, I'll watch you better yet. (3.1.46–48)

And, in the Folio, Lucentio continues, "In time I may believe, yet I mistrust" (3.1.49). In the modern text, Bianca says line 49 to Lucentio, apparently not hearing or disregarding Hortensio's "How fiery . . ." As the scene unfolds in all modern texts, she continues to sow the uncertainty she apparently has expressed in telling Lucentio neither to presume nor to despair. But in the Folio text, Lucentio, after voicing his suspicion of Hortensio ("How fiery . . ."), confesses his mistrust of Bianca. This is a big difference and is certainly significant in any discussion of Bianca's character in the Folio version.

In all versions of the modern text, Lucentio seems then to look ahead to the next two words in Ovid's poem, "*Illic Aeacides*" ("there was the offspring of Aeacus"), which inspire him to return to his insistence on the importance of lineage: "Mistrust it not, for sure Aeacides / Was Ajax, called so from his grandfather" (3.1.50–51). At this point, unless you have students with the knowledge of Ovid that the grammar-school-educated members of Shakespeare's audience would have had, you will just have to tell them that Lucentio is wrong and help them see how odd it is that he is wrong. Aeacides, a patronymic that could denote either Ajax or Achilles, refers in poem 1 of the *Heroides* to Achilles, and Lucentio's point would be stronger if he read the line that way. That is, if he takes Aeacides as a reference to Achilles, he would be likening himself to the unequaled heroic warrior of the *Iliad* rather than to Ajax, a lesser warrior in that poem and one who is often interpreted as somewhat thickheaded. (Ajax's name, pronounced *a-jakes* in early modern English, conceals a coarse pun, *jakes* being the word for privy, or water closet.) It is difficult to imagine why Shakespeare would not only have Lucentio make the mistake but also have Bianca notice it with no further comment:

> I must believe my master; else, I promise you,
> I should be arguing still upon that doubt,
> But let it rest. (3.1.52–54)

Her decision not to argue is doubtless why most editors of the modern text take no notice of it at all.

In the Folio text, however, Bianca is the one to misconstrue the line, and her apparent mistake makes her seem a reader after Shakespeare's own heart. As a rejoinder to Lucentio's "In time I may believe, yet I mistrust," her "Mistrust it not, for sure Aeacides / Was Ajax, called so from his grandfather" seizes on the ambiguity in Aeacides to pointed effect. Since early modern English audiences would have heard the *ass* in "Ae-*ac*-i-des" as well as the *jakes* in "A-*jax*," her mistaking the referent in the line would convey contempt for someone who promotes himself by referring to his pedigree. In the Folio, Bianca's cleverness is not lost on Hortensio, who in lines 52–54 takes the point, agreeing with his "master" (Bianca) that this Aeacides is no Achilles.

I ask students to suppose that Bianca means what she says at 2.1.11–12 when she tells Katherine that she has "never yet beheld that special face / Which [she] could fancy more than any other" and to suppose that Lucentio does not at this point change her mind about that, since in the Folio text nothing she says suggests that she does. In what spirit, then, might she "kiss and court" (4.2.27) Lucentio in the scene where Hortensio is tricked into giving her up on the condition that Tranio (as Lucentio) will do the same?

The first fifteen lines of 4.2 are another good place to give students parallel copies of the modern text and the Folio text (see appendix) and ask them what the lines as disposed in the Folio might convey about Bianca. You may need to tell them that they must figure out how and when Lucentio enters the scene (a relatively easy task, since it must be soon enough to have him hear Tranio's opening lines).

The best answer, I think, is the clever way my student playing Tranio staged it: Tranio and Lucentio enter together as if the latter has just told the man to whom Bianca is now betrothed the rumor about Bianca fancying Licio (Hortensio). This neatly supports the Folio's "me" over the modern text's "none" at 4.2.13. In the Folio, Hortensio reacts to Bianca's "kiss[ing] and court[ing]" of the disguised Lucentio by saying that this proves that the rumors about Bianca loving "me" (that is, Hortensio himself) are false. In the modern text, where line 4 ("Sir, to satisfy you in what I have said") is assigned to Hortensio, "me" makes no sense, so Hortensio points out the error of "[y]ou that durst swear that your mistress Bianca / Loved *none* in the world so well as Lucentio" (4.2.12–13; italics added).

A more difficult problem to solve (though it provides a good opportunity to consider the difference the punctuation of line 7 can make) is what would have to happen between Bianca and Hortensio that would inspire Lucentio to move in and claim her as "mistress of [his] heart" at 4.2.10. In the modern text, Bianca answers Lucentio's "Now, mistress, profit you in what you read?" with "What, master, read you? First resolve me that" (4.2.6–7). In the Folio, Hortensio asks the question of line 6, and Bianca's reply to him is, "What Master reade you first, resolve me that?"

If students have any success with this exercise, they will also enjoy exploring various ways to read the dialogue after the exit of Hortensio. Tranio speaks with affectionate familiarity:

> Mistress Bianca, bless you with such grace
> As 'longeth to a lover's blessed case.
> Nay, I have ta'en you napping, gentle love,
> And have forsworn you with Hortensio. (4.2.44–47)

Bianca's reply is ambiguous: "Tranio, you jest. But have you both forsworn me?" (4.2.48). *Both*? When Tranio assures her—"Mistress, we have"—Lucentio's completion of the line is a good example of how a reading may be conditioned by what the reader, Lucentio, desires: "Then we are rid of Licio" (4.2.49). He needs to think that Bianca's question concerns Hortensio, not Tranio.

I know no better way to introduce a discussion of the last scene of *The Taming of the Shrew*, and particularly of Katherine's last speech, than to suggest that as readers we are often influenced by what we need or desire a text to say. In my experience, asking students in what spirit Katherine delivers that speech and calling on them to justify their answers will quickly bring them to concede that their reading is influenced by what they want to believe about the relationship between Katherine and Petruccio and to consider the legitimacy of such a reading. I am content for them to argue for the meaning they need to find in the lines. Increasingly my goal in teaching is less to persuade students of a particular interpretation and more to help them become independent and imaginative readers who are able to exercise those qualities with subtlety and finesse. The action centered on Bianca in *Shrew* is a good testing ground for these skills.

NOTES

[1] *The First Folio of Shakespeare*, prepared by Charlton Hinman, was reissued in a second edition with a new introduction by Peter Blaney; this is the edition I cite in this essay. Online versions of F1 and other printed facsimiles of individuals plays in it are easy to find. Some versions preserve old spellings and punctuation but use modern fonts (see, e.g., Shakespeare, *Applause First Folio of Shakespeare in Modern Type*), a practice that eliminates the frustrations and the fun of the long *s*.

[2] The first distich is quoted in the scene and a reference is made to the first line in the second. Lines 33–36 of *Heroides*, poem 1, are "hac ibat Simois; haec est Sigeia tellus; / hic steterat Priami regia celsa senis. / illic Aeacides, illic tendebat Ulixes; / hic lacer admissos terruit Hector equos" (p. 12). Variations from this in Shakespeare's text could

reflect a different textual tradition for Ovid's poem or minor errors to be imputed to Shakespeare, the printer, or the speaker of the lines. Grant Showerman translates the lines: "Here flowed the Simois; this is the Sigeian land; here stood the lofty palace of Priam the ancient. Yonder tented the son of Aeacus; yonder, Ulysses; here, in wild course went the frightened steeds with Hector's mutilated corpse" (13).

APPENDIX

First Folio

TLN 1340–53

Hort. The base is right, 'tis the base knaue that iars.
Luc. How fiery and forward our Pedant is,
Now for my life the knaue doth court my loue,
Pedascule, Ile watch you better yet:
In time I may beleeue, yet I mistrust.
Bian. Mistrust it not, for sure *Æacides*
Was *Aiax* cald so from his grandfather.
Hort. I must beleeue my master, else I promise you,
I should be arguing still vpon that doubt,
But let it rest, now *Litio* to you:
Good master take it not vnkindly pray
That I haue beene thus pleasant with you both.
Hort. You may go walk, and giue me leaue a while,
My Lessons make no musicke in three parts.

TLN 1846–63

Enter Tranio and Hortensio:

Tra. Is't possible friend *Lisio*, that mistris *Bianca*
Doth fancie any other but *Lucentio*,
I tel you sir, she beares me faire in hand.
Luc. Sir, to satisfie you in what I haue said,
Stand by, and marke the manner of his teaching.

Enter Bianca.

Hor. Now Mistris, profit you in what you reade?
Bian. What Master reade you first, resolue me that?
Hor. I reade, that I professe the Art to loue.
Bian And may you proue sir Master of your Art.
Luc. While you sweet deere proue Mistresse of my heart.
Hor. Quicke proceeders marry, now tel me I pray,
you that durst sweare that your mistris *Bianca*
Lou'd me in the World so wel as *Lucentio*.
Tra. Oh despightful Loue, vnconstant womankind,
I tel thee *Lisio* this is wonderfull.

Modern Text (*The Norton Shakespeare*)

3.1.45–58

HORTENSIO The bass is right, 'tis the base knave that jars.
[*Aside*] How fiery and forward our pedant is!
Now, for my life, the knave doth court my love.
Pedascule,° I'll watch you better yet. *Little pedant*
BIANCA [*to* LUCENTIO] In time I may believe; yet, I mistrust.
LUCENTIO Mistrust it not, for sure Aeacides[6]
Was Ajax, called so from his grandfather.
BIANCA I must believe my master, else, I promise you,
I should be arguing still upon that doubt.
But let it rest. Now Licio, to you.
Good master, take it not unkindly, pray,
That I have been thus pleasant with you both.
HORTENSIO [*to* LUCENTIO] You may go walk and give me leave° awhile. *allow me leisure*
My lessons make no music in three parts.° *for three voices*

4.2.1–15

Enter TRANIO [*as Lucentio,*] *and* HORTENSIO [*as Licio*]
TRANIO Is't possible, friend Licio, that Mistress Bianca
Doth fancy any other but Lucentio?
I tell you, sir, she bears me fair in hand.° *leads me on*
HORTENSIO Sir, to satisfy you in what I have said,
Stand by, and mark the manner of his teaching.
[*They stand aside.*]
Enter BIANCA [*and* LUCENTIO *as Cambio*]
LUCENTIO Now, mistress, profit you in what you read?
BIANCA What, master, read you? First resolve° me that. *answer*
LUCENTIO I read that I profess,° *The Art to Love.*[1] *what I practice*
BIANCA And may you prove, sir, master of your art.
LUCENTIO While you, sweet dear, prove mistress of my heart.
[*They stand aside*]
HORTENSIO Quick proceeders,[2] marry! Now tell me, I pray,
You that durst swear that your mistress Bianca
Loved none in the world so well as Lucentio.
TRANIO O despiteful° love, unconstant womankind! *cruel*
I tell thee, Licio, this is wonderful.° *astonishing*

Reversing the Polarity: Teaching Textual Practices through *The Taming of the Shrew*

Laura Grace Godwin

My essay begins with a double negative. It is not the sort of twin negation that sends grammarians scavenging for red pens but, rather, the story of a doubly negative response engendered by my first encounter with *The Taming of the Shrew*.

I grew up an avid reader, but my passion waned by the time I reached high school, and I found myself increasingly disenchanted by a once-beloved pastime. Resentful at the "greatness" autocratically and at times seemingly arbitrarily accorded to works of literature, I was discouraged by the dilapidated state of the institutional tomes provided to me. Weary anthologies and dog-eared paperbacks, both with pedantic introductions and notes that I neither knew nor cared how to use, rarely captured my adolescent attention.

Nevertheless, at some point I internalized the oft-articulated (but rarely well explained) notion that Shakespeare was "the greatest writer in the English language" and "a 'universal' poet," who spoke "across time and national (even cultural) boundaries" (Garner 105). Though I was unconvinced of Shakespeare's greatness by a sophomoric (in all senses of the term) in-class reading of *A Midsummer Night's Dream* and enforced viewing of Zeffirelli's *Romeo and Juliet*, I had no reason to question his status as spokesman for "universal" values —until *The Taming of the Shrew*. Hoping for the exploits of a fiery female lead, I was horrified by the play's dramatization of what seemed to me the unchecked demonization and systematic suppression of women. Mystified why any school would require a reading that approved of men oppressing women, I grew more perplexed when my teacher and fellow students failed to share my dismay. When I expressed my views, I was accused of misreading the "love story" and taking Shakespeare's "comedy" too seriously.[1] Ultimately, my twentieth-century classroom was uncomfortably reminiscent of Shakespeare's sixteenth-century Padua, with me as Katherine the shrew. Initially ostracized, I was eventually silenced insofar as I was forced to regurgitate the consensus of my peers or risk an F for "failing" to understand the genre of the play. Frustrated, I literally and metaphorically placed Shakespeare on the shelf and avoided his works for years to come.

I relate this anecdote not to exorcise a traumatic formative experience but to preface a conviction that my negative response to the ideological content of *The Taming of the Shrew* was inextricable from my ignorance about and adverse reaction to the nature and history of the text provided to me in the classroom. Unaware that the play was a product of mediations between author and audience, I could only comprehend—and reject—the play for its patriarchal "Shakespearean" message. Years later, as I migrated to the other side of the desk and became an educator myself, I realized that as a student I had *not* misread the play, but that I *had* misunderstood the edition in which it was presented. My inability to use the tool I had been given hindered my understanding.

Educators have long understood the benefits of contextualizing Shakespeare. Classroom activities and printed editions provide relevant historical, social, and theatrical background to help students comprehend assigned readings, but if information about the provenance of the text is provided at all, it is often isolated and expressed in "dauntingly technical language" (Marcus, *Unediting* 72). In this essay, I advocate the instructor's dissemination of information about the play's bibliographic background in classroom discussions of *The Taming of the Shrew* and the creation of assignments that encourage students to explore early printed versions of Shakespeare. Some may object that in the crowded curricula of the secondary-school or undergraduate classroom, textual studies are too obscure to merit consideration. But just as no industrial arts teacher would expect students to build a bookshelf without being certain they could use a saw, so teachers of literature must not assume students can "build" an understanding of Shakespeare when ignorant of the customs underlying the creation of an edition. (Our knowledge of these customs has recently been assisted by the careful work of Lukas Erne; Peter Holland; and Tiffany Stern [*Making Shakespeare*].) Given widespread scholarly acknowledgment that many Shakespearean texts "varied between themselves enormously, invariably in terms of detail and often in terms of substance" (Holderness and Loughrey 5), educators do students a disservice by obscuring the instability of early modern plays under the mistaken belief that an awareness of textual variation will prove confusing or undermine comprehension. Already well acquainted with the concept of variant narratives through (for example) computer gaming or cinematic adaptations of well-known books, millennial students, once given a basic understanding of editorial practices, gain agency (and become more engaged in the reading) by learning to identify, interpret, and evaluate textual evidence for themselves. By facilitating student understanding of bibliographic vocabulary and textual tools that can be used in conjunction with online archives, educators can open new avenues for discussion and interpretation with each variant of a Shakespeare text.

Equipping students for bibliographic study begins with showing them the location and explication of resources housed within modern critical editions. In these resources, introductory material regularly states which "base text," or early edition, provides most of the dialogue in the volume. In the case of *The Taming of the Shrew*, editors invariably name the First Folio of Shakespeare's works, since that volume contains the first published version of the play that bears the author's name. It's important to alert students to basic facts about the First Folio that are often not clearly explained in editions. Students should be informed that the Folio, printed posthumously in 1623, is the first "complete" edition of Shakespeare, containing thirty-six plays, of which eighteen had not previously appeared in print. Students should also be taught that some scholars view the First Folio as the "authorized" version of Shakespeare, published "according to the True Originall Copies" of his work by colleagues who memorialized their friend's contributions in impressive folio format ("Title Page"). To make a folio, paper was folded once, yielding only four double-sided pages per sheet. Although material expenses were passed on to the customer, making the First Folio extremely expensive, the entire edition sold out within a decade of its initial print run, necessitating the Second, Third, and Fourth Folios in 1632, 1663–64, and 1685. Each subsequent folio, prepared by unknown yet not unskilled editors, made substantial changes to the edition or editions preceding it, and many of the emendations in these three folios are incorporated into modern editions.

How is a reader to know whether a word, line, or speech derives from the First, Second, Third, or Fourth Folio? Contemporary editions provide a vital but often unexplicated tool to assist readers in assessing words in front of them. Sandwiched between play text and footnotes is what Leah S. Marcus (crediting Thomas Berger) has dubbed the "band of terror," a group of characters she describes as "a bristling hedge of textual notes that are incomprehensible to the average reader and therefore serve as a forbidding barrier" (*Unediting* 72). The impenetrability of the code tempts disregard, but while ignorance may lead to the blissful notion that one is reading pure Shakespeare, a text-wise reader can gather valuable information easily from this "band of terror." Educators must draw students' attention to an editor's list of abbreviations, which serves as a key to understanding textual notes. In general, F designates a folio, and the number that follows it indicates which of the seventeenth-century editions supplied a given variant. (F1, for example, indicates the First Folio of 1623, F2 the Second Folio of 1632, and so forth.) Surnames that appear in the abbreviations and textual notes indicate a suggestion or emendation from one of the long line of eminent editors of Shakespeare, beginning with dramatist Nicholas Rowe in 1709.

A discussion of Rowe's lasting contribution to *The Taming of the Shrew* provides a useful illustration of the importance of textual studies. The First Folio, reproduced here with modern spelling, concludes:

PETRUCHIO. 'Twas I won the wager, though you hit the white,
And being a winner, God give you good night.
Exit Petruchio
HORTENSIO. Now go thy ways, thou hast tamed a curst shrew.
LUCENTIO. 'Tis a wonder, by your leave, she will be tamed so.
(229)

Compare this ending to that in a standard modern edition like *The Norton Shakespeare*:

PETRUCCIO. 'Twas I won the wager, though [*to* LUCENTIO] you hit the white,
And being a winner, God give you good night.
Exit PETRUCCIO [*with* KATHERINE]

HORTENSIO. Now go thy ways, thou hast tamed a curst shrew.
LUCENTIO. 'Tis a wonder, by your leave, she will be tamed so.
[*Exeunt*]

(5.2.190–93)

Leaving aside the disruptive instruction regarding Petruccio's delivery ("to Lucentio") and the unnecessary final order to exit the stage, the penultimate stage direction marks a startling departure from the Folio.[2] While the Norton editor does set off editorial interventions with square brackets, the uninformed reader might misconstrue these and assume that Shakespeare, rather than Rowe, required a dual exit.[3] While scholar-director Ralph Alan Cohen might find it "hard to quarrel" with Rowe's decision that Kate and Petruccio should leave the stage together as an expression of their just-demonstrated partnership (277), I would be inclined to disagree with Cohen's assessment, since certain ironic or resistant readings of Katherine's speech make it hard to see why she *should* exit with Petruccio. An assignment that leads students through a comparison between folio and modern editions provokes wildly divergent opinions about what should happen at this moment in the play. Students who read the play as a comic romance find a happy conclusion in Rowe's pairing, while others promote the Folio version and speculate about the implications of a solo exit for Petruccio. Suggestions that Katherine is unwilling or unable to leave the stage and remains emotionally or physically rooted to the spot where she has offered her hand as an object to tread upon lead invariably to in-class attempts to stage the moment and explore its potential. It is only through an alertness to textual variation, editorial invention, and the mechanisms used to detect both that these activities and the understanding they promote are made possible.

Astute readers of *The Norton Shakespeare* will have noticed that the "band of terror" is absent from their edition. Like many collected works, the Norton banishes textual notes to an appendix, making consideration of variants a more laborious task. Still, appendixes provide a better basis for bibliographic work than do many student editions that exclude textual discussion entirely. Faced with an edition that hides textual complexity, educators may turn to early texts in facsimile editions or a digitized First Folio made available online by the Schoenberg Center for Electronic Image (SCETI) at the University of Pennsylvania Libraries (*Mr. William Shakespeares Comedies*).[4] A cursory glance at the passage quoted above as it appears in original Folio form may cause the reader to recoil "before the intimidating display of linguistic and visual strangeness—antique type, non-standardised spelling [and] archaic orthographic conventions" like the long *s* and interchangeability of letters *u/v* or *i/j* (Holderness and Loughrey 2). Only a fool would deny the peculiarity of the Folio text, but for students accustomed to communicating via SMS language, orthographic flexibility is assumed. Equipped with a modern text and the ability to use it, students can read the Folio on their own and see exactly where historical and modern editors have deviated from it. No longer at the mercy of an impenetrable and invariable text, students move beyond passive readership toward active analysis and interpretation. Had I been aware that the Folio Katherine might refuse to accompany her smug tamer off the stage, my early response to *The Taming of the Shrew* would have varied significantly. At the very least, I might have been able to convert a disillusioned reading to a resistant one, thus opening a discussion rather than allowing myself to be silenced.

Even if we assume variant interpretations that would allow Katherine the choice "to exit or not to exit," readers, resistant or otherwise, are still faced with the patriarchal rhetoric of her final speech. Early folios and editorial emendations offer no variants significant enough to answer the question whether Katherine has been undeniably "tamed." A glance at the notes and appendixes of modern editions does, however, offer a further line of inquiry in the anonymous play *A Pleasant Conceited History, Called the Taming of a Shrew*, printed in quarto format twenty-nine years before the First Folio. Quartos, small books created by folding twice a sheet that was typically sized eighteen-by-fourteen inches, allowed a publisher to squeeze eight double-sided pages from a single piece of paper, thereby offering a less expensive product. Students might be informed that seventeen Shakespearean plays were printed in quarto (and one in smaller octavo) before the First Folio was a glint in publishers' eyes, and though they vary significantly from the texts as they appear in the collected works, many early quartos were used as copy texts for the Folio itself (McDonald, *Bedford Companion* 205). The authority of Shakespearean quartos is much debated, with some critics dismissing them as unauthorized publications or texts that reflect performance practice rather than authorial originals.[5] Scholars are especially uncertain about the relationship between the 1594 quarto of *A Shrew* and the 1623 folio version, *The Shrew*. Four hypotheses dominate the discussion: *A Shrew* is an early play by Shakespeare that he later revised as *The Shrew*; *A Shrew* is an independent play used by Shakespeare as a source for *The Shrew*; both the non-Shakespearean *A Shrew* and the Shakespearean *The Shrew* are based on a lost play; *A Shrew* is a revision or adaptation of *The Shrew* by Shakespeare or another playwright.[6] Whatever the relation between the two texts, informed textual comparison complicates and expands understanding of the general narrative that both *Shrew* works share. The *Shrew* plays are remarkably similar yet meaningfully distinct. Stephen Roy Miller, editor of the most recent edition of *A Shrew*, provides a summary of resemblances and divergences:

> Structurally, *A Shrew* is quite similar to *The Shrew* with three plot strands: the main plot of the taming of Kate the shrew, the subplot of the wooing of her sister(s) and the separate framing plot of a trick played by a lord on the drunkard, Sly. . . . However, despite the similar titles and many similarities of plot and occasionally of language, *A Shrew* shows many striking differences from *The Shrew*. *A Shrew* is just over half the length . . . and except for Kate and Sly, all the characters have different names. *A Shrew* is set in Greece, not Italy, it has a conclusion to the Sly frame tale not

> found in *The Shrew* and its subplot differs in many particulars from *The Shrew*, most notably in giving Kate two sisters instead of one.
> (Introduction 3)

Comparison of the texts might engender many classroom activities, but most germane to my discussion are those that might arise from a comparison of the texts' conclusions.[7]

The Shrew's Katherine's final speech is vastly different from that in *A Shrew*. *A Shrew*'s injunction to obey is based on religious grounds, while that in *The Shrew* rests its argument on a link between female disobedience and political treason. However, at the end of each recitation the wife offers to place a hand beneath her husband's foot. In *A Shrew*, a stage direction indicates that she does so, while *The Shrew*'s failure to provide an explicit stage direction leaves the moment open so that an actor can choose to make the offer without completing the gesture. Students can compare the two texts and discuss the implications of Katherine's varying arguments and actions, but teachers may also wish to draw on critical assessments of the moment(s) to foster discussion. Peter Berek argues that "the sexism of *The Shrew* is less automatic, and thus perhaps less offensive, than that in the bad quarto," and he compares the two speeches to support his traditional reading of gender ideology in the texts (96). Marcus counters that Katherine's speech in *The Shrew* endorses a view of women as passive, homebound possessions while *A Shrew*'s rhetoric offers women some agency. Marcus also observes that *A Shrew*'s Katherine may offer her hand as a step stool, saying, "in this version her masochistic gesture is acknowledged as excessive—performed to help her husband win the bet" ("Editor" 112). By drawing on these or other scholarly interpretations, educators can demonstrate how critics build cases for their arguments.

Given the uncertain provenance of *A Shrew*, many scholars are quick to dismiss it as the work of an inferior author or unscrupulous plagiarist. Regardless of one's perspective on the artistic and moral status of the author of *A Shrew*, his work may be used to fill in a significant blank in the Folio that determines interpretations of the play.[8] Christopher Sly is often forgotten or ignored in classroom discussions because he appears only at the beginning of *The Shrew*, but in *A Shrew* Sly remains onstage and concludes the piece convinced that he can "tame" his own wife. Graham Holderness has observed that the decision to include or exclude Christopher Sly is not a matter of an "ordinary playhouse cut: without Christopher Sly the *Shrew* becomes a different play" ("Text" 129). The continued presence of Sly casts the taming narrative into double doubt by exposing it as a fiction played by actors and by positioning the drunken tinker (who, significantly, "misunderstands everything he sees") as an eager graduate of Petruccio's taming school (Holderness and Loughrey, Introduction 15). While Marcus backs off from the suggestion that modern editions follow the practices of eighteenth-century editors who included *A Shrew*'s Sly materials in their editions of Shakespeare, I would argue that full consideration of the Sly framework offers yet another avenue for textual (and theatrical) exploration of the *Shrew* narrative and what I once viewed as its inherent misogynistic values.[9]

I do not wish to suggest that use of bibliographic techniques will "solve" *The Taming of the Shrew* for students who understood it as I did. If anything, consideration of textual variants has convinced me that the "problem" of the play is irresolvable. Ironically, it is the play's very intractability that compels me to explore its text with students. By teaching textual practices, I reject a "Petruccian" control over material resources that forces obedience and submission to "author-ity." I hope that my students, armed with an understanding of the processes that shape texts from pen to print and past to present, will find their own critical voices. Reversing the polarity I experienced long ago, I replace a double negative with abundant—and variant—positives.

NOTES

[1] The same predicament arises when teaching *The Taming of the Shrew*, for students primed to expect comedy sometimes have difficulty viewing the text from alternative perspectives. To begin a dialogue, students are provided with a series of quotations offering conflicting assessments of the play. Lengthy explications of the two positions described here can be found in Peter Berek's and Shirley Nelson Garner's contributions in *Bad Shakespeare*, while a useful list of pithy assessments is available in Michael Fynes-Clinton and Perry Mills.

[2] Hodgdon grapples with the implications of the final stage direction in "Who Is Performing 'in' These Texts(s)? or, *Shrew*-ing Around," an article to which this discussion is much indebted. The final exit (or lack thereof in the Folio) is also discussed by Ralph Alan Cohen in relation to a Folio-centric production he codirected in 1983.

[3] While the well-accepted idea of early modern corporate authorship lies somewhat beyond the confines of my discussion, I wish to remind the reader that in the period, "texts were open to penetration and alteration not only by Shakespeare himself and by his fellow actors but also by multiple theatrical and extra theatrical scriveners, by theatrical annotators, adapters and revisers (who might cut or add), by censors, and by compositors and proofreaders" (Werstine 312).

[4] Facsimile editions have been published by Norton (*First Folio* [ed. Hinman]) and Applause (*Applause First Folio*). In addition to its digitized First Folio, SCETI hosts a series of helpful online tutorials that "allow students to wrestle with major textual issues at their own pace" on the *English Renaissance in Context*.

[5] See McDonald (*Bedford Companion*) as well as Murphy for full histories of the debate over the quartos and folios. It is important to note that recent scholarship distinguishes between the authority of the playwright and the authority of the playhouse, and critics argue that texts drawn from authorial "foul papers" (rough drafts) reflect an author's initial thoughts while editions drawn from playhouse manuscripts, like promptbooks, are valuable as documents that may record the authorized versions of Shakespeare, playwright, and actor. Orgel (*Authentic Shakespeare*), as well as Greenblatt ("Dream"), has discussed the relative merits of playwright-playhouse authority.

[6] Debates regarding the provenance of the play are rehearsed in Miller's Cambridge edition of *A Shrew* as well as in major editions of *The Shrew*. Chapters by Marcus ("Edi-

tor as Tamer") and Miller also address the subject at length. The British Library hosts an online archive of quartos that, sadly, does not contain *A Shrew* (the only extant copy is housed at the Huntington Library in California). Nevertheless, the site contains a useful glossary of bibliographic terms ("Glossary"), as well as a consideration of the relationship between *A Shrew* and *The Shrew* by Liz Schafer.

[7] I would direct the reader to works by Hodgdon and Marcus as well as to McClintock's essay, in this volume, for additional materials to consider in classroom discussion and activities. Specifically, Marcus's chapter on *A Shrew* and *The Shrew*, like McClintock's essay, draws attention to characterization through an examination of an aside, unique to *A Shrew*, in which Katherine explains her decision to marry her "tamer," here called Ferando (Marcus 109). The speech stands in stark contrast to *The Shrew*, where Katherine insinuates she will wed Petruccio "over his dead body" but then appears humiliated when Petruccio fails to arrive at their wedding in a timely fashion. As Paola Dionisotti, Katherine in Michael Bogdanov's famed 1978 Royal Shakespeare Company production of *The Shrew*, observed, "All the crucial moments of the story for Kate, she's off stage" (qtd. in Rutter [1988] 1).

[8] Many critics and editors ridicule the anonymous compiler and consequently devalue *A Shrew*. The compiler found defenders in Marcus (who suggests, intriguingly, that critical animosity is evidence of a sustained antifeminism on the part of editors) and in Holderness and Loughrey.

[9] Marcus is right to point out that it "is not as though editors have been altogether fastidious in barring other questionable material from our standard editions: witness the parallel case of *Macbeth*, in which the witches and Hecate in 3.5 and 4.1.38–43 are, by strong editorial consensus, a non-Shakespearean interpolation, yet almost always kept in the playtext" ("Editor" 128).

CONTEXTS

The Taming of the Shrew as Introduction to a Shakespeare Course

Peter H. Greenfield

As an early, perhaps something of an apprentice, work, *The Taming of the Shrew* is an appropriate play with which to begin students' apprenticeships as readers of Shakespeare. The play's language is less dense, more accessible than that of the later plays, yet it does reveal intriguing subtleties. The main plot, involving the relationship between Katherine and Petruccio, is relatively easy to follow, but students can also begin to appreciate how Shakespeare shapes his multiple plots to develop themes. The sensitivity of students to gendered language and behavior makes them willing and able to see the significance of details of the language and action. The play's concern with the position of women in marriage provides students with an interpretive entry point, and the range of critical reactions allows students to take a similar range of positions with confidence.

The sequence of class sessions and assignments I describe here introduces students to the main activities we will engage in over the term: close reading, exploring options for performance, learning about the values and practices of Shakespeare's culture in order to try to understand the plays in relation to their time as well as our own, and enhancing our own understanding of Shakespeare through reading a range of critical responses. The aim is to offer students a taste of each of these activities and to develop each of them more fully when working on other plays (the three-day sequence described here is based on eighty-minute classes).

Day 1: Text and Performance

On the first day, I typically ask students to read through the end of act 2, skipping the induction for now. We begin by discussing what the students know about Shakespeare—his times, his theater, his dramaturgy—before focusing on the scene in 2.1 where Katherine and Petruccio first encounter each other. I read aloud Petruccio's soliloquy (2.1.166–79) before Katherine's entrance, noting that the language is not especially difficult. Of the individual words, only "rail" (168), "volubility" (173), and "banns" (178) are likely to be unfamiliar, and the first two are clear enough from context. Moreover, the "poetic" qualities of the speech consist entirely of similes worked out at some length: "Say that she rail, why then I'll tell her plain / She sings as sweetly as a nightingale" (2.1.168–69). We note that the iambic pentameter of the speech strikes our ears as a natural rhythm for English, so that students reading aloud only need to look for the sense, and the rhythm will take care of itself. (As a member of the group Actors from the London Stage once told my class, an everyday sentence like "I think I'd like a slice of carrot cake" is a perfect iambic pentameter line.) I then ask students to join me in reading aloud the whole confrontation between Katherine and Petruccio, with each person in turn taking a speech (or two lines of the longer speeches), and we go around the room until we reach the point when Baptista and the others enter. Though students read with varying levels of skill, the momentum picks up, and the exchanges of one-liners can be quite effective even in this unrehearsed reading.

At this point it is time to put the scene "on its feet" by asking two students to take the parts of Petruccio and Katherine. The rest of the class acts as director by committee. To begin, I let the two "actors" start the scene any way they like, stopping them after ten or fifteen lines. Unless they have had some acting training, students tend to stand in place and read the lines, so immediately the group can see the need to think about blocking the scene—partly to make it more interesting, but more importantly to help the audience understand the dynamic between the characters through visual signals. So we stop to consider what we already know about these two characters, looking for clues in earlier scenes. What are these characters like? What is each thinking at the beginning of and hoping to get from their encounter? Petruccio seems easy, since he has announced his intention to "wive it wealthily" for all to hear and shares his strategy for dealing with Katherine in the soliloquy that immediately precedes the encounter. But is he as supremely confident as his words suggest, or are they bluster covering some nervousness about his ability to handle "a fiend from hell" (1.1.88)? It is perhaps more common for productions to portray Petruccio as confident, but a number of productions have explored the possibility that he has misgivings.[1] Similarly, our view of Katherine shouldn't be limited by that of the Paduan men, who can see only the angry shrew. Is Katherine someone who genuinely wishes to be married but has found no man worthy of her among the graybeards like Gremio and ninnies like Hortensio? Or has she had it with men? Is she intrigued that a stranger wants to talk with her? or annoyed? Does she initially simply want to be rid of Petruccio or, conversely, feel some attraction—though she knows better than to let him know it?

The several possible responses to these questions lead to different ideas about how Katherine enters and Petruccio responds to her. We have sometimes spent an hour just on the different possibilities of Katherine's entry and the first two speeches. One of the most revealing strategies has been to tell the student playing Katherine that she is going to show her disdain for Petruccio by sweeping across the playing space with barely a look at him, aiming to exit on the far side. Petruccio then has to find a way to keep her onstage long enough to be able to do his wooing. He may simply grab Katherine as she goes by, but I urge Petruccio to try other tactics. Can he find a way to arrest Katherine by using the lines? If not, can he at least block her way? Thus, as Katherine attempts to step around him, we can see a connection between Petruccio's dodging back and forth to block her and the back-and-forth rhythm of "you are called plain Kate / And bonny Kate, and sometimes Kate the curst. . . ."

It isn't necessary to block the entire scene to get the point across, but it's useful to ask students to consider which actions are required by the lines, which are merely suggested, and which we find ourselves wanting to add despite the fact that there's nothing in the text that overtly calls for them. Only when Katherine strikes Petruccio, and perhaps when he raises a hand in response, does the script make certain actions explicit. Petruccio's "Come, sit on me" would seem to require an illustrative gesture, and his non sequitur about the world's reporting that "Kate doth limp" (2.1.183–84) suggests that he may have done something to make her limp at this moment. Most modern productions go much further in giving physical expression to the verbal battle on the page. One can underline the range of possibilities by showing video clips of contrasting performances. The 1980 BBC version with John Cleese and Sarah Badel contains remarkably little physical action and lets the verbal jabs do most of the work. At the other end of the spectrum are the wildly physical scenes in the 1967 Franco Zeffirelli film starring Richard Burton and Elizabeth Taylor and the 1976 American Conservatory Theater stage production with Marc Singer and Fredi Olster (*William Shakespeare's* The Taming of the Shrew), in both of which we barely notice the lines as Katherine and Petruccio pummel each other.

Overall, this first day's discussion establishes that being aware of the dramatic elements requires us to pay close attention to the language. The students realize that working with Shakespeare can be enjoyable if one combines imagination and close reading. In succeeding class sessions we will use the controversy over the play's depiction of women and marriage to provoke a deeper examination of the text and its context.

Day 2: Theme and Criticism

On our second day on the play, I ask students to read to the end and then to focus on the problem that this play creates for modern audiences. Does it insist that women's proper role is subservience to men—and that men are entitled to use any means to ensure their dominance? And, further, does the play thus intend to make humor out of a man's bullying and brainwashing his wife into submission? Or does the play suggest that Katherine and Petruccio attain a relationship not only of affection but also of mutual respect and equality? Or is the play a satire on male dominance or some other variation on or combination of these views? We will respond to these questions using a variety of perspectives, which will allow us to look not for the definitive answer but for the ways Shakespeare has shaped the story and character and language of his play to give a complex picture of married life.

The students write a one-page paper responding to the above questions, which I do not grade. They are directed to look especially at Katherine's final speech, which admonishes the other wives to obey their husbands. The students must determine whether this speech expresses the "message" of the play and should thus be taken at face value or whether we should read the speech ironically. What clues are there—in the language of the speech and in the language and actions of the characters earlier in the play—as to how we should interpret Katherine's final speech? These response papers provide the starting place for our class discussion and may be incorporated into the graded paper on this topic that I assign at the end of the unit.

I also provide students with brief quotations representing a spectrum of critical response to these questions. George Bernard Shaw's insistence that the play's ending is "altogether disgusting" (*Dramatic Opinions* 2: 364) is balanced by Martha Andresen-Thom's view that the play shows us "extraordinary individuals [who] learn to play with wit and wisdom the roles of sex and class that at once bind them and bond them" (141). Coppélia Kahn's brilliant reading turns the traditional perspective on its head, holding that the "play satirizes not woman herself in the person of the shrew, but the male urge to control woman" (*Man's Estate* 104). Katherine's submission reveals that "only a woman has the power to authenticate a man, by acknowledging him *her* master" (117).

The critical readings show that a wide range of interpretations are possible, even among those who characterize themselves as feminist critics. (Demonstrating the range may also be necessary if students have read the introduction to the play in one of the many recent editions in which the introduction is less an introduction than a critical interpretation of the play.) Students are free to take a similar range of perspectives, but they are also challenged to think through their responses to the play in relation to opposing ones. Students who initially have trouble articulating their perspectives can find clarity and language in the passages. In addition, students who initially resist discussing questions of gender because "we're past all that" are often forced to realize that we haven't achieved gender equality (as much as we might like to believe otherwise) when they see how some of their classmates react to the same material.

We begin discussion on the second day by reading Katherine's long speech aloud, again taking turns. I ask my students to do this in order to continue habituating them to reading and hearing Shakespeare's words and to focus their attention on the details of the speech's language. I ask first for reactions to the speech, pushing students to provide specific textual support for their responses. Do they think that Katherine means what she is saying? that Shakespeare means it? If, as most of them want to argue, neither Katherine nor Shakespeare means it, where are the hints in the text that we should not take Katherine at her word?

Many students see the speech as too hyperbolic to be sincere, but I press them to find more specific evidence. Someone will usually notice that lying "warm at home, secure, and safe" (5.2.155) is hardly Katherine's experience in Petruccio's house. Nor has Petruccio committed his body to "painful labour both by sea and land" (153), since her dowry—added to his inheritance from his father—means he will never need to do a day's labor in his life. Students often need to be prompted, though, to see the possible pun on "labour," which reminds us that the only "painful labour" in this marriage will be Katherine's in childbirth, a probable and dangerous event that she curiously leaves out of her description of a wife's duty. Sharp readers may notice the ambiguity in the phrase "honest will" when Katherine argues that a wife who is "not obedient to [her husband's] honest will" is "a foul contending rebel" (lines 162–63). The phrase may simply mean that she accepts that a husband's will is always honest, but if the actor puts extra emphasis on the word "honest," we are made to realize that a husband's will may also be dishonest and his wife thus released from any duty to obey. The line that effectively concludes Katherine's argument—"That seeming to be most which we indeed least are" (179)—opens the door to any number of ways that wives might seem to be other than what they are, linking the speech to the many instances of disguise, playacting, and other gaps between appearance and reality in the play.

We also imagine how the speech could be performed. Katherine may appear convinced of (or, in a darker reading, brainwashed regarding) the rightness of what she is saying, or she may make it clear she doesn't mean any of it. The simplest way for Katherine to do the latter is the exaggerated wink at the end of the speech employed by Olster (made famous earlier by Mary Pickford's wink at the end of an early twentieth-century filmed version of the play). In the 2000 Oregon Shakespeare Festival production, Robynn Rodriguez's Katherine stunned the audience by doing more than just putting her hand beneath Petruccio's foot. She threw herself full-length on the ground in front of him. A moment later she jerked her hand upward, sending Petruccio somersaulting backward over his chair, to a unanimous gasp of relieved laughter from the audience. Other approaches can suggest that very different relationships have developed between

Katherine and Petruccio. If they have come to a mutual, loving understanding, the speech may be played as a "privately shared joke" between the two of them, as it was for Sinead Cusack and Alun Armstrong in a 1982 Royal Shakespeare Company production (Rutter [1989] 22). Five years later at the RSC, Fiona Shaw took a nearly opposite tack. Her Katherine used the speech to take Petruccio and the other men on: "She's saying, 'I concede it. You own the lot. Feel good about it, boys?'" (Rutter [1989] 24).

Then we work backward, examining which elements of the rest of the play led students to their different readings of Katherine's crucial final speech. We consider the overall thrust of the action, but I emphasize close reading, using the students' sensitivity to gendered speech to get them to see the details of the language. Those who see a misogynistic Petruccio pounce on the speech where he claims that Katherine "is my house, / My household-stuff, my field, my barn, / My horse, my ox, my ass, my anything" (3.3.101–03). His extended metaphor about Katherine as falcon similarly objectifies her and rewards further analysis (4.1.170–76). Students quickly realize that, unlike a horse or ox, a falcon is never fully tamed and requires the handler not only to wear leather gauntlets to avoid being torn by its talons but also to hood the animal and tie it to its perch to ensure it won't leave when the handler isn't giving it full attention. An investigation into who kept falcons in Shakespeare's time leads to the recognition that it was only the aristocracy and that falcons, considered noble animals, were respected far more than an ox or certainly a dog. The complexity and ambiguity of this single analogy can serve as an illustration of the complexity and ambiguity of the play as a whole.

The moment at which Katherine finally capitulates is of course crucial to any reading of the play. What is the tone at that moment, when Petruccio forces her to call the sun the moon, then reverse herself at his bidding? Does she respond as someone brainwashed by a controller who has withheld food and sleep? Or is she playful, her response a return to the verbal one-upmanship of the wooing scene? If the latter, what clues do we find in her lines, and can we find Katherine using similar verbal tactics in her long speech at Bianca's wedding?

When our discussion of Katherine and Petruccio begins to lose momentum (which sometimes doesn't happen until the third day), I ask students to consider how Shakespeare's use of parallel plots affects our view of the play's central action. The parallels work partly by contrast, as when Lucentio's blind romanticism is juxtaposed against Petruccio's practical strategies, but mainly they work through addition. The disguises of Bianca's suitors and Petruccio's antic, costumed performance at the wedding make us suspect that Katherine is performing as well, both in her capitulation and in her lecture to the other wives—though the nature of her performance is, of course, very much open to debate.

The induction also offers intriguing parallels (whatever its problematic status in the text). The Lord's directing his household to treat the drunken tinker Christopher Sly as if he is a lord, with the page Bartholomew acting the part of

Lord Sly's wife, makes us even more aware of how role playing pervades *The Taming of the Shrew*. And what, for instance, might we make of the parallel between Kate and Sly, who is certainly shrewish at the beginning of the induction, but whose behavior moderates when he takes on the role of lord? How does it affect our reading of the main play to think of it as an entertainment chosen for Sly? Is Petruccio's taming of Kate to be understood as satisfying the desire of the onstage audience—Sly—for a male dominance he failed to achieve over the Hostess? Exploring the significance of any of these parallels provides rich topics for discussion.

Day 3: Context—Shakespeare's Time and Ours

On the third day of work on the play our goal is to understand the play's presentation of gender by placing that representation in historical context. Students know that women and men did not have equal status in Shakespeare's time, but those who have not studied the period tend to assume a straightforward misogyny because they are unaware of the extent to which existing views of women's position in society were examined and modified during the early modern period. The readings in the Bedford edition of the play, edited by Frances E. Dolan (1996), represent the diversity of perspectives in the period, ranging from learned tracts on women's legal rights and position in the household to popular ballads on shrew taming. I ask students to read the excerpts from "A Homily of the State of Matrimony" so they will get a sense of the official view—that of the Crown and the Anglican Church—of the ideal marriage relationship. Each student chooses one of the other readings to report on in class, giving us a description of the reading and then relating it to *The Taming of the Shrew*. (Having students post their descriptions on a course discussion board or wiki can make it easier for them to include in their essays contextual material other than the piece they reported on.) They realize that in parts of her long speech, Katherine is quoting the "party line" of the homily on matrimony almost word for word, while, on the other hand, Petruccio's taming tactics appear a good deal milder when compared with those of the husband of "A Merry Jest of a Shrewd and Curst Wife," who flays his wife's skin and ties her up in a salted horsehide. The diverse nature of these contextual readings leads students to recognize that women's position in marriage and society in Shakespeare's time was a matter for debate in the culture at large and a matter of negotiation for individual women and couples. We inevitably find that our conclusions from the previous class session undergo further revision.

The unit culminates with the students writing a three- to four-page essay addressing the play's treatment of women and marriage. Students now have far more material than they could possibly use in a paper of only three to four pages, but all of what they have learned will inform our study for the rest of the term. We continue the practice of close reading and the other methods for approaching Shakespeare's plays throughout the semester. Beginning with *The Taming of the Shrew*, students learn that each of these approaches and perspectives—close reading of crucial passages, examining performance options, and reading both contextual materials and criticism—is possible and necessary if we are fully to understand Shakespeare's plays.

NOTE

[1] A notable example was Jasper Britton's Petruccio in a 2003 Royal Shakespeare Company production. Britton emphasized the line reporting his father's death and especially stressed the following line—"And I have thrust myself into this maze" (1.2.50)—revealing a lack of confidence that he could find his way through that maze. His bragging and wildness in public were clearly intended to mask this insecurity, which he continued to show in private.

"To Serve, Love, and Obey": *The Taming of the Shrew* and Early Modern Marriage

Robert Matz

Can this marriage—or play—be saved? *The Taming of the Shrew* frequently shows up on the syllabi of Shakespeare courses or in English literature classrooms, in part because students readily identify with the situation of its battling lovers, Petruccio and Katherine. In my experience, student responses to these characters fall into two main camps. Those sympathetic to the play find Petruccio and Katherine to be moving toward mutual understanding and love as Petruccio, by mirroring Katherine's shrewish behavior, teaches Katherine to leave behind her immature or defensive anger. Students less sympathetic to the play maintain that Petruccio, having brutally "tamed" Katherine, reduces her by the play's end to speaking the platitudes of wifely obedience. Either side in this debate might invoke the historical remove of the play, those sympathetic to it suggesting that we cannot judge Petruccio's method of taming by our own more enlightened standards, those less sympathetic arguing that the play does indeed represent the brutal patriarchy of past times.

Both of these positions can contribute to an engaged debate about the play and its relation to its historical moment, but they can also fairly quickly lead the debaters to a stalemate. I find that placing this relation in a richer understanding of ideas about marriage during the early modern period offers an effective way to move the debate forward and to nudge students toward closer readings of the play. In addition, this approach helps students explore more generally how Shakespeare's plays relate to their historical moment, as well as how we characterize such moments. It also allows students to become familiar with some early modern nonliterary texts.

Both informal attitudes and formal law in the early modern period enjoined the wife's submission to her husband in marriage—"to serve . . . and obey," in the words of Katherine's notorious final speech on wifely duties (5.2.168). But marriage in the early modern period was also supposed to entail a loving and mutual relationship between husband and wife, the "love" that comes between "serve" and "obey" in the line just quoted. Early modern advice books can be quite lyrical on the subject of married love. Henry Smith, in his 1591 *Preparative to Marriage*, advises that the wife is neither the husband's head *nor* (*pace* Petruccio) his foot. Rather, just as Eve was made from Adam's rib, so the husband must set his wife at his heart: "If she must not match with the head, nor stoope at the foote, where shall he set her her [sic] then? He must set her at his heart, and therfore she which should lye in his bosome, was made in his bosome, and should be as close to him as his rib of which she was fashioned" (9).

To preserve this loving intimacy, William Whately, in his 1623 *A Bride-Bush*, offers a warning to husbands that might surprise readers who take *The Taming of the Shrew* to represent early modern orthodoxy:

> [B]eware of, "Do it or you had best"; and "you shall whether you will or no"; and "I will have it so, if it be but to crosse you." O no, much more comely for an husbands mouth are these words, "Good wife"; "I pray you"; "let it be so"; "I intreate you"; "doe me the kindnesse to doe this or this." Doubtlesse in crossing, a man shall crosse himselfe most at length. (163)[1]

"In crossing, a man shall crosse himselfe most": these injunctions to be kind and loving rather than cross toward the wife did not come from a protofeminist concern about women. Rather, both the church and state wanted marriages to succeed. The state wanted good order and marriage as a civic institution to preserve it. So did the church, which also wanted marriage to fulfill its purpose as sacred institution, rather than to become, as the subtitle of *A Bride-Bush* describes the bad marriage, "a little hell."

Students can find this idea of married love and the tensions between it and the expectation of wifely obedience to the husband in "A Homily of the State of Matrimony." This homily, still widely available in print editions and on the Web, was one of the twenty-one homilies that ministers in the state-run churches of early modern England were enjoined to read to their congregations.[2] The "Homily of the State of Matrimony" (1563) was intended as a sermon appropriate for the occasion of a marriage (Klein 12). Students encountering this homily will discover a more complicated text than they might expect. (Indeed, because some students so expect to find a grim doctrine of patriarchal authority they have trouble at first seeing this complexity.) The homily assumes that the woman is the "weaker vessel" who ought to obey her husband. But it also takes pains to urge husbands not to abuse their authority. The homily is particularly keen to warn against the pride or wrath that will create dissension in marriage:

> For this folly is ever from our tender age grown up with us, to have a desire to rule, to think highly by ourselves, so that none thinketh it meet to give place to another. That wicked vice of stubborn will and self-love is more meet to break and to dissever the love of heart than to preserve concord. (14–15)

The warning against the "desire to rule" is not addressed just to the wife (15), as a reader of *The Taming of the Shrew* might suspect, but to persons who are married. In fact, husbands are especially warned that, because of their superior position, they need to take care:

> This precept doth particularly pertain to the husband. For he ought to be the leader and author of love in cherishing and increasing concord, which

> then shall take place if he will use measurableness and not tyranny, and if he yield some things to the woman. (16)

Of course, women still need to obey, and they are advised not to take advantage of their husband's kindness: "As concerning the wife's duty. What shall become her? Shall she abuse the gentleness and humanity of her husband and at her pleasure turn all things upside down? No surely" (17). Even so, the wife is promised that if she behaves kindly to her husband, she will run her marriage anyway. The homily quotes an unnamed poet: "'A good wife, by obeying her husband, shall bear the rule,' so that he shall have a delight and a gladness, the sooner at all times to return home to her" (17).

The problem is this: the homily wants to preserve the husband's authority in marriage while at the same time promoting marriage as a loving fellowship between the husband and wife. The tension between these goals divides the text, which not only stresses the husband's authority and his forbearance but also stresses the wife's obedience and promises her that she can still rule the roost. This tension is perhaps most evident in the homily's advice on whether it is ever appropriate for a husband to beat his wife. The short answer is no: "yet I mean not that a man should beat his wife. God forbid that, for that is the greatest shame that can be. . . ." The longer answer is that while men are enjoined not to beat their wives, the homily (and early modern law) does not forbid it or offer an effective remedy to women who are hit. When we complete the previous quotation past its ellipses we find that for the husband to hit his wife "is the greatest shame that can be, not so much to her that is beaten, as to him that doeth the deed" (21). Not much sympathy for the wife there. Wives who are subject to physical abuse by their husbands are provided only this rather unhelpful consolation: "if by such fortune thou chancest upon such an husband, take it not too heavily, but suppose thou that thereby is laid up no small reward hereafter and in this life time no small commendation to thee if thou canst be quiet" (21). On the one hand husbands are told in no uncertain terms that they should not hit their wives; on the other hand, wives who have abusive husbands are told to bear their abuse with patience, in order to earn praise in this life and their reward in heaven.

Modern readers are likely to find troubling the homily's emphasis on wifely forbearance. But they should not, therefore, discount the homily's corollary emphasis on husbandly kindness as irrelevant to orthodox attitudes about early modern marriage—or to *The Taming of the Shrew*. Rather, I suggest we can read the tensions in the narrative of Shakespeare's play through these tensions in ideas concerning early modern marriage. For one thing, the play is more uncomfortable with Petruccio's behavior toward Katherine than it might first appear. Petruccio does not clearly represent early modern attitudes about the husband's behavior in marriage.[3] He does not even clearly represent proper behavior in the play. Skepticism about Petruccio's behavior is best seen in what is often taken to be his clearest expression of early modern patriarchal orthodoxy:

Nay, look not big, nor stamp, nor stare, nor fret.
I will be master of what is mine own.
She is my goods, my chattels. She is my house,
My household-stuff, my field, my barn,
My horse, my ox, my ass, my anything,
And here she stands, touch her whoever dare.
I'll bring mine action on the proudest he
That stops my way in Padua. Grumio,
Draw forth thy weapon, we are beset with thieves.
Rescue thy mistress if thou be a man.
Fear not, sweet wench. They shall not touch thee, Kate.
I'll buckler thee against a million. (3.3.99–110)

As we have seen, early modern marriage ideals were opposed to this kind of humiliating subjection of the wife. Petruccio may be spouting traditional or proverbial wisdom, but it is a wisdom challenged, not endorsed, by the authority of the church and state, and certainly by the world of the play. Indeed, Petruccio is being outrageous. His proverbial speech no more represents early modern orthodoxy regarding male authority in marriage than his haphazard and slovenly dress represents early modern fashion (3.2.41–57, 105–06).

Students can see that Petruccio does not simply represent orthodox male authority by considering as well to whom he is speaking when he warns "look not big, nor stamp, nor stare, nor fret." It is not to Katherine. Petruccio is arguing with Baptista and the wedding guests, who expect the newly married couple to join them at a wedding feast. Petruccio warns these men not to intervene with his intention to leave with Katherine before the feast begins: "I'll bring mine action on the proudest *he* / That stops my way" (italics mine). Petruccio's words and behavior, that is, are seen as wrong not just by Katherine but also by other men, if only because fathers (and family friends) have an interest in protecting the daughter. But this conflict does not divide only father and husband. It also divides Petruccio's rhetorical stance, which strikingly shifts in this passage from a language of ownership to one of chivalric protection. As we would expect from a reading of the homily, Petruccio does not in any simple way represent how men are supposed to behave toward their wives. Even his launch into the language of chivalry ("Fear not, sweet wench. They shall not touch thee, Kate. / I'll buckler thee against a million") seems defensive, as if Petruccio is trying to claim he, and not the men whom he is opposing, is Katherine's loving protector. Hence the rapid shift of Katherine from "ox" to knight's lady.

Students can consider Petruccio's unorthodox stance in the play in generic terms as well. Often the plot of a comedy allows the release of a character's subversive energies, such as when, in *A Midsummer Night's Dream*, Hermia rebels against her father's command that she marry Demetrius. In *The Taming of the Shrew*, however, comic rebellion works to the disadvantage of the woman, since the comedy lies in Petruccio's willful disregard of expectations that the husband will treat his wife with love, kindness, and respect. The certitude with which

Petruccio asserts his objectifying authority over Katherine—a certitude that might lead us to believe that Petruccio is speaking what everyone in the early modern period believed—is rather an index of his strong challenge to early modern belief and an expression of his comic unruliness and foolery. I like to imagine this passage as spoken by John Cleese, not in his 1980 role as Petruccio in the BBC production but in high Basil Fawlty or Monty Python fashion.

Of course, comedy allows people to say or do things they would like but are ordinarily not allowed to do, since "it's only a joke." And members of an audience—both modern and early modern—may well laugh with Petruccio rather than laugh at him. Shakespeare has it both ways. Petruccio's "taming" is more transgressive than we might first think, but these first thoughts are not wrong either. Official church teaching on marriage is against Petruccio, but the energies of comedy are on Petruccio's side. We are meant to enjoy his character and frequently led to see the world of the play from his point of view. In this way, *The Taming of the Shrew* expresses some of the same ambivalences as the homily. It does not directly endorse a husband's abusive behavior toward his wife, but neither does it rule such behavior out. It is worth noting, however, that the comic aspects of the play make this abuse quite a bit more attractive than the homily does. Indeed, one could argue that Shakespeare's play challenges the orthodox stance against abuse by trying to make that abuse funny.

The description by Petruccio's servants Grumio and Curtis of Petruccio as a "shrew" provides another opportunity to consider *The Taming of the Shrew* in relation to early modern attitudes toward marriage, for this description implies similar divides between love and obedience, between mutuality and male authority. Student readers of the play are often delighted to discover statements by characters that Petruccio is "more shrew than she" (4.1.71) or that he "kills her in her own humour" (4.1.161). These statements suggest that Petruccio is really the man for Katherine. He is tough enough to demonstrate to Katherine her unattractive shrewishness by mirroring it, and he is tough enough to handle her. From this point of view, Petruccio's taming becomes a kind of attractive mutuality. It seems only natural that the two feistiest characters in the play are made for each other. Moreover, explicit statements of Katherine's and Petruccio's mirroring personalities are complemented by their spirited exchanges, such as when in act 2 they first meet and trade funny insults (2.1.181–272). Students who see happy sparks flying between Petruccio and Katherine use this exchange as evidence that Petruccio is not simply a brute who tames Katherine. This observation shows recognition of a more complicated dynamic between these two characters. But this dynamic, I suggest to my students, provides another way for Shakespeare to have it both ways, in the manner of early modern ideas about marriage. From this perspective, the play depicts two "shrews" who, made for each other, will enjoy a mutual love based on their shared sass. As for the ending of the play, Katherine's speech can be construed ironically in order to suggest that these two spirited lovers are having a last laugh together.[4]

In response to this reading of the play, I emphasize that what looks like mirroring really is not. Petruccio cannot become "more shrew than she," or, rather, if he does, his shrewishness has a meaning opposite to Katherine's, not like it. A shrewish man is not the same thing as a shrewish woman. When Katherine, as a woman, behaves like a "shrew" she departs from the norms of womanhood. She is too aggressive. When Petruccio, as a man, behaves like a shrew he exercises a version of masculinity, however contested by official ideology (as in the homily). Shrewishness is inappropriate for Katherine but not for Petruccio—at least up to a point. Thus, for example, although husbands who beat their wives were, not surprisingly, more frequent in early modern England than wives who beat their husbands, popular literature condemned the latter more frequently than the former (Shepard 136–37).[5] Relatedly, their shrewish behaviors are not equal either. For Katherine, as a woman, shrewishness is limited to sulkiness and sharp words. She has no other power. Petruccio can be sharp or sulky too, but, because he is the male master of his house, he can deny Katherine food and sleep and, by hitting his servants, signal to Katherine she could be next (that Petruccio never does quite hit Katherine keeps the play comic and Petruccio's behavior from fully crossing the line against hitting one's wife). The ideological trick of the play is to provide the illusion of increasing mutuality between Katherine and Petruccio—they are both shrews—even as Petruccio's mirroring behavior actually increases their gendered difference. In this way, I suggest to students, the play "solves" in narrative, but not in reality, the tensions between mutuality and male authority in early modern marriage.

Another reason to provide this context when teaching *The Taming of the Shrew* is to raise some larger literary critical and historiographical issues at the beginning of the term (when this play is usually taught). Introducing students to the vexed question of early modern marriage allows me to emphasize the importance of finding tensions and even opposing ideas in a text. Students often find this advice difficult for a couple of reasons. First, study aids such as SparkNotes tend to provide students a simple "theme" to read and remember, and that's what they expect from me. Second, when we teach students writing, we emphasize the virtue of clarity, so they have a hard time understanding that works of literature remain compelling in part not because they are clear but because they incorporate the energies of multiple perspectives and desires. This energy, I add, is not necessarily benign. In discussing how the play incorporates opposites, I introduce a definition of ideology that emphasizes its quality of illusorily smoothing over actual social contradiction—the "trick" I described above. I argue that *The Taming of the Shrew* encourages male authority and violence even as it disguises both in a fiction of mutuality that makes obedience look like love. Kiss me, Kate.

Examining early modern marriage advice while reading *The Taming of the Shrew* also provides an occasion to get students thinking about how they understand history. Students often assume that all people in the past believed the same things. I take the opportunity provided by a discussion of early modern marriage ideas to remind them that people in the past no more held a single point of view on an issue than people do now. Could the class describe a single current belief about gender roles? No. And neither could early moderns. Even the orthodox doctrine of the marriage homily would provide a quite fuzzy road map to the just-married couple. Further, when students imagine the early modern period, they often envisage this single point of view to be much more brutal than that held in our apparently more enlightened times. When they understand that views on the relationships between men and women were mixed in the early modern period, with some ideas sounding quite modern, they can also begin to think about how our "modern" ideas may be mixed as well and can see the ways that we have not ceased being early modern. In this respect, one could consider, for example, Phyllis Rackin's reception history of *The Taming of the Shrew*, which notes that the play became popular only in the twentieth century because it resonates with contemporary anxieties about gender roles (51–62).

Finally, in discussing the relationship between the play and its historical context, I also try to challenge the idea of Shakespeare as our contemporary, a feminist forefather, a cultural rebel, or a purveyor of near godlike wisdom. For if both early modern ideas about marriage and *The Taming of the Shrew* reflect a similar divide between mutual love and male authority, Shakespeare's play appears to serve women less well, both by muting male aggression in the name of comedy and by hiding the rifts plainly visible in a text such as the "Homily of the State of Matrimony" under the illusions of ideology. Nor, I think, can Shakespeare be said to be a superior analyst of the human mind. It's worth noting in this respect that the homily advises against Petruccio's intention to "tame" Katherine by being as violently belligerent as she is: "But if thou shouldest beat her, thou shalt increase her evil affections, for frowardness and sharpness is not amended with frowardness but with softness and gentleness" (23). Petruccio never goes so far as to beat Katherine, but he does believe, and the play suggests, that sharpness can best be amended by sharpness. In my own experience, it is the homily that's right, not Shakespeare's play. Students may also think that sharpness is better corrected with softness and gentleness. But their expectation that they will find the truth in Shakespeare's play keeps them from trusting their experience, especially if they believe that the early modern period had no better alternative to Petruccio's belligerence, his effort to become "more shrew than she." These observations lead the class to new questions. Should we be concerned if Shakespeare's play offers a *less* progressive view of marriage than early modern culture at large, a *less* perceptive sense of human behavior than we can find in the merely "historical" "Homily of the State of Matrimony"? Does the play have to be progressive or true in order to be great? If not, why do we continue to hold the play in high esteem? Should we?

NOTES

[1] I have added the quotation marks in this passage.

[2] Klein's modern edition of the homily, which I cite, is fairly accessible. Students might also consult the Web version at www.anglicanlibrary.org/homilies/bk2hom18.htm.

[3] For interesting insights on this point, see also Rackin 51–58.

[4] An ironic reading of this last speech recalls the promise of the homily that the wife who accommodates her husband will end up ruling him. Such irony, however, is hardly a triumph of love over obedience, for two reasons. First, the uncertainty of irony in the speech just expresses the drive in the play to smooth over contradictions in early modern attitudes toward marriage by allowing an audience to experience the speech as ironic—or not. Second, even if the speech is performed with heavy irony, the power of female charm has its limits, while the male fear of female deceit apparently does not. Just ask Desdemona.

[5] Shepard sums up this point nicely: "Ideas of men's controlled self-government exerted a frail, or at least a highly selective, hegemony, both in terms of their limited impact as well as in terms of the contradictions contained in official attitudes toward violence" (151). For an example of this "frail" control in Shakespeare, we could think of Othello. As Ruth Vanita has observed, Lodovico may be shocked at Othello's behavior toward Desdemona, but he does nothing to stop it. And he admires Iago for being valiant (346, 347).

"The Woman Is a Weak Creature": The Homily of Matrimony and *The Taming of the Shrew*

Peter C. Herman

"A Homily of the State of Matrimony," first published in England in 1563 and then republished twenty-two times by 1640, formed part of the two official compilations of sermons, one of which was supposed to be preached every Sunday. Given that church attendance was mandatory in early modern England, it is highly likely that nearly everybody in the country heard these sermons—often considered the voice of orthodoxy—at least once. Certainly, the Homily of Matrimony is often trotted out as an example of early modern views on women (see, e.g., McDonald, *Bedford Companion* 256–57). Teaching the homily presents the same problem as teaching the thorny topic of gender in *Paradise Lost*. Just as students in the Milton class often get stuck on "He for God only, she for God in him," thinking Milton an irredeemable misogynist, so students presented with the homily often do not get past "For the woman is a weak creature, not endued with like strength and constancy of mind" (174).[1] And yet the homily can serve as a guide to a more complex view of gender in early modern England as well as in *Shrew*. Instead of assuming that the homily takes a purely negative view of women or that it exclusively reproduces the "Pauline insistence on female submission" (McDonald, *Bedford Companion* 257) and thus constitutes a static backdrop for teaching *The Taming of the Shrew*, we can make the homily's contradictions and vacillations the foundation for a greater understanding of both Shakespeare's play and his culture.

I begin this project by asking the class how the homilist defines marriage and its purposes. They quickly point out that at the start, the homilist defines marriage as a union "instituted by God" whose main function is to "bring forth fruit, and to avoid fornication" (172). The first two points generally accord with their expectations: marriage is of more than casual importance in the early modern period, and its purpose is the channeling of sexuality into a socially approved relationship (i.e., sex itself is not bad, but sex outside of marriage is). The homily's description of marriage, however, as "a perpetual friendship" (172) usually surprises the class, who have assumed that in the early modern period, men were all-powerful and considered women their physical and intellectual inferiors. A "friendship," however, implies equality and mutuality. (Giving a short talk on the history of companionate marriage at this juncture is often a good idea.)[2] The real fun, however, begins when I ask the class, "So what was the state of marriage in early modern England?" A few minutes of further reading produces an answer: "It was a battlefield." The class's attention settles on this key passage: "We see how wonderful[ly] the devil deludeth and scorneth this state, how few matrimonies there be without chidings, brawlings, tauntings, repentings, bitter cursings, and fightings" (173). It often comes as something of a shock to the class when they realize that the point of the homily is not so much the praise of marriage as the denunciation of such violence within the marriage.

Two points follow that challenge preconceived notions about Shakespeare's culture: neither the church nor the secular government approved of domestic violence or considered it a minor issue, and the description of domestic violence in the homily is surprisingly evenhanded. Many critics and historians (e.g., Boose, "Scolding" and "Taming"; Underdown) have emphasized the patriarchal nature of Shakespeare's society: how those in authority (obviously, mainly men) sought to crush into submission unruly, disobedient women, or, as Katherine calls them in her infamous last speech, "froward and unable worms" (5.2.173). The homily, however, suggests that the picture may be more complicated. Evidently, early modern women resisted, or at least gave as good as they got and got as good as they gave. The question I ultimately raise is what the homily concludes about this situation.

At that point in the lesson, I ask the class to back up and look at the language of the whole homily more closely. Whom precisely does the homilist address, when does the homilist address them, and what does the homilist say? The first surprise is that the homilist begins not by addressing women alone but by addressing both husbands *and* wives. And after bluntly describing the war zone of early modern marriage, the homilist refuses to assign blame to one particular sex. Instead, the reader finds a procession of third-person plural pronouns:

> Yea, *they* would not give place to the provocation of wrath, which stirreth *them* either to such rough and sharp words. . . . [It is] a miserable thing to behold, that yet *they* are of necessity compelled to live together, which yet cannot be in quiet together. . . . *[T]hey* will not consider the crafty trains of the devil, and therefore give not *themselves* to pray to God.
>
> (174; my emphasis)

When the homilist says, "Learn, thou, therefore, if thou desirest to be void of all these miseries" (174), "thou" refers to both parties in the marriage, not just one side.

Mirroring, perhaps, the course of contemporary marriage therapy, after the homilist finishes his initial comments to the battling couples, he then addresses remarks specific to each gender. When we come to this part of the tract, I often split the class by gender and have the men summarize the homilist's remarks to wives while the women take the remarks to husbands. There is no avoiding, nor should one avoid, how the homilist's initial remarks to women unambiguously endorse the misogynist belief in female inferiority. After quoting Paul's description of the wife in 1 Peter 3 as "the weaker vessel" (174), the homilist drives the point home: "For the woman is a weak creature, not endued with like strength and constancy of mind; therefore, they [women] be the sooner disquieted, and they be the more prone to all weak affections and dispositions of mind, more than men be; and lighter they be, and more vain in their fantasies and opinions" (174). (Depending on how annoying the male students want to be, they will often deliver their summary with considerable relish.)

But then, the class discovers that if the homily endorses women's inferiority, that still does not mean it is an unqualifiedly masculinist document. After suggesting that husbands, taking female frailty into account, "ought to wink at some things, and must gently expound all things, and to forbear" (175), the homilist denounces the machismo (an anachronistic term, but accurate nonetheless) that leads to so much domestic violence:

> Howbeit, the common sort of men doth judge that such moderation should not become a man. For they say that it is a token of womanish cowardness and therefore they think that it is a man's part to fume in anger, to fight with fist and staff. Howbeit, howsoever they imagine, undoubtedly Saint Peter doth better judge what should be seeming to a man, and what he should most reasonably perform. For he saith reasoning should be used, and not fighting. (175)

In fact, the homilist attempts to redefine masculinity so that it doesn't include violence: "And yet a man may be a man, although he doth not use such extremity" (175–76). Nor does the homilist restrict himself to denouncing wife beating. "*But* what say I? Your wives? No, it is not to be borne with that an honest man should lay hands on his maid-servant to beat her. Wherefore, if it be a great shame for a man to beat his bond-servant, much more rebuke it is to lay violent hands upon his free-woman" (180).

This pattern repeats itself for the rest of the homily. On the one hand, the homilist consistently enjoins wives to obey their husbands (e.g., "This let the wife have ever in mind, the rather admonished thereto by the apparel of her head, whereby is signified, that she is under covert or obedience of her husband" [177]). Yet with equal consistency (or inconsistency), the homilist balances his emphasis on female inferiority against a validation of women's perspectives and an attack on the male propensity toward hitting people. After, for example, the homilist reminds women how "ancient women of the old world called their husbands lords," he endorses their imagined response: "But peradventure she will say that those men loved their wives indeed. I know that well enough, and bear it well in mind" (177). The homilist fully understands, in other words, that sixteenth-century husbands do not compare well with those "of the old world" and so perhaps are not as worthy of their wives' adulation. Furthermore, after telling women that they should follow Sarah's example in calling their husbands "Lord" (177), the homilist turns to men and reminds them that they should be grateful that women marry at all, given the costs and dangers:

> Truth it is, that they [women] must [e]specially feel the grief and pains of their matrimony, in that they relinquish the liberty of their own rule, in the pain of their travailing [laboring to give birth], in the bringing up

> of their children. In which offices they be in great perils, and be grieved with great afflictions, which they might be without, if they lived out of matrimony. (177)

As the homily continues, the vacillation between the two positions increases in intensity. Each time the homilist enjoins women to deal with their situation by either prayer or patience, he seems to realize the implications of what he is saying and quickly delivers a correction. And then, realizing the implications of the correction, he corrects the correction, leading to a dizzying procession of qualifications and counter-qualifications. For example, after telling women that they must endure with Christian patience "an extreme husband" in anticipation of the reward in heaven, the homilist immediately says: "Yet I speak not these things that I would wish the husbands to be sharp towards their wives" (178). And after telling both parties to mind their own affairs rather than their partner's ("Let not, therefore, the woman be too busy to call for the duty of her husband . . . [and] let not the man only consider what belongeth to the woman" [180]), the homilist offers this series of suggestions, each qualified by the next:

> *But*, as I have said, let either party be ready and willing to perform that which belongeth [e]specially to themselves. For if we be bound to hold out our left cheek to strangers, which will smite us on the right cheek, how much more ought we suffer an extreme and unkind husband? *But* yet I mean not that a man should beat his wife. For God forbid that, for that is the greatest shame that can be, not so much to her that is beaten as to him that doth the deed. *But* if by fortune thou chancest upon such a husband, take it not too heavily, but suppose thou that thereby is laid up no small reward hereafter, and in this lifetime, no small commendation to thee, if thou canst be quiet. *But* yet to you that be men, thus I speak: let there be none so grievous fault to compel you to beat your wives . . .
>
> (180; my emphasis)

In sum, the "Homily of the State of Matrimony" depicts a vastly more confused and contradictory picture of early modern thinking regarding gender than most teachers allow. At the same time that the homilist insists on female subservience and inferiority ("the woman is a frail vessel" [181]), he recognizes the tremendous cost and risk to women when they get married. They not only lose their freedom, they might lose their lives giving birth. As for men, the homilist wastes no opportunity to denounce their propensity toward violence and explicitly tries to redefine masculinity away from fuming and fighting with fist and staff. Yet the homilist seems unsure of precisely what position he wants to take, since he follows each statement with "but" (as does Paul; see the procession of qualifications in 1 Corinthians 7.1–7).

When I ask my students how the homily alters or guides their understanding of the play, they usually respond with two observations. First, they note that the play represents the violent landscape of early modern marriage as described by the homilist. The genders in this play are at war, and thus Shakespeare's plot would have seemed very familiar to the original audience. Students can imagine somebody hearing the "Homily of the State of Matrimony" on Sunday morning and seeing *The Taming of the Shrew* a few days later (plays were not performed on Sundays). They also note how Katherine very clearly does not comport with the ideals for feminine behavior set out by the homilist. Patience and prayer do not seem to be in her repertoire of behaviors.

However, just as the homily looks critically at both genders, so does this play. Drawing the class's attention to the homilist's denunciation of masters beating servants, I ask them to look at Petruccio's first appearance. When Petruccio enters the stage in act 1, scene 2, he and Grumio engage in a very funny argument over the precise meaning of the command "Here, sirrah Grumio, knock I say" (1.2.5). Grumio pretends incomprehension ("Knock, sir? Whom should I knock? Is there any man has rebused your worship? [1.2.6–7]), but my point is not so much that Petruccio's meaning is not self-evident as that, fed up with his stubbornly clever servant, Petruccio proceeds to "lay violent hands" upon Grumio: "Faith, sirrah, an you'll not knock, I'll ring it / I'll try how you can sol-fa and sing it. [*s.d.*] *He wrings him by the ears*" (1.2.16–17 [*Mr. William Shakespeares Comedies*, sig. S6r]). Nor is this instance of violence unique. By Gremio's later report, Petruccio has given the cleric marrying him and Katherine "such a cuff / That fell down priest, and book, and book, and priest" (3.3.36–37), and later we see him kick the servant taking off his boots (4.1.128). This is all very funny slapstick, whether seen or reported, but the comparison of these moments with the homily lends them a darker overtone. Students quickly note that if Katherine contravenes the ideals of female behavior set out by the homily, Petruccio contravenes the homilist's ideals of masculine behavior, however comically, by acting as if "it is a man's part to fume in anger" ("Homily" 175).

Using the homily as a guide for teaching Katherine also allows for a more complicated appreciation of both. Certainly, Katherine fails to embrace the homily's ideal of feminine obedience, and so, using those parts of the homily as their guide, students would think that Katherine's behavior puts her outside the pale of acceptable feminine norms. However, as we have seen, the homily is not altogether unsympathetic toward the plight of women in early modern England, and its sympathetic passages give further point to the two passages in the play in which Katherine justifies her behavior. When Petruccio refuses to go to the bridal dinner, Katherine demands that they proceed, but she couches her contrariness in resonant terms: "I see a woman may be made a fool / If she had not a spirit to resist" (3.3.91–92). Later, Katherine demands her right to speak as she sees fit: "I am no child, no babe. / Your betters have endured me say my mind, / And if you cannot, best you stop your ears" (4.3.74–76). Katherine, in short, demands agency. Certainly, these lines contradict the part of the homily enjoining women to submit their will to their husbands', but they harmonize with the homilist's recognition that marriage not only costs women "the liberty of their own rule" but also causes them to feel "grief and pain" at their loss. Putting these passages together in the classroom allows students to understand that Shakespeare's play and the homily are not always at odds with each other and that each is more complicated than a superficial reading would suggest. Both *The Taming of the Shrew* and the homily—and by extension, early modern culture generally—recognize the *costs* of patriarchy even as they seem to endorse the Pauline belief in female inferiority and subordination.

Asking students to compare the homily's overall sense of marriage with Petruccio's also provides an unexpected perspective. Immediately following Katherine's declaration of her determination to resist Petruccio's plan to deny her her own bridal dinner, Petruccio delivers his famous speech on woman as object rather than person:

> I will be master of what is mine own.
> She is my goods, my chattels. She is my house,
> My household-stuff, my field, my barn,
> My horse, my ox, my ass, my [any thing],[3]
> And here she stands, touch her whoever dare. (3.2.218–22)

When students are asked to compare Petruccio's reduction of his wife to the status of an object with the homily's statements about women, they usually first notice that this speech provides a concrete example of a woman losing "the liberty" of her own rule. Once a human being, she is now his "goods," his "chattels"—an animal, an object, no longer a subject. This insight often leads to a discussion of how Petruccio's speech conflicts with the homilist's definition of marriage as "a perpetual friendship" (172), how they need "to knit their minds together, that they be not dissevered by any division of discord" (173). Even at his most insulting toward women (when, for instance, the homilist asserts that "the woman is a weak creature" [174]), the homilist never denies that women belong to humanity. The wife may be "under covert or obedience of her husband" (177), but she is not the husband's dog. Petruccio even goes beyond (or below) the standards established by the Tenth Commandment: "Neither shalt thou covet thy neighbor's wife, neither shalt thou desire they neighbor's house, his field, nor his man servant, nor his made, his oxe, nor his asse, nor ought that thy neighbor hath" (Deut. 5.21 [*Geneva Bible*]). While the Norton's gloss rightly notes that Petruccio's catalog of possessions alludes in a general way to this text, the wife in the biblical text retains her humanity, whereas Petruccio reduces his spouse to property. This distinction brings us to how the homily can guide class discussion of Katherine's infamous final speech.

When charged by Petruccio to "tell these headstrong women / What duty they do owe their lords and husbands" (5.2.134–35), Katherine responds with an extensive oration (forty-three lines) that puts the relationship between husband and wife in explicitly political terms:

> Thy husband is thy lord, thy life, thy keeper,
> Thy head, thy sovereign, one that cares for thee
> . . . .
> And craves no other tribute at thy hands
> But love, fair looks, and true obedience—
> Too little payment for so great a debt.
> Such duty as the subject owes the prince,
> Even such a woman oweth to her husband,
> And when she is froward, peevish, sullen, sour,
> And not obedient to his honest will,
> What is she but a foul contending rebel,
> And graceless traitor to her loving lord?
> (5.2.150–51, 156–64)

Certainly, these lines comport with the homilist's assertion that wife is to husband as child to parent or servant to master. Women, the homilist claims, should no more point out their husbands' faults than a child should correct his or her parents ("if they should tell us again our duties, we should not think it well done" [178]). But significant differences emerge as well.[4] The most important shift, students quickly note, is that the homilist speaks in terms of religion ("For thus it is most reasonable to obey God, if they wilt not suffer thyself to transgress his law" [178]), while Katherine invokes secular politics. But Katherine's language, instead of aligning Katherine with political orthodoxy, suggests that she may be going too far in her prescriptions of female subservience. True, this speech draws on the common analogy between the household and the commonwealth, but the relationship between subject and sovereign, whether domestic or state, in sixteenth-century England was more reciprocal, less one-sided, than Katherine seems to allow. Thomas Smith, in *De Republica Anglorum* (1583), for example, while allowing for differences in gender roles and endowments, describes husband and wife as mutual rulers and subjects: "each obeyeth and commandeth [the] other, and they too together rule the house" (590; see also Jordan). When placed next to the homily (and related texts), Katherine's final speech, like Petruccio's lines objectifying women, goes beyond the accepted norm, thus inviting a skeptical reception.

The question for class discussion, of course, is whether Katherine's extremism reflects her broken spirit or her irony. This is not to say that Katherine and Petruccio are always at odds with both each other and the homilist. The homilist urges husbands to "forbear" (181) in the face of provocations, and that is exactly what Petruccio initially plans, and indeed does: "Say that she rail, why then I'll tell her plain / She sings as sweetly as a nightingale. / Say that she frown, I'll say she looks as clear / As morning roses newly washed with dew" (2.1.168–71). And Petruccio and Katherine's mutually improvised joke played on the befuddled Vincentio in 4.6 provides a marvelous example (albeit not the one the homilist has in mind) of minds so knitted together "that they be not dissevered by any division of discord" (173).

Using the homily as a guide to teaching *The Taming of the Shrew* allows the class to capture the full complexity of both the play and early modern conceptions of gender. The convolutions and contradictions of the homily demonstrate that the convolutions and contradictions of *The Taming of the Shrew* arise from more than Shakespeare's complex imagination. Rather, the play mirrors Elizabethan England's difficulties with defining the proper roles for men and women. In an early essay, Jean E. Howard wrote that Shakespeare's comedies are not designed to "solve problems, but to make us live with a heightened sense that the problematic is the inescapable element in which we live and move" ("Difficulties" 126). Using the homily to teach Shakespeare's play admirably fulfills that goal for both Shakespeare's culture and our own.

NOTES

[1] All references to *The Taming of the Shrew* and the homily are to Dolan's 1996 edition of Shakespeare's play.

[2] See Haller and Haller; Wright 205–27; and Powell as foundational sources. See also Todd for a critique of this concept.

[3] To emphasize how this speech degrades Katherine, I have adopted the Folio's splitting "anything" (which emphasizes possibility) into two words, "any thing" (Shakespeare, *Mr. William Shakespeares Comedies*, sig. T2v), which limits the range to objects.

[4] The homilist's point is not so much blind obedience as not using someone else's faults to excuse your own, and the point applies as much to men as to women ("for when we be admonished of our duties and faults, we ought not then to seek what other men's duties be. For though a man had a companion in his fault, yet should he not thereby be without his fault" [178]).

Music, Ovid, and the Renaissance Classroom in *The Taming of the Shrew*

Joseph M. Ortiz

The main action of *The Taming of the Shrew* begins, as most college courses do, with a syllabus. Having just arrived in Padua, Lucentio announces that he will "haply institute / A course of learning and ingenious studies" (1.1.8–9). His servant Tranio is quick to offer suggestions about the proposed course of study, lest it prove too dry and academic:

> Let's be no stoics nor no stocks, I pray,
> Or so devote to Aristotle's checks
> As Ovid be an outcast quite abjured
> . . . .
> Music and poesy use to quicken you;
> The mathematics and the metaphysics,
> Fall to them as you find your stomach serves you.
> No profit grows where is no pleasure ta'en. (1.1.31–33, 36–39)

My Shakespeare students, most of them English majors, often find a fellow feeling with Tranio here, since many of them profess to have little "stomach" for mathematics and since some have experienced firsthand the trimming of music education from American public school systems. Students unfamiliar with Ovid are likely to wonder about his inclusion here, although those who have read even a little of the *Metamorphoses* know full well that Ovid is no "stoic." I think it is important, however, to try to recuperate some of the strangeness of Tranio's remarks. Music and Ovid, as Shakespeare was fully aware, were not always taught for "pleasure" rather than "profit" in Renaissance England, and the academic presentation of music and Ovid could be as leaden and monotonous as anything found in Aristotle. Tranio's conspicuous attempt to include them in the Paduan curriculum thus begs the question: what is to be learned or gained from studying music and Ovid? And, for me, this question is inextricably bound up with another: what is to be learned or gained from reading *The Taming of the Shrew*?

When teaching the play, usually as part of my college's standard Shakespeare course and occasionally in advanced courses on Renaissance literature, I foreground the idea of education as a possible topic for analysis. I point out to my students that Padua was well known in Renaissance Europe as a center of higher learning; Lucentio's visit to Padua is not very different from a study-abroad semester at Oxford. I also discuss briefly the play's critical and theatrical history, in which there has generally been much anxiety about what the play "teaches" through its unabashed displays of sexism and its apparent sanction of domestic abuse. (I almost always show a clip of Elizabeth Taylor's performance as Katherine in the 1967 Zeffirelli film version, noting that Taylor once said in an interview that she believed Katherine is a truly converted woman by the end of the play and that her final speech should be performed without a hint of irony.) In addition, during the first class session on the play I spend a significant amount of time on the induction, a structural element that appears in no other Shakespeare play and that foregrounds a number of concepts relevant to the problem of education. For example, when the Lord announces his plan to transport the sleeping, drunken Sly to his house and dress him in lavish clothes, he asks his servants, "Would not the beggar then forget himself?" (sc. 1, line 41). What precisely, I ask, does the Lord want Sly to forget? Is it possible to forget one's social class? And, as a corollary, is it possible to "learn" a new social identity? Although the answers to these questions vary from class to class, my students generally agree that the induction is likely to influence the way we respond to Katherine's transformation from shrew to obedient wife in the main action of the play. In other words, the induction teases out our assumptions about the possibilities and limits of education, especially when the goal of education is the fashioning of social and gendered identities.

Music and Ovid are useful topics for unpacking the play's complex engagement with education, not least because they were often at the center of Renaissance debates over the value of certain kinds of knowledge. As Jonathan Bate has shown, the question of how to teach the poetry of Ovid—as Christian or moral allegory, as a set of rhetorical exempla, as a model for poetic invention, or as a textbook for the learning of Latin—remains unsettled in early modern England (43). The presence of multiple Ovids in the Renaissance reflects a fundamental disagreement about the value of classical poetry and about the aims of humanist education in general. A similar heterodoxy can be seen in the several approaches to music in the period. English books on practical music instruction started appearing with unprecedented regularity in the 1590s, although the older habit of teaching music as a branch of mathematics or speculative philosophy persisted well into the seventeenth century. The ideological nature of these differences in music education is nowhere more apparent than in the careers of John Bull and John Taverner, both professors of music at Gresham College between 1596 and 1610. Bull, a well-known organist and composer, centered his Gresham lectures on musical demonstrations, often using his own compositions as examples. By contrast, Taverner, whose main qualification for the post was a character recommendation from his former professor at Oxford, focused almost exclusively on etymological, historical, and literary topics in his music lectures, going so far as to wish publicly that other music instructors (i.e., Bull) "had laboured in that historicall search, which if they had done, they might have added much to their owne glory and our knowledge" (lecture 4). Clearly, for Taverner, true knowledge of music is gained by reading, not hearing. Likewise, when the Elizabethan polemicist Stephen Gosson writes in *The Schoole of Abuse* (1579) that "if you will bee good Scholers, and profite well in the Arte of Musicke, shutte your fidels in their cases, and looke up to heaven" (sigs. 4A4v–5A4r), he is not so much acting the part of a cranky Puritan as he is taking sides in an ideological debate over forms of teaching.

That *The Taming of the Shrew* speaks to the debates over music and Ovid is suggested by the play's several examples of musical and literary instruction, most of which are memorable for their utter failure. For example, there is Hortensio's attempt to teach Katherine the lute, an endeavor that ends with his head being forced through the instrument's sound hole:

> I did but tell her she mistook her frets,
> And bowed her hand to teach her fingering,
> When, with a most impatient devilish spirit,
> "Frets, call you these?" quoth she, "I'll fume with them,"
> And with that word she struck me on the head,
> And through the instrument my pate made way,
> And there I stood amazèd for a while,
> As on a pillory, looking through the lute,
> While she did call me rascal, fiddler,
> And twangling jack, with twenty such vile terms,
> As had she studied to misuse me so. (2.1.147–57)

Katherine's decision to use the lute as a bludgeon comes as little surprise, given that Hortensio's lesson requires her to conform her physical body to an established set of rules—in this case, literally to bend her fingers and place them on the correct places on the lute's fingerboard. In this respect, Katherine's refusal to play the lute correctly both figures and constitutes her resistance—at least in the first half of the play—to prescribed models of feminine behavior. At the same time, Hortensio's description of Katherine's rebellion as "studied" portrays her willful misuse of musical terms and her inspired use of the lute as a "pillory" to provide a counterlesson to Hortensio's orthodox approach to music. As such, Katherine's noisy, violent response makes apparent—with painful consequences for Hortensio—the reality of music as a physically embodied activity, rather than a set of easily codified rules.

Shakespeare stages a more complex scene of instruction in the lessons given to Bianca by her would-be tutors. Here, both Ovid and music are subject to a dizzying display of willful distortions. Lucentio is the first instructor, and he begins his Latin lesson by parsing lines from Ovid's *Heroides*: "'*Hic ibat*,' as I told you before—'*Simois*,' I am Lucentio—'*hic est*,' son unto Vincentio of Pisa—'*Sigeia tellus*,' disguised thus to get your love—'*hic steterat*,' and that Lucentio that comes a-wooing—'*Priami*,' is my man Tranio—'*regia*,' bearing my port—'*celsa senis*,' that we might beguile the old pantaloon" (3.1.31–36). As Heather James has pointed out, although the Latin text is a seemingly innocuous passage from Penelope's letter to Ulysses, Lucentio's mock translation of the lines is clearly inspired by the conventions of Roman new comedy, in which a young man overcomes rival suitors and forbidding fathers in order to win the love of a desirable girl (69). In this way, Ovid's *Heroides* is both an instrument and veil for Lucentio's amatory plot. Bianca, in her reply to Lucentio, which corrects his parsing of Latin phrases and implies her own guarded encouragement of his advances, shows that she understands well the traditional forms of Latin instruction—in which master and pupil rehearse ad nauseam the grammatical forms of classical quotations—as well as the underlying motive of this particular instructor.

A similar pretext characterizes Hortensio's music lesson, which follows almost immediately:

> *Gam-ut* I am, the ground of all accord,
> A—re—to Plead Hortensio's passion.
> B—mi—Bianca, take him for thy lord.
> C—fa, ut—that loves with all affection.
> D—sol, re—one clef, two notes have I,
> E—la, mi—show pity, or I die. (3.1.71–76)

Here, Hortensio teaches the notes of the musical scale using the solmization method (a combination of letter names and syllables), an extremely popular way of teaching music in Renaissance Europe that was often described in instructional texts. For example, Thomas Morley's *Plaine and Easie Introduction to Practicall Musicke* (1597), one of the earliest published music primers in England, begins with the scale of music, which Morley tells his reader must be learned "forwards and backwards" before anything else can be studied (6). Of course, like those of Lucentio's Latin lesson, the motives of Hortensio's teaching are amatory rather than academic, a fact that Bianca clearly perceives: "Call you this gamut? Tut, I like it not. / Old fashions please me best. I am not so nice / To change true rules for odd inventions" (3.2.77–79). Bianca's rebuff of Hortensio, while unmistakable, is articulated through legitimate claims about musical teaching, and the sexual competition between her suitors is played out through references to actual contemporary debates about music:

> HORTENSIO. But, wrangling, pedant, this Bianca is,
> The patroness of heavenly harmony.
> Then give me leave to have prerogative,
> And when in music we have spent an hour
> Your lecture shall have leisure for as much.
> LUCENTIO. Preposterous ass, that never read so far
> To know the cause why music was ordained!
> Was it not to refresh the mind of man
> After his studies or his usual pain? (4–12)

Characterizing music as "heavenly harmony," Hortensio echoes much speculative writing on music in the period, while Lucentio, following writers like Gosson and Taverner, strongly reinscribes the distinction between *musica mundana* (cosmological harmony) and *musica practica* ("performed music"). In any case, the scene of instruction quickly devolves into a series of sexual insults thinly disguised as musical advice: "Spit in the hole, man, and tune again" (39). I often have my students read aloud the entire scene in class, suggesting to them that if something sounds like a dirty joke, it probably is.

For all its bawdy humor, Bianca's lesson in *Shrew* is a parody, not a travesty. Moralizing interpretations of music and Ovid were alive and well in the Renaissance classroom, where the impulse toward allegory was often strongest. By staging music and Ovid as obvious pretexts for flirtation and bawdy, Shakespeare merely reverses the prevailing trend: he gives us a demoralized Ovid and a demoralized music, effectively sending up Renaissance educational practices. To give my students a sense of the topicality of Shakespeare's scenes of instruction in *Shrew*, I provide some background on Renaissance Ovidianism and music theory. For example, my students are simultaneously horrified and relieved (for themselves) to learn that grammatical drills in Latin like the one rehearsed by Lucentio were absolutely normal and frequent in the Renaissance classroom. Likewise, a page from the *Ovidius Moralizatus*—I use my own translation of the beginning of Pierre Bersuire's interpretation of the Apollo and Daphne episode—is usually enough to convince my students of the liberties taken by Christian allegorists. For music, I pull extracts from a number of sources to illustrate the general approach taken by writers on speculative music: the story of Pythagoras in Macrobius's *Dream of Scipio*, illustrations of Pythagoras in Gaffurio's *Theorica musice*, and musical-astronomical diagrams in Robert Fludd's *Utriusque cosmi . . . historia*, among others. Especially in Shakespeare courses that also include *The Merchant of Venice* or *Twelfth Night*, I generally devote part of a class session explaining the mathematical basis of musical harmonics (occasionally using my own clarinet to demonstrate), noting how this mathematical approach helped bolster universalizing claims made about music during the period.

My point in providing this historical background—which can be abbreviated or expanded depending on the particular course—is to give my students a sense of the ways in which a seemingly narrow subject, like music theory or classical poetry, can be (and was) used to teach and ingrain a vast range of ideas, beliefs, skills, and behaviors and that these "ends" of instruction almost always reflect the particular motives or ideologies of persons and institutions. Along these lines, in order to help my students theorize education for themselves, I recently developed an interactive class assignment in conjunction with reading *Shrew*, in which I asked some students to "teach" music or language. I asked the student-instructors, who were preselected based on information they provided about themselves on an earlier quiz, to develop a twenty-minute lesson on music or a foreign language, which each of them would teach to two or three fellow students as part of a group activity during class. The instructors were free to take any approach to their subject, though they were told that their "students" would be asked to demonstrate something they had learned to the rest of the class. Afterward, the "pupils" were required to submit written answers to the following questions:

> Briefly describe the lesson. What was your instructor trying to teach?
> How would you characterize the knowledge that was taught? Was it a body of information? a physical skill? something else?
> How would you describe your instructor's approach to the subject? What method did he or she use to help you learn the subject?
> What is most difficult about the subject for you? Do you think it would be harder or easier for others? If so, why?
> Is learning music or a language different from learning literature? Explain.

On the whole, the activity was successful. The instructors collectively devised a wonderfully various and substantive set of lessons, including the complete alphabet in American Sign Language, basic conversational phrases in Japanese, methods of chord playing on an acoustic guitar, and the history of the lute, to mention only a few. More important, in their written responses to the assignment my students were able to articulate several fine points about different types of learning. For example, some were particularly eloquent on the difference between conceptual and motor learning: "ASL is both a body of knowledge and a set of physical skills. Being a language, it has a large body of rules, symbols and syntax. But the actual use of the language requires fine control over motor function and a good deal of muscle memory." Many students were very candid, including one who addressed directly the relation between education and pain: "Playing chords on the guitar hurt my fingers. My left index finger is still sore." I compiled the student responses and organized them under theoretical categories (conceptual vs. somatic learning, visual vs. aural learning, memory knowledge vs. critical knowledge, etc.), and I distributed them to the class as a record of their collective observations about the educational experience.

Armed with this set of theoretical frames for thinking about education, we turned our attention to the beginning of 4.1, in which Petruccio's servants prepare for his arrival with Katherine. I chose this scene for its seeming innocuousness, although almost any scene in the play would have done. The scene initially comes off as a moment of lowbrow comic relief, but my students quickly identified it, like the gravedigger scene in *Hamlet*, as a scene of instruction, in part because of its several references to "taming":

> CURTIS. Is she so hot a shrew as she's reported?
> GRUMIO. She was, good Curtis, before this frost; but thou know'st, winter tames man, woman, and beast, for it hath tamed my old master, and my new mistress, and myself, fellow Curtis.
> (4.1.17–21)

What Grumio and Curtis (and possibly Katherine by now) have learned, according to my students, is the extreme vulnerability of human beings to the physical elements and—as a corollary—the need for "fellow" beings to help provide a defense against harsh conditions. In other words, they have learned the usefulness of social structures—of having servants to fire the wood, masters to provide clothes—for daily life. Moreover, the effectiveness of this lesson is directly proportional to its status as a physical process: Grumio's experience of having his lips "freeze to [his] teeth" and his "tongue to the roof of [his] mouth" forcefully impresses on him the demands placed on him by seasonal change (5–6). He "know[s]" winter because he has physically felt it.

The relationship between learning and physical sensation, or between learning and pain, directly bears on the passage that follows, in which Grumio describes Petruccio and Katherine's journey. Grumio frames his narrative with the language of education ("a sensible tale," "*inprimis*" [4.1.54–56]), yet the method of his storytelling is one that immediately inspires the audience's pleasure:

> But hadst thou not crossed me thou shouldst have heard how her horse fell and she under her horse; thou shouldst have heard in how miry a place, how she was bemoiled, how he left her with the horse upon her, how he beat me because her horse stumbled, how she waded through the dirt to pluck him off me, how he swore, how she prayed that never prayed before, how I cried, how the horses ran away, how her bridle was burst, how I lost my crupper, with many things of worthy memory which now shall die in oblivion, and thou return unexperienced to thy grave.
>
> (4.1.61–70)

Jeanne Addison Roberts, as well as Grace Tiffany (*Erotic Beasts* 85), has argued that Shakespeare's repeated references to horses in *Shrew* speak to his fascination with human transformation, especially as informed by Ovid. While I am persuaded by this reading, my students—most of whom are from upstate New York and some of whom have actually lived on or near a farm—are more likely to point out that a horse is a very, very heavy thing. Thus, for Katherine to find herself "with the horse upon her" is a very physical lesson indeed, not likely to be easily forgotten. As readers of the episode, we may be inclined (after we have stopped laughing) to pay attention to the metaphoric significance of horses, especially if we have read our Ovid. On the other hand, as my students have suggested, Katherine more immediately learns here the limits of her strength and the insignificance of her desires. She learns that her body is in fact "soft, and weak" (5.1.169), at least relative to a horse's. Subsequently, having made distinctions about the different kinds of learning in the play, my students are slightly less interested in the question of whether Katherine is truly sincere at the end of the play (a point on which they are perennially divided) than in the question of *what* she learns and the forms in which that learning takes shape.

Music and Ovid are not the only approaches through which to untangle the play's complex representation of educational practices. At the same time, the performative nature of music and the discursive promiscuity of Ovidian poetry put unusual pressure on any educational model that attempts to enlist music and Ovid. This may partly explain why Shakespeare returns to music and Ovid, often in conjunction, in plays from *Titus Andronicus* to *The Tempest*. As a final demonstration of Shakespeare's tendency to resist interpretive closure, especially when it comes to questions of learning, I show my students the ending of the anonymous *The Taming of a Shrew*, in which Sly pointedly announces that he has learned how to tame his own wife by watching the play. What, I ask them, has Shakespeare's Sly—whom we do not see at the end of *Shrew*—learned? Perhaps, they suggest, he has fallen asleep, which he seems on the verge of doing by the end of the first scene. Again, we see that learning, whatever its content, requires a physical, wakeful presence. Only once while teaching *Shrew* did I have an actual example of this fact to use as a demonstration. Although I was annoyed, the slumbering student made an excellent teaching tool.

“To Teach Both Sexes Due Equality”

Todd M. Lidh

Katherine's final speech in 5.2 of *The Taming of the Shrew* is easily one of the most controversial moments in Shakespeare. Is she serious? broken? sarcastic? playful? knowing? brainwashed? satisfied? seething? sincere? And perhaps more pressing, How do you teach that moment? As Ervin Beck notes, “This speech has been used to support opposite interpretations of the play. If Kate indeed places her hands under Petruccio's foot, then patriarchal dominance is confirmed. Most critics, however, have assumed that Petruccio does not allow Kate to do so. Her speech is, after all, only an offer” (10). As Ann Thompson, editor for the New Cambridge edition of the play, astutely remarks in the introduction, “[t]he relationship between Petruchio and Katherine is obviously the heart of the problem; in no other Shakespearean comedy does a single relationship dominate the play so thoroughly” (25).

Few contemporary productions offer an interpretation codifying the patriarchal relationship between Katherine and Petruccio and giving his wooing-and-taming method an unquestioned seal of approval. Instead, interpretations have in one way or another incorporated an ironic commentary on Kate's submission speech. A case in point: in a 1990 Central Park production starring Morgan Freeman and Tracey Ullman, Kate made her final deferential speech while kneeling and helping Petruccio off with his boots. Petruccio sat on a stool, “looking very pleased with her comments. As she finished, she upended him and he landed on his back, first shocked, then amused. Then the two of them walked off together arm in arm, having ‘played a joke’ on the rest of the people on stage” (van den Berg).[1] In other productions of the late twentieth and early twenty-first century, Katherine in this scene has been played as a mental patient, a sadist, a co-conspirator with her gambling husband, or some other sort of schemer.[2] How do I as a teacher balance what's on the page and what's currently on the stage? After all, my students are unlikely to see a contemporary performance with Katherine delivering her speech without irony or anger or amusement—and yet there's nothing in the text itself that necessarily indicates something other than a conventional interpretation, in which she means what she says.

One solution I have found is to ask them to read another play.

There's a Sequel?

John Fletcher's lesser-known *The Woman's Prize; or, The Tamer Tamed* may seem like an unlikely addition to a traditional Shakespeare course. Fletcher's play, written sometime from 1604 to 1614 and thus at least twenty years after *Shrew*, makes a number of changes to Shakespeare's play: the locale shifts from

Padua to London, eliminating whatever "exoticness" may have existed as a result of the earlier play's mainly Italian setting; any connection to the induction material is nonexistent; Petruccio is the only recognizable character (both Tranio and Bianca appear in Fletcher's play, but neither seems familiar); and, most shockingly, Katherine has died, even going unnamed. However, for students and teachers struggling with how to interpret Katherine's final speech, Fletcher's *The Woman's Prize* is far more than a sequel, a continuation, a counterblast, an adaptation, a spin-off, a burlesque, or even a "calculated intertextual glance."[3] After all, it is the only contemporary response from within Shakespeare's own playing company by the playwright who collaborated with him on *Henry VIII*, *The Two Noble Kinsmen*, and (some believe) a lost play called *Cardenio*. *The Woman's Prize* focuses squarely on the theme of a tamer and a shrew, but from a different perspective. In Fletcher's play, while there is still taming to be had, it is Petruccio who is tamed by his new wife, Maria.

The change is appreciated by my students, who always exhibit some ambivalence about the ending of *The Taming of the Shrew*. As one student put it, a marriage that a woman is forced to enter and to behave subserviently in does not end happily ever after. In some fashion, it appears Fletcher felt similarly and therefore chose to revisit the story's infamous tamer, Petruccio, and to put him in decidedly different circumstances with a vastly different outcome. In class, students have described Shakespeare's Petruccio as conceited, arrogant, violent, chauvinistic, and even as a Neanderthal. While there is some grudging agreement that his methods appear to be successful, rarely are students satisfied with the ending of Shakespeare's play. Indeed, my students don't feel completely happy about any of the couples by the end of the play. Thus, there is some surprise and validation when students read Moroso's speech from Fletcher's play:[4]

> What though his other wife,
> Out of her most abundant stubbornness,
> Out of her daily hues and cries upon him—
> For, sure, she was a rebel—turned his temper
> And forced him blow as high as she?
> . . . .
> For yet the bare remembrance of his first wife—
> I tell ye on my knowledge, and a truth too—
> Will make him start in's sleep, and very often
> Cry out for cudgels, cowl-staves, anything,
> Hiding his breeches, out of fear her ghost
> Should walk and wear 'em yet. Since his first marriage
> He is no more the still Petruccio
> Than I am Babylon.
>
> (1.1.16–20, 31–38)[5]

This description near the beginning of the play as well as ongoing references to Katherine throughout the play "revise" the ending of *The Taming of the Shrew* in a fundamental way. In Fletcher's play, Katherine has not been tamed, however much Petruccio would like everyone around him to believe that she has. According to Fletcher, Petruccio's design to tame Katherine was temporary at best and very likely never successful. In fact, his efforts actually reinforced her shrewishness. Shakespeare's ending may actually support Fletcher's conclusion that Kate was never tamed. Margie Burns notes that

> Kate's big speech to the audience seems at first to endorse a downplaying of the woman's role. Its immediate impact in the theater, however, certainly does not downplay *her* role, and like many other readers, I think it proceeds through—and succeeds theatrically by means of—intentional though extemporaneous irony. . . . [H]er eyebrow-lifting overenthusiasm, the vivid language she uses to delineate women's weakness, all support the strongest possible reading of her part at this juncture. (45–64)

However, Fletcher himself suggests no motivation for Katherine's actions at the close of Shakespeare's play. Instead, he returns to the earliest descriptions of her by Gremio and Hortensio in *The Taming of the Shrew*: "a devil" (1.1.121); "Mark'd you not how [she] / Began to scold, and arise up such a storm / That mortal ears might hardly endure the din?" (1.1.171–73); "a shrewd ill-favor'd wife" (1.2.60); "Her only fault, and that is faults enough, / Is that she is intolerable curst / And shrewd and froward, so beyond all measure" (1.2.88–90). Fletcher borrows this language in describing Katherine as a shrewish married woman in her life with Petruccio after *The Taming of the Shrew* ends. Petruccio did not tame "Katherine the curst"; rather, as he states in *The Woman's Prize*, "did Heaven forgive me, / And take this Serpent from me" (3.3.165–66).

Despite Moroso's comments, it often takes a class discussion or two before students realize that Fletcher offers an unambiguous interpretation of how Katherine and Petruccio's marriage evolves following the close of Shakespeare's play. After all, most of Fletcher's drama focuses on Petruccio's second marriage, so students initially spend their time comparing and contrasting the taming techniques used by Shakespeare's Petruccio and Fletcher's Maria, the lucky second wife, instead of looking closely at how Fletcher reimagines both Katherine and Petruccio. Likewise, it is possible that Fletcher may not have "revised" Katherine's character at all. The portrayals of Katherine in years of productions of *The Taming of the Shrew* may have come much closer to the way Katherine is described in *The Woman's Prize*. I suggest this in the light of Burns's analysis and because of Fletcher's depiction of Katherine in his play. So it is not that far-fetched when modern versions attempt to show Katherine as still strong-willed, having withstood Petruccio's machinations (or "torture" as one student put it). In fact, these portrayals of Katherine may be consistent with what was seen on Elizabethan and Jacobean stages. Fletcher's sequel can provide a helpful perspective on the final scene in *The Taming of the Shrew*, and nowhere was this fact more evident than in a recent production of Shakespeare's play by one of my classes.

Using Performance as Discovery

I periodically ask my students to put on a scaled-down version of one of the plays we read in a semester, and one group selected *The Taming of the Shrew*. After having read *The Woman's Prize* and participating in a weeklong discussion of both plays, the students struggled to be true to Shakespeare's words while also reflecting the additional contextual information they had gleaned from reading Fletcher's work. They were keenly aware that most people watching their production would be unfamiliar with the sequel and would, instead, rely wholly on their interpretation of Shakespeare's play in performance. Yet the students also believed that Katherine's final speech could not be given with absolute sincerity. As they struggled to come up with a solution, the young woman playing Katherine also struggled with the enormousness of the speech, which is both long and dramatically crucial.

Ultimately, serendipity provided the solution. In rehearsal, the young man playing Petruccio jokingly handed the woman playing Katherine a copy of her speech (she didn't have it memorized yet). But at that moment, the cast realized they had their solution: Katherine reads the speech verbatim as given to her by Petruccio. While the sentiments are orthodox and conventional, she is just as surprised as anyone—on stage or in the audience—with what she is reading. Most important, however, she is a fully conscious participant with her husband in winning his wager, providing "commentary"—verbal and nonverbal—as she works her way through this lengthy set of rebukes, observations, and instructions.

What excited my students above all was that they felt part of a long-standing theatrical tradition and had some contemporary support for their interpretation. Productions that take Katherine's speech at her word ignore the contextual information provided by Fletcher's sequel, which suggests that she remains shrewish throughout her marriage to Petruccio. Fletcher's play helps students see that there may have been some desire for an untamed Kate at the end of the play in the early modern period, just as there is for many in our own. In reading the two plays and then attempting to mount their version of *Shrew*, my students discovered a way to show the relationship between Petruccio and Katherine as it is reflected in Fletcher's *The Woman's Prize*.

Reinterpreting the End of Shrew

Ultimately, what is freeing about coupling these two plays is that when we do so, students are allowed to look more comprehensively at the husband-wife relationship instead of either having to accept the final speech in Shakespeare's play at face value or finding some way to justify an alternative interpretation. As Maria says in the epilogue to *The Woman's Prize*:

> The Tamer's tam'd, but so, as nor the men
> Can finde one just cause to complaine of, when
> They fitly do consider in their lives,
> They should not raign as Tyrants o'r their wives.
> Nor can the women from this president
> Insult, or triumph: it being aptly meant,
> To teach both Sexes due equality;
> And as they stand bound, to love mutually. (1–8)

Fletcher's point is clear here. No one should view his play as a husband's vindication for mistreating or dominating his wife. Instead, the goal is "[t]o teach both Sexes due equality" and "to love mutually." What becomes apparent in class discussion of the epilogue to Fletcher's play is that Shakespeare's play, when we read or stage it in isolation, has a different dramatic purpose, and the mutually exclusive interpretations of Katherine's final speech ensure that one sex or the other comes out "on top." At the conclusion of *The Taming of the Shrew*, either Petruccio emerges as the successful tamer who achieves his marital and monetary goals or Katherine emerges as a savvy spouse who manages to outwit or outlast her domineering husband.

Fletcher's continuation of the story gives students a third option: the possibility of imagining that at the end of *The Taming of the Shrew* both husband and wife believe they have foiled the other and therefore continue to fight for dominance for the remainder of their marriage, a result that only offers ongoing misery for one, premature death for the other. In the realm of Shakespearean comedy, there need not be a satisfactory, logical, or even palatable resolution—*Measure for Measure* and Isabella's unspoken reply to the Duke's offer of marriage, *A Midsummer Night's Dream* and Demetrius's continued drug-influenced love of Helena, or *The Merchant of Venice* and Shylock's forced conversion to Christianity, to name a few. In these plays, Shakespeare only hints at future troubles. Clearly the playwright of this sequel had other intentions. While not attempting radically to alter English society—his prologue specifically cautions (or reassures) the audience, "The end we aim at, is to make you sport; / Yet neither call the city nor the court" (15–16)—Fletcher puts into sharp relief how troubling inequality is in a married relationship. His "solution" necessitates killing off Shakespeare's heroine and turning the tables on Shakespeare's hero. Doing so casts a retrospective shadow over the final scene in *The Taming of the Shrew*, but students can alleviate interpretative concerns with the insight provided by Fletcher's "battle without blood" (prologue 3). They have seen how Fletcher, Shakespeare's contemporary and successor, characterized the famous relationship between Petruccio and Katherine.

Thus, when my students had Katherine read a note from Petruccio as her final speech, it was evident to everyone in the audience that, while he was continuing his attempts to control her actions and thoughts, her participation was hesitant and increasingly incredulous. Certain moments from the speech in 5.2—"painful labor" (153), "so great a debt" (158), and "I am ashamed that women are so simple" (165)—were all delivered with rolled eyes and rising voice, as if she could not believe she was saying them out loud or that anyone would have written them in the first place. Other students in the class, after seeing the original "solution" offered by their classmates, found themselves thinking more critically of the conclusion. One particularly skeptical student wrote that the happy union of Kate and Petruccio is only achieved once the wife subjugates herself to the husband; Fletcher's removal of Kate from his play allows another female character to teach an altogether different lesson than that found in Shakespeare's work.

Beyond Shakespeare

Including *The Woman's Prize* in conjunction with *The Taming of the Shrew* demonstrates that questions about marriage, the duty of wives, and power in the early modern family in general are not (and never were) limited to Shakespeare's *The Taming of the Shrew*. Not surprisingly, his fellow playwrights dealt with these same social issues and treated similar questions within their works. Part of what I want my students to understand is that this debate went well beyond the playhouses: "The English Renaissance continued and even intensified the age-old debate about women" (Henderson and McManus 20). "Women were told over and over and over that they were inferior, that they had lesser minds, that they were unable to handle their own affairs" (Hull 140). A bit later in the same decade that produced Fletcher's sequel, the anonymously authored *Swetnam the Woman-Hater* (1618) played its part in fueling some heated pamphlet exchanges (the *hic mulier*, or "man-woman," controversy specifically, which was sparked by a popular anonymous pamphlet criticizing women who wore masculine garb).[6] But playwrights and others had been dealing with this issue in various ways before and after Shakespeare. Allowing students to discover this reality opens the discussion about substantial social issues then and now, as they learn how Elizabethans and Jacobeans addressed these questions.

NOTES

1 As Frank Rich, then the theater critic for *New York Times*, put it, "Her climactic speech championing wifely duties is delivered with just the right twinkle of irony and is capped by an ingeniously managed physical gag that allows Kate to have her man and her feminist independence, too."

[2] Elizabeth Schafer's *The Taming of the Shrew* provides an informative sampling of productions ranging from 1844 to 2001; not surprisingly, Schafer devotes ten pages of her introduction to playing Katherine (with particular emphasis on her speech in 5.2) as well as eighteen notes on lines in this final speech.

[3] Terms are taken, respectively, from Munro 283; Gayley 83; R. Baldwin 377; McKeithan 58; Squier 120; Cone 65; and M. Smith 39.

[4] I'm curious about the proximity of names of Fletcher's Moroso and Jonson's Morose from *Epicoene* (1609), considering *Epicoene*'s play reversion and then subversion of gender roles. Morose not only desires a silent woman and then finds himself cursed with one who cannot and will not cease talking but also finds that he has actually married a boy—a revelation that manages for once to silence the Collegiate Ladies. Jonson himself addresses the nature of writing on such a controversial subject and for whom such works are intended: "Truth says, of old the art of making plays / Was to content the people; and their praise / Was to the poet money, wine and bays. / But in this age a sect of writers are, / That only for particular likings care, / And will taste nothing that is popular. / With such we mingle neither brains nor breasts; / Our wishes, like to those make public feasts, / Are not to please the cook's taste but the guests" (Prologue 1, 1–9).

[5] Quotations from *The Taming of the Shrew* cite Daileader and Taylor's edition.

[6] Linda Woodbridge goes one step further: "King James' attempt . . . to enlist the support of literature in his campaign against aggressive women was, as far as can be judged from extant plays, a signal failure. We can account for the drama's new image of women, forged during the hic mulier years, by positing increased pressure by female playgoers. . . . For generations, literature had sought to modify women's behavior by praising Grissils and damning shrews; during the hic mulier years, women forced the drama, at least, to provide models more to their taste—Katherine of Aragon, the spurned wife who stands up for herself; Maria, the rebellious wife whose insubordination is celebrated; the Duchess of Malfi, the widow allowed a sex life with no authorial condemnation. Whether any insubordinate wife was ever celebrated by any living creature in the real world is finally a secondary question: a real world whose literature admits to her celebration as an imaginative possibility is capable of celebrating her in the flesh eventually" (*Women* 267).

Kate, the Commonplace: The Framing of the *Shrew*

Joseph Ricke

When it comes to teaching *The Taming of the Shrew*, I don't think anything can take the place of a historicized class(room) consciousness. That goes for the teacher, the students, the assignments, the exams, and the suggested topics for essays or presentations. One hopes that, by now, our encounters with *Shrew* are soaked in a rich historical context and that these encounters are set up to model not only a historicized reading of an individual Shakespearean text but also the problematic and contested meaning of historical understanding. And of course we want that understanding to be shaped by more than the traditional metanarratives of Western patriarchal culture and literary scholarship (here overgeneralized to make my point): Shakespeare is great; Shakespeare is the result of an evolutionary process; Shakespeare always transformed his sources into something better; where Shakespeare appears racist or sexist, our interpretation must be wrong; Shakespeare relates to history in such a way as to shine a light on all that is best, brightest, and most "modern" in Renaissance England.

The "new history"—or the synchronic exploration (and, in some cases, the deconstruction and reexploration) of "literary" texts, cultural artifacts, letters, ballads, sermons, legal and civic documents, broadsides, and courtesy and behavior manuals—provokes us to uncover the evidence in these sources of the lives and voices of those who have been hidden or silenced or defamed in the traditional narratives. That very important work, though, should be placed in a more robust diachronic context. For me and for the work I do in the classroom, the push-pull between the synchronic and the diachronic (especially a history of performance as part of that larger "history") produces what I hope is an engaging and balanced critical stance. We cannot, like Thomas More, "step in among the players" whose world we long to enter (William Roper, qtd. in Greenblatt, *Renaissance Self-Fashioning* 29). But we may perhaps, by attending to the genre of "shrew plays" (narrowly defined), have a better sense of where we are when our interpretive cue comes.

The Ubiquitous Shrew

It is important for students to see that "shrews" were everywhere in medieval and early modern England—in historical documents, literature, and popular culture. As Frances Dolan claims, "Ballads, folktales, jokes, and plays about outspoken, assertive women suggest that the English found disorderly women simultaneously threatening and fascinating" (3). The diachronic context helps students understand that this was not just a symptom of some cultural paranoia about women, as so much of the critical material implies. The new popularity of ballads and pamphlets about shrews almost certainly had more to do with the new popularity of ballads and pamphlets themselves than with "shrew hysteria" as such. Dolan's description of the popularity of the shrew character in Renaissance England could just as easily be applied to medieval culture. In fact, ignoring the diachronic element may artificially turn historical readings into hysterical ones. "Shrews" were indeed a hot topic in the 1590s, as they had been in the 1490s and the 1390s, when Chaucer's Wife of Bath first emerged on the scene. (Shrews were a hot topic for the first readers of the book of Proverbs, for that matter.) In her Norton Critical Edition of the play, Dympna Callaghan reminds us that "the problem of male authority and women's resistance to it . . . is hardly unique to Shakespeare. . . . The theme of unruly women and male tyranny . . . has indirect literary precedents and was an already well-established theme in classical and medieval literature" (preface ix).

To help make this clear, the teacher can draw on a number of helpful sources. One rich and readily available resource (also online, thanks to TEAMS—the Consortium for the Teaching of the Middle Ages) is Eve Salisbury's anthology of medieval texts, *The Trials and Joys of Marriage*. It includes satire, fabliaux, secular lyrics, didactic treatises, and homiletic matter and spans the late thirteenth century to the early sixteenth century. These texts, many of them comic, reflect a surprising variety of views, an ongoing cultural dialogue (related to the medieval *querelle des femmes*, or debate about women) about gender roles and marriage. According to Salisbury, "These texts challenge and, in some cases, parody, satirize, and critique the institution of marriage. In so doing they allow us to interrogate the traditional assumptions that shape the idea of the medieval household" (1).

Not only does this earlier nondramatic material suggest a richer context for understanding the medieval and Renaissance cultural dialogue about shrewish women, but a wealth of specifically dramatic material (which Salisbury omits) should, but too often does not, inform our discussion of Shakespeare's play. As many feminist critics (most notably Boose) have insisted, Shakespeare's *Shrew* should be seen in the context of contemporary cultural practices such as shaming, bridling, ducking, and carting (Gremio, for example, recommends "cart[ing]" Kate in 1.1.55). But the specific relation of *The Taming of the Shrew* to these contemporary concerns is difficult to calculate accurately, since it is part of a well-established tradition of shrew plays. To introduce our students to this tradition is to ask them to question the traditional mystification of the great liberal humanist Shakespeare, who saw beyond the sexist practices of his day. It relocates Shakespeare in a more dialogical and diachronic understanding of history, especially the history of popular representation of shrews.

The massive evidence for this tradition, especially in the drama, is all but ignored by both Dolan and Callaghan in their influential editions, both of which, ironically, stress historical contextualization. Although this shrew story has been approached as an anomaly or as the result of a unique cultural hysteria about women, Shakespeare's play is (and can be in the classroom) framed by a rich tradition traceable from the garrulous wife of the biblical Proverbs, through the *querelle des femmes* carried on by medieval authors like Chaucer and Christine de Pizan, down to the dramatic versions of strong, defiant women popular in England throughout the fifteenth, sixteenth, and seventeenth centuries. The shrewish woman was brought to life in a variety of dramatic situations from a variety of perspectives, providing a rich genre-specific context for Shakespeare's play, in such characters as Noah's wife (in several plays), Gill of *The Second Shepherds' Play* (from the Towneley Cycle), the defiant mothers of Bethlehem resisting Herod's soldiers (in, e.g., the York Cycle's *Slaughter of the Innocents*), the Mary Magdalen who argues with the risen Christ (in, e.g., the York play *The Appearance of Christ to Mary Magdalen*), the Virgin Mary (arguing with an obviously stereotypically henpecked Joseph in York plays like *Joseph's Trouble about Mary* and *The Flight into Egypt*, not to mention her rather argumentative tone toward Jesus on the cross in the York play *The Death of Christ*), Tyb (in Heywood's *Johan Johan*), and Zantippa (in Peele's *Old Wife's Tale*). This continued both during and after his career with characters like Moll Cutpurse (in Middleton and Dekker's *The Roaring Girl*), Maria (in Fletcher's *The Tamer Tamed*), and, at least to some degree, the no-longer-silent woman/boy in Jonson's *Epicoene*.

It is no wonder, then, that Shakespeare turned his attention to strong women who posed threats to the patriarchal social structures reflected in his plays. Engaging this rich dramatic context, too, can become a "teachable moment" about more than this play and about more than gender issues. Shakespeare tapped into popular topics—whether the subject was weak, effeminate kings; usurious Jews; magicians; or long-lost twins (or spouses or parents or children). As Dolan writes, "Presenting Shakespeare's play as one text among many, this [edition] is as much about sixteenth- and seventeenth-century debates about marriage, women, and domesticity as it is about *The Taming of the Shrew*" (preface viii). I affirm the decentering of Shakespeare as our solo shrew expert. But I contend that considering his plays in a context of other, and especially earlier, plays (without ignoring other forms of social history) gives us an even richer sense not only of how the drama interacted with culture over several centuries but also of how those dramatic representations of gender persist and have been adapted, interpreted, transformed, and performed in a variety of ways over time.

I also want students to see that Shakespeare himself has more than one "go" at shrewish women (whatever we make of his relation to *The Taming of a Shrew*). Certainly in *Love's Labour's Lost*, Rosaline and the Princess are shrewish in their argumentativeness, in the joy they get out of mocking the (rather silly) men who want them, and, finally, in their resistance to husbands (in this case, would-be husbands). In fact, Boyet, their male attendant, refers to them in language typical of the shrew play. He asks about "curst wives" who "strive to be / Lords o'er their lords" (4.1.35; 36–37). The witty Princess responds, "Praise we may afford / to any lady that subdues a lord" (38–39). A little later, Boyet declares, probably to the audience (a typical dramatic practice in shrew plays), that "The tongues of mocking wenches are as keen / As is the razor's edge invisible" (5.2.256–57). In *Much Ado about Nothing*, which has more structural resemblance to *The Taming of the Shrew* than does *Love's Labour's Lost* (which has a more typical, though disrupted, romantic pattern), Shakespeare paints perhaps his most attractive portrait of the argumentative, resistant, and male-baiting shrew. Beatrice, whom the men call "shrewd" and "curst" but "merry," is certainly attractive to Benedick (see his dialogue with Claudio in 1.1.130–64), Don Pedro, and her uncle, Leonato. Further, like Katherine in *The Taming of the Shrew*, she is balanced (or at least arguably so) by an equally shrewish masculine character, the loud, talkative, resistant-to-marriage, and Beatrice-baiting Benedick (whose opposition to marriage is certainly interpreted as something just as unnatural and antisocial as Beatrice's).

In my one-semester Shakespeare course, we work through a "shrew cycle" over a period of two weeks or so. I ask the students to read *Shrew*, *Love's Labour's Lost, and Much Ado about Nothing* (we do *The Winter's Tale* later in the term). We supplement that in the classroom with readings from *The Trials and Joys of Marriage* as well as student performances of shrew plays from "cut" and lightly simplified versions. Although the exact scenes we perform vary from year to year, they include passages from one of the medieval plays about Noah and his wife, arguments between Gill and Mak from *The Second Shepherds' Play*, the depiction of Joseph as a henpecked husband from *Joseph's Trouble about Mary* in the York cycle, one of the Herod plays, and scenes from the three Shakespeare plays.

The Dialogical Shrew

Wide exposure to dramatic shrews challenges not only simplistic notions of gender but also, more significantly, our modern simplistic notions of the medieval and early modern dialogue about gender. In fact, the dialogical shrew poses a distinct challenge to the idea of innate female shrewishness. Students can see that the traditional formulas (that a loud woman equals a lewd woman and, similarly, that a strong woman is an evil to be avoided or punished) are often undercut in performance. For example, most shrews are chaste—either monogamous wives or virgins. Likewise, many shrews are shown to have pretty good reasons for acting the way they do, and they usually let us know what those reasons are as they engage in a dialogue about their own shrewishness. As it turns out, shrews are usually "motivated" by weak, stupid, or brutal men. At least they say so. Part of the energy of shrew plays is the way they call for our (possibly gendered) interpretive activity, provoking further dialogue, appropriation, and reinterpretation. The focus in modern editions, like Dolan's and Callaghan's, on later revisions or adaptations (like Fletcher's) is appropriate but misleading without an acknowledgment that Shakespeare's version is already revisionary.

The kinds of motivations of which I speak are those usually voiced directly by the shrews in question. And, most of the time, they are complaints about their husbands (Noah, Mak, Johan, Petruccio, Lucentio), fathers (Baptista), suitors (as in *Shrew* and *Love's Labour's Lost*), other powerful and lethal men (Herod, soldiers, Leontes, Claudio), or braggart soldiers-bachelors (Benedick). Usually, these complaints are rather specific, and often it is at least relatively unclear just how we are to take them. We may choose to interpret them as general "bitchiness" attributed to women in stereotypical (especially farcical) representations, but that must be qualified, to some degree, by whatever we know about the men in the play who are the subject of the complaints.

Kate, of course, seems to complain about everything. But her complaints about her father's favoritism ("A pretty peat!" [1.1.78]) and her sister's Machiavellian role playing ("Put finger in the eye, an she knew why" [1.1.79]), not to mention her continual shaming at the hands of the idiotic men whom her father allows to ridicule her ("I pray you, sir, is it your will / To make a stale of me amongst these mates?" [1.1.57–58]), either ring true or at least call for further consideration of her situation. After the head-spinning "wooing" scene, we can hardly blame "shrewishness" for her complaint: "Call you me daughter? Now, I promise you, / You have showed me a tender fatherly regard, / To wish me wed to one half-lunatic" (2.1.277–79).

If these complaints are at least ambivalent, in many other cases a complaining woman's complaint, even when configured by a masculine voice in the play as "shrewish" or "scolding" or "curst," sounds either quite reasonable or simply correct. Noah's wife and Mak's wife, Gill, are typical shrewish characters from the mystery plays, yet both of them verbalize their anger over their husbands' laziness and failure to do their part in support of the household economy. In the Towneley play, Noah's wife draws battle lines between herself and her spouse in terms of work, specifically verbalizing her resistance to her pious spouse over his failure to provide (*Noah*, lines 274–86). When she directly addresses the women in the audience about good-for-nothing husbands, one wonders how dialogical the response may have been. Gill, Mak's wife in the Towneley *Second Shepherds' Play*, similarly complains that her no-good husband keeps interrupting her work at the distaff. Interestingly, many critics assume that this must be interpreted in an antifeminist manner and that she is probably lying. After all, she is a shrew, according to her husband (a notorious sheep thief). In Shakespeare, we see many similar scenes of feminine complaint with what are at least arguably understandable motivations. Among these are Beatrice's negative assessment of Benedick; the women of *Love's Labour's Lost*, whose shrewishness extends to their final criticism of masculine folly and delay of marriage that the play appears to affirm; and, in *The Winter's Tale*, Paulina's shrewish behavior both on behalf of Hermione and, ultimately and ironically, on behalf of the emotionally sick Leontes.

One surprising version of the dialogical shrew is what I call the "saintly shrew." This is especially relevant to Shakespeare because of the many dramatic characters, especially in the mystery plays, who are configured as "shrews"—loud, rebellious, defiant, and unruly, especially by the words and actions of male characters—and yet who seem to represent or at least be on the side of justice, goodness, even God. This "saintly shrew" usually comes as quite a shock to students, who think they pretty well have figured out that to be "shrew" in a text or play means necessarily that the shrewish character is the butt of the humor and the object of criticism of the play or the culture that produced it. Clearly, in a good many works, things are a bit more complex than that. Some of these examples demonstrate that the negative attitudes toward women embodied in the shrew tradition can themselves sometimes be the butt of the humor and the object of criticism.

Before looking at dramatic examples, I point students toward the unlikely source of medieval saints' lives. The best discussion of these is Karen Winstead's chapter "Unruly Virgins and the Laity" in her book *Virgin Martyrs: Legends of Sainthood in Late Medieval England* (64–111). Because of the obvious interpretive bias in favor of the saint in hagiography, the fact that the saintly shrew (my term) "defies society and humiliates her [male] adversary" poses a problem for any one-size-fits-all shrew theory (65). Further, Winstead argues that, despite orthodox intentions, such narratives might challenge "traditional relationships of dominion and subordination—for example the authority of husbands over wives" (66). These "vituperative saints" (75), whose abusive tongues would be culturally offensive in a different context, are often the victims of horrific violence at the hands of vicious, demonic men. And since the perpetrators insistently call attention to their masculinity and the saint's womanhood, "the Middle English hagiographers present their stories as gender conflicts" (76). In other words, it is not at all clear that the masculine voice that both constructs and opposes the shrew is always on the side of reason or the angels.

In the mystery cycles and beyond, we see this saintly shrew character rendered dramatically. The mothers of Bethlehem, for example, in a number of Herod plays are configured as shrews by their speech (they talk like shrews), their actions (they act like shrews), but, especially, by the words of others—namely, soldiers. In various plays they are called "false witches," "brawls," "wood" ("mad"), "queans" ("shrewish"), "whores," "bawds," and the like (Herod even calls baby Jesus a "shrew" in the Chester play [Harris 370]). Of course, we see them primarily as mothers who are protecting their children. As such, they are heroines, saints, or at least sisters of Mary, the great exemplar of suffering and lament. Thus, their representation undercuts the traditional understanding of loud, rebellious, violent women, which it also underscores (but perhaps only to those in the audience who find themselves identifying with brutal Herod and his murdering soldiers). Represented by their child-slaughtering opponents with the typical traits of the antifeminist version of unruly women, they nonetheless must be seen as sympathetic shrews—throwing a wrench or a distaff into the words of Herod's power machinery. Opposed to demonic power, they don't hesitate to mock, shame, curse, resist, and strike (with pots, pans, and distaffs) their hypermasculine enemy. Here, the performance might be said to call into question the demonization of shrews by the simple fact that their opponents look so ignoble or stupid or weak, depending on the context.

Among many other examples are Mary Magdalene, the sisters Mary and Martha, and Sarah (usually an offstage shrew). In at least one play, Abraham addresses the audience directly, much like henpecked Noah does, afraid of what Sarah will say or do to him when he gets home after slaying their son. Most surprising, perhaps, is the way the York plays depict Mary, the mother of Jesus, in stereotypical shrewish situations, dialogue, and actions. Although Mary is more passive than most shrews, the plays adapt the comic tradition to portray Joseph as a henpecked husband. Mary's relationships with her handmaidens ("gossips"), whom Joseph accuses of "carping" and "gabbing," also associate her with traditional shrewish characters (*Joseph's Trouble*, lines 140–41). In the York play *Flight into Egypt*, Mary grouches loudly and continually when Joseph tells her that they must flee to Egypt (lines 94–191). By performing the role of the henpecked old January character, Joseph calls into question the patriarchal interpretation of such gender(ed) conflicts. After all, Mary is Mary!

Shakespeare depicts a saintly shrew in the character of Paulina in *The Winter's Tale*. Although the "virgin martyr" part of the story is displaced onto the defamed but chaste (if not celibate) Hermione, destroyed by the accusations of the hypermasculine and Herod-like Leontes, Paulina becomes the play's central female character as she confronts abusive male power. She is also inarguably the (shrewish) voice of reason, goodness, and love in the play. Resisting Leontes's misogynistic "reading" of Hermione (1.2.110–20), Paulina must also resist Leontes's traditional understanding of her defiant tongue. Against Leontes's assertions that her rebellious spirit represents an aberration, an out-of-control irrationality, and a danger to the community, Paulina says and shows that shrews can, indeed, do good work. By defending the weak and persecuted, by sheltering them over time (as we are to learn), and even by charitably working (by the "strong medicine" of her tongue) toward the healing of misogynistic Leontes, she unsettles simplistic readings of the defiant woman. Interestingly, too, Leontes accuses Paulina of being a midwife. Midwives in medieval and early modern cultural representations were a sort of shrewish feminist health-care provider, although in antifeminist rhetoric they are almost always depicted as gossipy, garrulous, shrewish, and generally annoying to men. (see both *Titus Andronicus* 4.2 and *The Winter's Tale* 2.3.158–61).[1] If Paulina is presented in the classroom as she is in the play as a variety of "shrew" (so-called by a paranoid male authority figure whose heart and head are both obviously in the wrong place), students may discover the dialogue about gender in shrew plays to be much richer and more complex than they would have imagined. By the end of the play, not only has the shrew definitely not been tamed, but her role as teacher and leader has been affirmed by Leontes, who entreats her, "Good Paulina, / Lead us from hence" (5.3.152–53).

The Gendered Shrew (Mannish Women, Shrewish Men)

As a man (one of my many titles) who happens to be a feminist (another one), I have an interest in the dialogue about gender, past and present. Certain literary and dramatic (and "folk") representations of gender are dialogical in that, you might say, they allow both sides to speak and offer the opportunity to view not just gender but the argument about gender from multiple perspectives. A masculine character and voice may speak about "the weaker vessel" from a position of pride and authority, but other characters and voices may respond or even drown him out (or may not, as the case may be). Further, his actions, the way he goes about showing himself to be "strong," may be contradictory, self-refuting, or just plain idiotic. And even that is open to interpretation by a particular audience in a particular time and place. One popular medieval sermon exemplum from Jacques de Vitry tells of a certain demon who, disguised as a man, marries a rich man's daughter. Her shrewish behavior, however, makes him flee. Before departing, he reveals the truth: "I come from hell. And there I have never endured such discord. I'd rather be in hell than live with this shrew any longer." This exemplum seems, on the surface, designed, like the antifeminist tradition from which it springs, to denigrate strong women and to reinforce patriarchal attitudes and practices. Yet it resonates with a sense of the unsettling power of shrews. They unsettle not only hell, as the preacher no doubt intends, but the authorized version of woman as weaker vessel as well. If we look clearly, we can find case after case in medieval and early modern literature (including Shakespeare) of the frightening specter of strong (mannish) women and what that fear says about the supposed "natural" superiority and strength of men.

Although Lynda Boose is absolutely right to insist that "the impulse to rewrite the more oppressively patriarchal material in [*The Taming of the Shrew*] serves the very ideologies about gender that it makes less visible by making . . . less offensive" ("Scolding" 181–82), the play (like other shrew plays) "contains" much more than oppressive patriarchal material. When teachers, theorists, and performances repress the other realities of shrew plays—their interrogation of masculinity and their dialogical representation of shrews and sheep, strong women and weak men, angry women and bad men—they downplay and efface a feminist subtext that is also part of the tradition. When teaching a class that focuses on medieval and early modern shrews, I usually give at least one presentation that includes excerpts from Natalie Zemon Davis, especially her argument that early modern popular cultural depictions and "performances" of the "woman on top" had the potential at least to pose a challenge to abusive authority. Speaking specifically of so-called festive and shaming practices like charivari and skimmingtons, she claims, "the women are full of life and energy, and they win much of the time" (134–35). She further argues that women held "a temporary period of dominion, which is ended only after she has done or said something to undermine authority or denounce its abuse" (135). Of course, it is that "temporary period of dominion," ending, one might say, in a final submission scene at a sister's wedding banquet or on the ark, on which most modern audiences and readers cannot help choking. In performance, however, the shaming of or resistance to certain masculine assumptions and characters is not necessarily erased by a final taming or submission. The end of a play is not the "end" of a play, except to

Aristotle. This is certainly true in the medieval cycle plays and arguably so in the porous, disunified dramaturgy of Shakespeare and his contemporaries. Davis argues that "topsy-turvy play had much spillover into everyday 'serious' life. . . . Play with the various images of woman-on-top . . . kept open an alternate way of conceiving family structure" (143). Although such considerations must not be overstated, at the risk of understating the harsh reality of misogynistic thought and practice, it seems appropriate to say that, in some cases at least, these plays and practices reveal what Jean Howard (speaking of Shakespeare's *Shrew*) called "the constructed nature of patriarchy's representation of the feminine" ("Crossdressing" 435).

Another helpful scholarly work that shows how the feminine could be given a voice in traditional stories, plays, and "jests" is Pamela Allen Brown's *Better a Shrew Than a Sheep*. Although *Shrew* critics repeatedly point to a few popular misogynistic stories and ballads about unruly women such as the "Merry Jest of a Shrewd and Curst Wife Lapped in Morel's Skin for Her Good Behavior" (anthologized, for example, in both Callaghan's and Dolan's editions), Brown points to hundreds of examples of "jests" in which women's voices in fact respond in mockery to men, as in most of the shrew plays. Explaining what she calls Beatrice's "countertradition of antimasculinist [mockery]" in *Much Ado*, she argues that "her arsenal is no less ancient than Benedick's, but it is far less visible because it has been so rarely named as female satire with roots in social practice" (9). She locates five "markers" (one or more of which characterizes most "jests" that appeal for mockery of the masculine):

> A woman is the laugh getter through her words or actions; the fiction mentions an internal audience that includes women who approve the actions of the laugh getter; a male, often a husband, father, cleric, or unwanted suitor, is the butt of laughter brought down on him through the agency of a woman or women; a woman solves a riddle a man cannot solve or succeeds at a seemingly impossible task; a woman who has carried out a clever trick is not subjected to internal criticism or a dour concluding moral. (9–10)

Of course, although *Love's Labour's Lost*, *The Winter's Tale*, *The Tamer Tamed*, and perhaps York's *Joseph's Trouble* may point toward a countertradition, shrew stories, plays, and cultural practices almost always get around to some kind of taming, submission, or containment. Cleary, this fact must not be ignored. But as teachers we are not fair to our students or to shrew plays if we subject the plays to an Aristotelian interpretive framework that doesn't fit them. Interpreters, usually readers, who insist that the concluding action of a shrew play unfolds its ultimate, complete, and authoritative "message" confuse the final thing in a series with the most important thing. Such unifying absolutism is simply not true to our experience of much medieval or early modern drama (or jokes or other expressions of popular culture). Instead, it reflects a residual

Aristotelian bias still prevalent when new historicists turn their attention away from theory and toward texts and performances. Of course, even Shakespeare's play doesn't really conclude with its concluding events and "message." We have Fletcher's "sequel," not to mention Shakespeare's later shrews (like Beatrice and Paulina), and an entire history of performance.

The medieval drama scholar Theresa Coletti, writing in an earlier MLA volume (*Approaches to Teaching Medieval English Drama*), helped set the stage for a reconsideration of the dramatic shrew tradition in England by drawing our attention to the "frequent use of the unruly woman, who emerges as a commanding figure" in the mystery plays (81). The shrew-play tradition in medieval and early modern drama reveals that the shrewish woman is part of the deep structure of the world that both produced and was produced by those plays. Shakespeare's Katherine, one of the earliest of many Shakespearean examples of shrewish women, is best studied in the context of that larger tradition, which I have tried to highlight in my classroom and in this essay.

NOTE

[1] Books that discuss the midwife's early modern reputation include Paster; Bicks; and Evenden. For more information on medieval midwives and shrews, see Schaus; Neufeld.

"Practise Rhetoric in Your Common Talk": *The Taming of the Shrew* as an Exercise in Rhetorical Strategy

Margaret Dupuis

As Lucentio arrives in Padua to take advantage of the intellectual wealth the city and its great university have to offer, his servant Tranio counsels him not to bury himself in books. Instead, Tranio urges Lucentio to enjoy his studies, since "[n]o profit grows where is no pleasure ta'en" (1.1.39). In modern pedagogical parlance, Tranio is saying that we tend to learn best when we are engaged in our subject matter and understand its relevance to daily life. Among the topics that Lucentio plans to study is rhetoric, a standard part of any curriculum during Shakespeare's lifetime. On this topic, Tranio advises Lucentio to "Practise rhetoric in your common talk" (1.1.35)—to use rhetorical principles in daily conversation, rather than merely to memorize figures and rhetorical strategies in isolation.

At the same time that Lucentio and Tranio appear in Padua, another young gentleman named Petruccio arrives with the express purpose to "[w]ive it wealthily in Padua" (1.2.72), an enterprise that will surely require the art of persuasion. Interestingly, Petruccio's servant Grumio (Tranio's counterpart) also speaks of rhetoric, or, as he says, "rope-tricks" (1.2.107). Petruccio apparently has no problem practicing rhetoric in his common talk, for, as Grumio informs us, his master's rhetorical skill will outmatch that of the infamous although as yet unseen "curst Katherine" (1.2.178). Grumio tells Hortensio:

> O' my word, an she knew him as well as I do she would think scolding would do little good upon him. She may perhaps call him half a score knaves or so. Why, that's nothing; an he begin once he'll rail in his rope-tricks. I'll tell you what, sir, an she stand him but a little he will throw a figure in her face and so disfigure her with it that she shall have no more eyes to see withal than a cat. (1.2.103–10)

The figures Grumio refers to are rhetorical figures, linguistic devices used by a speaker to achieve an intellectual or emotional effect on the hearer. Grumio maintains that Petruccio will triumph in a war of words by throwing figures as weapons in Katherine's face. Thus, within the first two scenes of the play proper, the stage is set for the audience to recognize this as a play in which characters, with varying degrees of success, "practise rhetoric," the art of persuasion, "in [their] common talk." One fruitful approach to teaching *The Taming of the Shrew* is thus to present the play as an exercise in rhetorical practice, as Shakespeare's attempt to have fun with the conventions and perhaps even to lampoon some of the more formal and formulaic aspects of rhetoric in his time.

As Tranio and Grumio signal, the play abounds with characters who attempt to persuade others to bend to their wills. Shakespeare's rich comedic language invites examination on many levels, including an analysis of how the characters in this play use rhetoric, the art of persuasion. The purpose of this essay is to illustrate how attention to the rhetorical nature of *The Taming of the Shrew* (and all drama) can awaken in students a new awareness of the power of dialogue. Most important, a speaker needs a listener, and students should learn to look beyond the obvious and intended audiences.

Attention to the rhetorical aspects of the play helps relieve the sometimes fraught arguments over how to teach the thorny issues of gender and the politics of wife taming, thereby diffusing some of the anxiety experienced by instructor and students during the study of this play. After all, Shakespeare is hardly the first to tackle the topic of how a husband should deal with a shrewish wife. From folktales about disobedient wives to the Wakefield Master's Uxor, wife of Noah, to a sixteenth-century anonymous ballad that details the horrific and brutal subjugation of an unruly wife, stories of taming a shrew were ubiquitous.[1] We can look at *The Taming of the Shrew* as Shakespeare's "take" on this well-worn trope. However, unlike earlier authors, Shakespeare creates a character whose avowed wife-taming tool is his tongue, not brute force. It is ultimately Petruccio's power to persuade Kate that will determine his success or failure at the sport of shrew taming.[2]

Students in the twenty-first century rarely receive formal rhetorical training. Nevertheless, they can understand and are interested in rhetorical strategy as it is applied in the world around them—for example, by advertising agencies to gain brand loyalty among customers. Increasingly, students rely on the rhetorical practices of Internet communication through social networking, e-mail, and other sites. More to the point, however, they can readily relate to language games that romantic relationships entail: the tropes, the banter, and the art of persuasion. In fact, students in my introductory Shakespeare classes are particularly drawn to the verbal fireworks between Kate and Petruccio. This attraction to the language of the play ignites students' interest in a closer examination of what kinds of rhetorical strategies the two main characters use to achieve their goals and whether those strategies are successful. Instructors who incorporate performance when teaching this play will find that requiring their students to pay close attention to the rhetorical skills and tactics of various characters will enable the students to find the motivation necessary to give voice to the characters they embody when performing a scene. It may be useful for these instructors to point out the similarities between rhetoric as the delivery of an oration and the rhetorical nature of drama. Both require a speaker and an audience, and both attempt to educate, persuade, and entertain. When students understand what their characters need or want from other characters, they become more invested in their roles and their delivery becomes more convincing.

The power of rhetoric to sway emotions and drive behavior and thereby effect change was a subject of keen interest throughout Europe in the sixteenth century. During the medieval period, the study of rhetoric was divided into several highly specialized disciplines, and this fragmentation shifted focus away from the content of an argument to an emphasis on verbal forms. In the fifteenth century, the works of classical rhetoricians such as Isocrates, Aristotle, Cicero, and Quintilian were rediscovered. By the sixteenth century their ideas had been thoroughly incorporated into the curricula not only at Cambridge and Oxford but also at hundreds of newly established grammar schools throughout England. Grammar-school students encountered a standardized curriculum with the objective of teaching spoken and written Latin. Training in rhetoric was emphasized for the older students and formed the culmination of their education. English-language grammar-school textbooks on rhetoric were published for the first time in the sixteenth century. One text commonly studied at the time was Thomas Wilson's *The Arte of Rhetorique* (1553), the earliest complete English account of the Ciceronian theory of oratory comprising the five arts of rhetoric as set forth in *De inventione*: invention or discovery, arrangement, style, memory, and delivery. The study of rhetoric in the sixteenth century, however, focused almost entirely on invention and style. The classical rhetoricians whose work was studied saw their art as an elaboration on and extension of natural eloquence, the unexamined but powerful ability of persuasion native to many everyday speakers. They believed that eloquence had a civilizing effect and that, along with the faculty of reason, oration distinguished man from other animals. Their thinking inspired in sixteenth-century rhetoricians a drive to make rhetoric less stilted and more relevant to everyday situations. In 1548, John Jewel, prelector in humanities and rhetoric of Corpus Christi College, Oxford, delivered an oration to the entire college condemning the "inane, futile, and trivial" ornamentation by which rhetoric had come to be known (qtd. in Plett 70). In essence, Jewel argued that it is more important to speak intelligibly, simply, and clearly, or in Tranio's words, "to practise rhetoric in your common talk," than to weigh down one's communication with artful figures of speech.[3]

In addition to a resurgence of interest in classical rhetoric, the Protestant Reformation and the new emphasis on guidance from the Word of God on how to conduct one's daily life had begun to change expectations about how husbands should love (and thus treat) their wives (presumably, following Ephesians 5.25–33, as Christ loved the church). As a result, men were encouraged to use less violent means of controlling their wives, while women were exhorted to obey their husbands as they would the Lord. This new emphasis on verbal correction instructed husbands and wives to deal with marital discord in a more humane way. The Reformation's reliance on the power of the written and spoken word to effect profound change in the lives of believers, with the correspondingly lessened emphasis on good works, in turn helped renew respect for rhetoric and oratory, especially as resources for preaching the gospel using plain and simple speech. Among the theologians who wrote on the topic, Philipp Melanchthon, an ardent proponent of the Reformation, published a discourse on rhetoric in 1519 in Basel. The prominent Cambridge theologian and contemporary of Shakespeare William Perkins (1558–1602) published *The Art of Prophecying* in Latin in 1592 (it was translated into English in 1607). *The Art of Prophecying* is a treatise addressed "To the Faithfull Ministers of the Gospell" demanding "a speech both simple and perspicuous, fit both for the peoples understanding and to express the Majestie of the Spirit."

While many instances in *The Taming of the Shrew* can be useful in a discussion of how characters use rhetorical strategies, this essay looks at three significant scenes that highlight the war of words between Katherine and Petruccio: their first meeting in 2.1, their battle over food and clothing in 4.3, and, finally, Kate's long speech in 5.2. One approach for examining how persuasive the characters are is to divide the class into three groups, making each group responsible for one scene. The students analyze the rhetorical strategy of each speaker in the scene, judging each on the logic of the argument, the speaker's tone, how well he or she uses various figures of speech, and, finally, whether the character succeeds in accomplishing his or her desired goal.

The Wooing Scene (2.1.168–316)

As Petruccio anticipates his first meeting with Katherine, he makes "battle plans" for the war of words he is preparing to wage. Students will quickly notice that all of his strategies are rhetorical: "Say that she rail, why then I'll tell her plain / She sings as sweetly as a nightingale" (168–69). He clearly hopes that his contrariness and blatantly absurd observations will so confound Katherine that she will be rendered speechless. Even before meeting her, Petruccio anticipates that Katherine will refuse his marriage proposal—"If she deny to wed, I'll crave the day / When I shall ask the banns, and when be married" (177–78)—but that is as far as he gets in his plans before Katherine enters.

The next ninety-three lines (180–272) are a prime example of stichomythia, a rhetorical device popular in early modern comedy, which involves the rapid-fire give-and-take of verbal abuse, with one speaker often taking verbal cues from the other. So, for example, when Petruccio declares, "Myself am moved to woo thee for my wife" (192), Kate responds, "Moved? In good time. Let him that moved you hither / Remove you hence. I knew you at the first / You were a moveable" (192–94). Petruccio and Kate's puns on "move" and "moveable" are examples of the rhetorical figure known as syllepsis, in which the speakers exploit nuances and meanings of the same word. When students comment on the tone of this exchange, they generally see it as a contest between equals in which both Kate and Petruccio give as good as they get. Some students notice that Petruccio controls the dialogue, keeping Kate off-balance so that most of her conversation is in response to him. In fact, she eventually seems to be exasperated by Petruccio's linguistic ability, asking, "Where did you study all this goodly speech?" (255). When the students come to the question of whose rhetorical strategy prevails, they conclude that Petruccio wins not through superior argument but by trickery. He effectively silences Kate when he announces that they have agreed that she will be froward in public yet conformable in private. Baptista is all too willing to accept Petruccio's explanation for the apparent disparity between Petruccio's claim that he has won Kate's heart and her protestations to the contrary. The students acknowledge that Petruccio wins the war of words, not by "throw[ing] a figure in her face," as Grumio predicts, but by giving his audience (Baptista) what he wants to hear. They concede that although Petruccio plays the wooing game with all its rhetorical flourishes, the outcome is already determined:

> And therefore setting all this chat aside,
> Thus in plain terms your father hath consented
> That you shall be my wife, your dowry 'greed on,
> And will you, nill you, I will marry you. (2.1.260–63)

When the students realize that the outcome is a foregone conclusion, they understand that Petruccio's strategy for wooing Katherine has actually failed—she is not won over by him. But he does achieve his goal of marrying Kate because he is able to win over Baptista, who will give his daughter (and her dowry) away. While the banter between Kate and Petruccio is entertaining for the audience, Petruccio's actual rhetorical success comes when he is able to convince Baptista that " 'Tis bargained 'twixt us twain, being alone, / That she shall still be curst in company" (2.1.296–97). Once the students discover that Petruccio's wooing of Kate was a mere formality and that the more important rhetorical strategy was to win Baptista's approval, they begin to understand that Kate cannot choose her husband but that her marriage is a contract between Baptista and Petruccio. Nevertheless, from Petruccio's perspective, winning Katherine's hand in marriage is only the beginning of his challenge, for, once married, he must find a way to live with her in "peace . . . and love and quiet life" (5.2.112).

The Struggle over Food and Clothing (4.3)

Any careful analysis of this scene makes it difficult not to resent Petruccio and sympathize with Kate. Her requests for food are reasonable by any standard, and Grumio's quibbles over the condition of the meat (which he eats in front of Kate) can only come across as cruel. Kate, who has been described as untamed and irrational, is the only character in this scene whose speech operates within the conventions of normal dialogue. She begins with the observation that the more wrongs that are done to her, the more spiteful Petruccio becomes. She continues to ask for food, arguing on the basis of her class and her basic human needs—all points of a well-ordered, logical rhetorical appeal. However, Grumio responds with feigned concern to Kate's logical argument, offering a series of teasing suggestions for dishes that are served up in tantalizing description only and not in fact. Grumio has been trained by his master to play the rhetorical game that Petruccio has devised to tame his new bride. Instead of using overt physical violence, he eloquently employs the weapons of rhetoric. Ultimately, Kate has no choice but to play the game, but in order to do so, she must first recognize that there is in fact a game under way, and then she must deduce the rules of the game. The rhetorical strategy Petruccio uses to tame Kate is the destabilization of the basis of her discourse by inverting the standard system of signs and signifiers. By the end of the scene, Petruccio tests Kate to discern whether she is a witting participant in his rhetorical game by challenging her perfectly rational belief that it *is* two o'clock in the afternoon. She fails the test and Petruccio stomps offstage, declaring that "[i]t shall be what a clock I say it is" (189).

Now that Petruccio has denied Kate food, he turns to the matter of her wardrobe. Students usually see the exchange between Petruccio and the Haberdasher and the Tailor as an extremely amusing scene with many suggestive references, and indeed that is how most productions portray it. In a humorous display of the rhetorical device known as *tapinosis* (debasing someone through undignified language), Petruccio uses metonymy to reduce the tailor to the tools of his trade: "thou thread, thou thimble, thou yard" (106–07). He proceeds to shrink the Tailor verbally, going from calling him a "yard" to "three-quarters, half-yard," and, finally, a "quarter nail" (or "two and a quarter inches"; 107). However, when students see the scene from Katherine's point of view, they react differently to the humor. Most will agree that there is less at stake when she doesn't get to wear the latest fashions to Bianca's wedding than when she was denied meat. Nevertheless, when they examine Petruccio's verbal assault, first on the tradesmen and then on Katherine—"Well, come, my Kate. We will unto your father's / Even in these honest, mean habiliments" (163–64)—many students begin to identify his contrariness with emotional abuse. They often are offended that Petruccio couches his rejection of Kate's new clothes in pious platitudes:

> For 'tis the mind that makes the body rich,
> And as the sun breaks through the darkest clouds;
> So honour peereth in the meanest habit. (166–68)

They react negatively to what they see as Petruccio's abuse of rhetoric, his twisting of language to achieve an end, often taxing credulity. Students are usually divided between seeing Petruccio as a hypocrite for pretending to have moral reasons for refusing to give Kate what she wants and needs and considering him a pragmatist whose wily use of language will eventually enable him to accomplish his goals.

And then there is the question of why Shakespeare includes Hortensio in this scene. As every rhetorician knows, rhetoric is empty without an audience to hear the argument. Although Kate is the obvious target of Petruccio's verbal strategy, she will eventually become a player of the game. Shakespeare places Hortensio in this scene for no other apparent reason than to admire Petruccio's rhetorical skill and to witness its taming effect on Kate. Just as in the framing device of the induction, where Christopher Sly provides an audience for Shakespeare's larger rhetorical project, in this scene Hortensio supplies the audience for Petruccio's rhetorical contest. Because Hortensio is not in on the game, he is still operating under the everyday assumptions about logical discourse. Like the audience, he is sympathetic to Kate's appeal for fair treatment and is impatient with Petruccio's inversion of normal verbal signification. He, like Kate, cannot imagine a world in which Petruccio can command the sun, even though it would serve both Kate's and Hortensio's purposes to do so.

Katherine the Orator (5.2)

Critics have long noted the irony that Katherine not only has the longest speech in the play (forty-four lines) but also more or less gets the last word. This is significant in a play that focuses so keenly on the power of language to persuade others. Students will notice that Kate's language in this speech is formal, abounding in metaphors. It uses many standard rhetorical flourishes, such as alliteration, anaphora, and parallelism, and it is spoken in iambic pentameter. In short, her language in this speech sounds nothing like the Kate we have heard before. Until now, she has spoken her mind in a fairly conversational tone, or, as in the stichomythic exchanges of the wooing scene, has parried Petruccio's verbal thrusts with skillful and somewhat stylized responses. Consequently, students are surprised by the high-flown language of her long speech, which is delivered in the style of an oration. Wayne Rebhorn points out that Grumio's warning that Petruccio will "disfigure" Katherine with his "rope tricks" (1.2.105–10) implies another meaning of "disfigure," that is, to disguise (327). Rebhorn argues that at the end of the play, Katherine wears the mask of an orator, a disguise that allows her to participate in Petruccio's rhetorical game. It may not be the "real" Katherine, but at least she has gained some agency in an otherwise oppressive situation.

When students go beyond analyzing the tone of Katherine's speech to consider its content, they are struck by how little her words correspond to her experience of marriage as it has been related to us throughout the play. She bases her argument first on a division of labor, speaking of the husband's duty "To painful labour both by sea and land, / To watch the night in storms, the day in cold" (153–54), while a wife leads an idyllic existence "warm at home, secure and safe" (155). Her characterization of wives as women of leisure hardly corresponds to her marriage to Petruccio, who deprives Katherine of food and sleep and, perhaps more important, takes away her freedom to speak her mind. The second premise for her appeal to the other wives is on the basis of women's physical weakness:

> Why are our bodies soft, and weak, and smooth,
> Unapt to toil and trouble in the world,
> But that our soft conditions and our hearts
> Should well agree with our external parts? (169–72)

She reprimands the other wives for their scornful glances and unkind looks, entreating them not to jeopardize their beauty, their reputations, or their amiable natures (140–49), considerations that heretofore did not seem to merit Katherine's attention. In the face of such apparent inconsistencies, students must decide how to interpret Katherine's final speech. Is it sincere? Is it ironic? Has Katherine been brainwashed? Whatever they decide, students need to base their conclusions on the full range of Katherine's rhetorical moves.

Finally, it is helpful for students to consider the intended audience for Katherine's oration. Although she addresses the other wives directly—"Fie, fie, unknit that threat'ning, unkind brow" (140)—the women are not alone on stage. Students have argued cogently that Katherine's real, and perhaps only, audience is Petruccio. This is Katherine's final exam in Petruccio's wife-taming academy, and she passes the test with flying colors. It is a public performance of her newly learned rhetorical skills in the game that Petruccio devised when he set out to woo her, a game in which language bears little or no resemblance to reality. And just as Petruccio, when wooing Katherine, paints a verbal picture of her as the woman he would like to marry, it may be that in her final speech Katherine is challenging Petruccio to live up to the image of what a husband should be.

NOTES

[1] For a more extensive history of medieval and early modern literary shrews, see Ricke, in this volume.

[2] Rebhorn provides an extensive and useful discussion of Petruccio's rhetorical skills.

[3] For a thorough history of rhetoric during the early modern period, see Vickers (ch. 5); Howell. Other helpful references on the topic include Donawerth; McDonald, *Shakespeare*; Newman; and Parker.

Fifteen Women and Nick Sly, the Astrophysicist: Staging Critical Engagements with *The Taming of the Shrew*

Alice Dailey and Shawn Kairschner

Most English department Shakespeare in Performance courses operate according to specific disciplinary assumptions. Borrowing from what are understood to be the staging practices taught and executed in theater departments, such courses aim to uncover textual meaning—to "bring Shakespeare to life" in ways that conventional literary study cannot. Accordingly, working through performance challenges like blocking, doubling, exits, and entrances is thought to help historicize the plays by illustrating the practical challenges faced by Shakespeare's company of actors. This approach to Shakespeare in Performance conceives of the relation between textual studies and stage work as unidirectional. The working practice of theater is understood as secondary, a device for illuminating the nuances of or profitably historicizing a foundational text. Conversely, theater-department Shakespeare offerings—acting classes in particular—tend to emphasize the physio-emotional work of locating Shakespeare's words in the performer's voice and body but frequently fail to consider the critical or historical implications of that embodiment. Both of these models register disconnection from more literary English department offerings such as upper-division Shakespeare seminars, in which students are encouraged to subject texts to rigorous critical scrutiny and to analyze them using an array of secondary materials.

But what happens when we begin the study of Shakespeare with close literary-textual work and then translate that work into the practice of embodied theatrical production? This essay reflects on just such an interdisciplinary experiment: a cross-listed English-theater-honors course at Villanova University in spring 2008 that culminated in a public production of *The Taming of the Shrew*. Instead of using the mechanisms of performance to acquire a sense of what a Shakespeare play tells us when it's "on its feet," this course—team-taught by two faculty members, one each from English and theater—reconstellated text, criticism, and performance. Using the disciplinary tools of both English and theater to study and stage *The Taming of the Shrew*, the course suggested not only how the work of literary scholarship can animate dramatic production but also how acts of interpretation become dramatic content.

The class began much like an advanced undergraduate or graduate-level English course: with close reading of the play and attention to its critical and cultural history. We worked from the Arden Shakespeare, Second Series (Arden 2) edition of *Shrew*, edited by Brian Morris, and from Frances Dolan's Bedford Texts and Contexts edition. In the opening weeks of the semester, students read and reread the play, becoming fluent with its language, characterization, structure, and thematics. We then moved into a survey of the literary-critical tradition and performance history. This reading was supplemented by a selection of the primary texts collected in Dolan's edition, with particular attention to those that situate *Shrew* in early modern discourses on domestic hierarchy, the duty of wives, the sport of falconry, and the practice of shrew taming.

Our readings and discussions, along with the students' own growing intimacy with the play, quickly brought the class to understand that staging *Shrew* would require them to reach some conclusions about the question of its misogyny, especially as regards the final scene. The issue of misogyny took on particular relevance for this group because of the lopsided gender makeup of the class. It comprised fifteen women and one man, Nick, our titular astrophysics major. As they approached the question of how they would stage the play, the class became aware of the implications of participating in a *Kiss Me, Kate*–style production as an overwhelmingly female cast. Because our use of the one male actor would inevitably be politically charged, it must therefore be thoughtful and strategic. Should Nick be cast as Kate? Should he be our Petruccio? What would the implications of these choices be in the production's broader interpretive framework?

To approach these questions, the class organized the critical history of the play into an interpretive binary in which an idealizing, romantic-comic reading of Kate's transformation was contrasted with one that sees her final submission as an expression of dehumanized brokenness. The class set Brian Morris's introduction, which claims that "When [Petruccio] wins the wager and [Kate] gives the final monologue, the love relationship triumphs" (147), at the romanticizing end of the critical spectrum. They set Stevie Davies's Penguin Critical Studies volume on *The Taming of the Shrew*, which they had read in its entirety, at the other end. Surveying the play's production history, critical history, and cultural context, Davies contests idealized readings like Morris's, concluding that at the end of the play, "Kate's life is finished, because she concedes her voice" (23).

These critical sites organized our conversations about what to stage and how to stage it. More specifically, they organized the class's thinking about the political implications of performing this particular play with their particular bodies in front of their professors and peers at Villanova. In this way, the students' knowledge of *Shrew*'s critical and performance history lent force to the process of dramatic embodiment they would be undertaking. With their knowledge came awareness that physically and vocally inhabiting the subject positions of the play instead of merely discussing those positions in class meant becoming participants in a preexisting public conversation with its own competing ideologies. This awareness did not produce a unified response. On the contrary, even students who identified themselves as "feminist" found themselves divided between intellectual or philosophical objections to the play's misogyny and the emotional attractions of the romantic-comic tradition. The course's pedagogical imperative—to teach the class to embody fully the political implications of Shakespeare's text—foregrounded precisely this tension. The course's interdisciplinary practice thus realized the value of textual embodiment in ways that are typically inaccessible both to courses in Shakespearean acting, which produce technically proficient but politically unaware performances, and to conventional Shakespeare seminars, which foster detached intellectual engagement.

With this interpretive tension not fully resolved, the group generated four possible production plans that would stage varying degrees of dissent from and accommodation of patriarchal readings of the play. These ranged from a heavily metatheatrical production that would use the Christopher Sly frame to emphasize the constructedness of gender roles to a darker, more frankly brutal dramatization of Kate's taming. From these outlines, the group decided on a production whose primary critical focus would be the investigation of the complexities of gender construction, principally the degree to which the culture of the play demands that men as well as women acquiesce to delimited gender roles. Further, we hoped that our production might wrestle with the play's messy, uncomfortable history in criticism and performance rather than offer a resolution that the students themselves had not fully experienced. Once they had decided to pursue these interpretive foci, the students began the work of editing the script. Each of six small groups was assigned a section of the play to cut, with the goal of shaping the script to sharpen the questions our production would pursue. The finished text, about half the length of the original play, efficiently told the story while retaining the moments that spoke most forcefully to the core issues that we had collectively decided to explore.

Given the students' interpretive interests, we cut all of the Sly frame's dialogue and eliminated its plot—a drunkard is fooled into thinking he is a lord watching a play in a fine house—but retained the character of the onstage voyeur. Thus Christopher Sly, unkempt tippler, became Nick Sly, the "director" of the production and an advocate for a romantic-comic reading of the play. We recognized that an interpretive battle of the sexes wherein a male director forces a masculinist interpretation on female actors is ultimately a reductive endeavor. However, the group accepted this problematic schema as a necessary corollary to their broader goal: to stage a production using only women's bodies in order to destabilize biological gender and to render transparent the constructedness of gender roles. To do so, Nick had to be excluded from the Paduan play world. The original purpose of casting Nick as the director was therefore not to establish a locus of masculine interpretive authority but, rather, to denaturalize the physical, sexual, and social authority that characters like Petruccio and Baptista enjoy as the prerogatives of the male body. By doing so, we hoped to show that such authority is achieved, enacted, and performed at great cost to both genders. Thus, even as we cast Nick in a directorial role and began to develop stage business in which he inculcated patriarchal interpretation, the group knew that, by the time the curtain came down, he would end up playing Kate.

In two public performances on the Villanova campus, we staged the play as a "run-through" by a new student theater group, the Villanova Shakespearience. Our Sly, like Shakespeare's, functioned as an active interpreter who embraced the play's tradition of *audiens interruptus*. The performance opened with Nick's welcoming the audience, asking them to turn off their cell phones, explaining who the new student group was, and reminding them that they were about to witness a rehearsal run of the play. He cautioned the audience that, because it was a rehearsal, there might be instances in which he interrupted the cast to offer comments or to make corrections. The play then began with Nick sitting off to the side, in the audience.

We established the convention of *interruptus* by having Nick offer a couple of brief scansion notes in the first act. In act 2, scene 1, he more forcefully made his presence known. As the actors playing Kate and Bianca began to perform the opening of the scene, with a genuinely hurt and bewildered Kate asking serious questions of a distracted, imperious Bianca, Nick stopped them. Telling them, "No, no—you've got it backward," he took the stage to offer interpretive advice: "Bianca is innocent . . . clueless. She's the ingenue. Our sympathy is with her. Kate's the antagonist—the devil, the bitch."[1] He then asked them to do the scene again from the top. On the second time through, the actors played Kate and Bianca as Nick had instructed. In full view of the audience they went upstage, quickly conferred, and then entered again, this time with a fierce and angry Kate leading on a helpless Bianca by her hair. The scene was played with Kate standing and Bianca on her knees, a fistful of her hair still in Kate's hand. At the end of the exchange, on her line, "If that be jest, then all the rest was so" (2.1.22), Kate threw Bianca to the ground, whereupon Baptista and the suitors entered. By performing two versions of the scene, we were able to stage a long-standing critical debate. The first iteration of the scene posited Kate as the innocent object of the scheming Bianca—a set of choices that threatens a critical tradition relying on an interpretation of Kate as a bullying harpy desperately in need of "taming." Our decision to have Nick voice the romantic-comic critical tradition staged the degree to which this tradition requires rigorous disciplinary enforcement—in this case, by a director.

Nick interrupted the performance again at the end of the sun-and-moon scene (4.5) and once more at the end of 5.1, after the actress playing Kate resisted Petruccio's public demands for a kiss. (There was no kiss. Rather, Nick, clearly frustrated, asked the actors to move on.) We decided that as the "run-through" progressed, some of the female students, embodying both masculine and feminine subject positions, should become increasingly uncomfortable with Nick's interpretation, to the point where they announced their discomfort, borrowing directly from the specific language of the scholarly debate (in the script below, those borrowings are indicated by italics).[2] This came to a head in the play's final scene. As the actor playing Kate began her monologue, Nick repeatedly interrupted her to offer interpretive corrections. The rest of the actors in turn silenced him, demanding that she be allowed to finish. After she performed the monologue as a deeply moving lamentation, Nick threw down his script, insisting that her interpretation was wrongheaded. This resulted in a different form of *interruptus*, an extended debate among Nick and the entire cast that used language from Morris and Davies as well as that of the students:

NICK. NO!! That's all wrong! You're playing it like a tragedy and it's a comedy! *When Kate accepts her status, she enters into the enjoyment of its rights and privileges. A dutiful wife gets to lie "warm at home, secure and safe" and all she has to give him is "love, fair looks, and true obedience"* (Morris 145).

STUDENT 4. But that's not all she has to give him. *It's bad enough that he denies her food and sleep, but now he appropriates her tongue—he takes her speech. She's nothing but a...a...a ventriloquist's dummy* (Davies 12, 11).

STUDENT 5. *Even her tongue is under his jurisdiction* (Davies 12).

NICK. Again, you're missing the point! *When he invites her to speak here, publicly, it's a mark of his trust in her—of his love* (Morris 147). Think back to the play's metaphors of falcon taming.

STUDENT 6. But don't you think there's something . . . disturbing about those metaphors? I mean, *they make Kate an animal while Petruccio gets to be a human being* (Davies 94).

STUDENT 7. But she's not an animal; she's a person.

STUDENT 8. It's dehumanizing.

STUDENT 9. It's just a metaphor.

STUDENT 10. But aren't the metaphors important? You know—isn't it important how people describe each other? It's not like language doesn't have any bearing on the action here. Look at Kate: everyone calls her a shrew.

STUDENT 8. Which, by the way, *is also a kind of animal* (Davies 94).

STUDENT 10. And then it's okay to do all these things to her because she doesn't count.
STUDENT 7. And that's supposed to be comedy?
STUDENT 11. Yeah, I don't think it's very funny.
STUDENT 8. Or romantic.
STUDENT 5. This play is giving me the creeps.
NICK. You're taking this far too literally and too seriously.
STUDENT 12. Yeah, I mean, Shakespeare isn't some kind of misogynist.
STUDENT 13. So—what? You're saying that *Shakespeare can't have meant what he seems to be saying, and that therefore he can't really be saying it* (Davies 43)?
NICK. I'm saying that *they subtly grow, interact, and achieve the equality of a true love-relationship* (Davies 43).[3] What this speech tells us is that *Kate and Petruccio have made their peace, and that she's in love with him and he's in love with her* (Morris 147).
STUDENT 14. *So not only does Petruccio tame his shrew but she's supposed to proclaim it publicly and be happy with it* (Davies 16)?
STUDENT 3. You're saying that *women desire to be mastered* (Davies 27)? This is what the speech tells us?
STUDENT 11. I think what this speech tells us is that *Kate's life is finished. Shakespeare has killed her off* (Davies 23, 41).
NICK. Look: *when Grumio comes for her, she obeys her husband's command. It's not a broken-spirited compliance. It's a duty she does and a gift she offers freely—one that Petruccio values highly because the cooperation of a woman like Kate is genuine and exciting. When he wins the wager and she gives the final monologue, the love relationship triumphs* (Morris 147).

At the end of this exchange, Nick came onstage to face the audience and performed the entire monologue. While this was happening, the rest of the company gradually began taking off their costume pieces and—some with great reluctance—left the playing space, no longer willing to participate. The show ended with Nick completing his rendition of the speech on bended knee, with his hand on the ground awaiting Petruccio's foot. When there was no response, he turned to realize that he was alone onstage. In a provocative reversal, a submissive Kate was gendered male, and Nick ended the performance by enacting the very disciplinary structures he had advocated. The production dramatized Nick's submission to his own interpretive framework, demonstrating that in such a reading, nobody triumphs: the romantic-comic tradition requires both genders to engage in acts of submission.

By developing a theatrical production that grew out of their literary and historicist work, students did more than consider the relation between interpretation and staging. They discovered that critical interrogation could become an embodied practice. The initial transition from textual study to performance had taken place at the semester's midpoint, when we took the class on a spring break trip to the Blackfriars Playhouse in Staunton, Virginia. In addition to seeing four of the Actors' Renaissance Season plays—which were, like our own production, collectively developed—the students took part in a series of seminars and workshops with the American Shakespeare Center's actors and artists. By the time the students arrived in Staunton, they had already engaged in a series of literary investigations as well as in myriad exercises designed to help actors locate Shakespeare's words in their bodies and breath.[4] Yet these two pedagogical strands had thus far remained discrete. On our last day in Staunton, they were brought together as the members of the group assumed their roles for the first time on the Blackfriars stage.

The students returned to Villanova after the break and spent the remainder of the semester learning to inhabit physically their enriched critical understanding of *Shrew*. This was a new and formative experience. They discovered that the physio-emotional commitment to the world of the play that is required for a scene to succeed necessitates a commitment to the value structures of the given play world, however racist, misogynist, xenophobic, or otherwise problematic they might be. As we have suggested, the students had widely divergent reactions to embodying the various denizens of Shakespeare's Padua and, by extension, were ambivalent about which critical understanding of that world and its values they favored. As is evident in the production's concluding *interruptus*, we sought to stage this ambivalence and its attendant complexities. The debate presented an opportunity for the students to express at once their dislike of the patriarchal reading of the play—"they make Kate an animal"—and their reluctance to relinquish such a reading: "Shakespeare can't have meant what he seems to be saying."

The production strove to carry this sense of ambivalence through to the final tableau. Neither side emerged victorious at play's conclusion; what was dramatized, rather, was a critical impasse. By ending the play with Nick alone onstage, the production allowed the romantic-comic critical tradition a voice and a space within which it could resonate, even as other actors were leaving the space in protest. This choice registered the fact that Nick's interpretation was not the remnant of a benighted misogynist past but a forceful contemporary presence. And indeed, the accuracy of this assumption was confirmed at the end of the semester, when we received the students' final papers. We had asked them to produce academic essays on *Shrew* using the critical materials we had encountered in class. The results were fascinating. Several students—all of them women—used Morris to support a romantic-comic reading of the play. In this, they reflected the critical tradition on which they were asked to draw; although most modern women's critical responses to the play are characterized by some degree of feminist critique, this has not always been, and does not necessarily continue to be, the case. Our students' postperformance critical engagement not only served as evidence of the play's capacity to yield a wide variety of critical interpretations but also suggested that the critical conversation surrounding the play continues to be acutely relevant. Instead of producing a single reading, the class experienced physically the ambivalence of the play—an ambivalence that demonstrates the continuing currency of *The Taming of the Shrew* for students, teachers, scholars, and practitioners of Shakespeare.

NOTES

[1] The students developed this line in rehearsal.

[2] The borrowings from Davies and Morris take the form of direct quotation, approximate quotation, and paraphrase. The students' objective was to use the language of the debate while naturalizing it into spoken conversation.

[3] This phrasing is Davies's characterization of the literary-critical tradition that reads the play as a romantic comedy (43).

[4] These exercises were borrowed largely from the work of Linklater.

Students Stage *Shrew*! The Theater as Classroom

Cynthia Lewis

"The thrill I felt when I connected with the audience," wrote one student in my Performing Shakespeare course, "was unparalleled by any character discovery or theatrical advance I had made in class." Such a statement is as good as it gets for a college teacher hoping to show students that the very best way to explore and learn a play is to put it on the stage. The year was 1995; the play was *The Taming of the Shrew*. This was the fifth incarnation of a course I had been offering every two or three years since 1983. English 452—Performing Shakespeare—began with *Much Ado about Nothing* as a pedagogical experiment combining scholarship and practical performance to teach a single Shakespeare play over a full semester's span. The course culminates in several public performances.

The group in question, composed of seventeen undergraduates, met for the first several weeks as a typical academic seminar. They read and discussed *The Taming of the Shrew*, as well as copious scholarship on the play, all the while formulating the core questions about the play that they imagined their production would address.[1] During the same period, they also learned the basics of original stage practices and of "playing Shakespeare," as the title of John Barton's book, which has long been a staple of the class, refers to the conventions of performing an Elizabethan stage script. By the seventh week of fifteen, the students had cast the play, each taking on at least one role. Then, they entered into rehearsal, testing onstage the various options they had encountered around the seminar table. The theater became their second classroom.

Although every Performing Shakespeare production incorporates several original practices—a three-quarter thrust stage, a lit house, and the absence of a fourth wall, for example—each class makes most of its decisions for itself. Starting with the script alone, the students eventually decide on and create their costumes, music and dance, set, publicity, and, most important, interpretations of a play's various controversial features, whether specific cruxes or overall tone. The Elizabethan ensemble model thus frames a course whose main aims are to teach one play from the inside out, to acquaint students with early modern stage and theatrical history, and, foremost, to develop a community whose artistic accomplishment depends on shared endeavor. The last of those goals emerges most prominently at semester's end, "the more delayed, delighted."[2]

Each time Performing Shakespeare takes up a new play, I also teach that play in my upper-division Shakespeare survey class, a course that is not without performance elements but that is a more traditionally "literary" undertaking. Teaching the same play in both classes inevitably points up how approaching it through performance can differ from a conventional literary approach. In the case of *The Taming of the Shrew*, Performing Shakespeare students came up with the usual questions for a literature class: questions about Petruccio's taming tactics (who is the *real* shrew in *Shrew*?), about Bianca's passive aggression (who *is* the real shrew in *Shrew*?), about the desirability of marriage in such a highly commodified market as Padua, and about Katherine's final set piece, to name a few. But time and again my Performing Shakespeare students' performances and journals registered revelations that surpassed those of my survey class members, many of them concerning shifts in genre, tone, and meaning.[3]

At the beginning of the semester, many Performing Shakespeare students welcomed the challenge of shaping concord from the discord of farce and romantic comedy, slapstick and rhetorical wit, self-conscious artifice and realism, sexism and satire of the same. By the end, few still harbored illusions that the play can be understood according to any single, overarching conception. A text that in the classroom and even in literary criticism may seem as conformable as any household Kate will in rehearsal quickly defy efforts to smooth over disjunctures. One student, writing in her journal, observed that Shakespeare "forces us to interweave genres and to think without the luxury of categories"—in itself a kind of luxury, however discomforting.

The students ultimately recognized that the only way to cope with the play's inconsistencies was to allow them to surface rather than to suppress them. This realization began in rehearsals, through repeated encounters with the unexpected. Those who initially were inclined to see the entire play as lighthearted quickly found occasion to take a more sober view of, for example, Petruccio's comparison of Katherine and a "haggard" (4.1.174). Conversely, students whose vision of the entire play was influenced early on by their sensitivity to its sexual politics and dark commentary on marriage were suddenly struck by its humor. In regard to some of the group's performance choices, one student conceded in her journal, "I really approve of the physical jokes and movements which make this play plainly a farce. I am surprised by how funny this play *really* is when finally put on stage."

The students' willingness to let the script guide them line by line increased over the course of the rehearsal period. The actor who played Petruccio testified to how such surrender to the script worked for him and Katherine in the wooing scene (2.1), which is often characterized by more extreme physicality than these two students eventually included:

> This scene proved to be a problem all the way up to dress rehearsal. Finally, though, I believe it worked. The point at which it began to gel was, I believe, when [Katherine] and I realized that we did not have to speed through it, we did not have to add anything to clue the audience in, we did not have to run around and tackle each other. Shakespeare's words do the work, and if we can deliver them, then we can carry the scene. "Play it naturally," he probably would have told us, "and it will work." We did that, and after a few run-throughs, aspects of our characters and our relationship started to pop out of our heads like the animals out of the soil in *Paradise Lost*. Petruccio wants to marry Kate for the money, but

> you know, he does find her attractive and spirited. Kate does not want to be told what to do, but here is someone paying attention to her, and what nice eyes!

Rather than choose one viewpoint over another or attempt to reconcile each character's mixed motives, the actors learned to perform incongruity. If, to cite another example, Katherine is scandalized by Petruccio's tardiness and bizarre apparel at her wedding in 3.3, she also hankers to be married to him. Two opposing motivations assert themselves, as Katherine is simultaneously angered by Petruccio's lack of respect for her, his bride, and favorably struck by his complete suitability for her. A "jolly, surly groom," Petruccio boasts an eccentricity that matches Katherine's own (3.3.84).

The class realized during their performances that audience members might respond as selectively to *The Taming of the Shrew* on stage as the class had while discussing the play. Throughout the rehearsal, however, the students became ever more tolerant of multiple interpretive approaches and ever more willing to experiment with as many as possible. Rather than jettison their critical readings once they entered into the theater, for instance, they returned frequently to these readings as crucial reference points. "Dismissing the literary criticism on *Shrew* as the work of scholars holed up in university libraries without any feeling for the practicalities of the play in performance would be inaccurate," one student wrote. "As much as I wanted to move on from so much criticism into rehearsals, even later on we kept revisiting some of the critics' main points."

Petruccio's characterization caused one notable problem of coherence for the class. Here, a word about one of the main ways this English class differs from a conventional theatrical venture is pertinent. In Performing Shakespeare, characters' roles are, to an extent, the property of the entire ensemble. While no one tells an actor how to perform a role, each role is up for class discussion like any other element of the play. In the past, a few students with more theatrical than literary background have found this feature of the course frustrating, but most adjust to it readily. In the case of this play, the students discussed Petruccio tirelessly, and the actor playing the part was perhaps the most enthusiastic participant in the conversation. He strove mightily with the "falcon taming" soliloquy in 4.1 and eventually came to view it as an extension of the character's improvisational approach to Katherine's taming. "I think Petruccio is feeling the process out as he goes along, game by game," the student remarked. "I think the key to understanding this monologue is right there in the last lines: 'He that knows better how to tame a shrew, / Now let him speak: *'tis charity to show*' " (191–92; emphasis added by student). The student went on to read the line as genuine, not meaning "I know what I'm doing better than any of you!" Rather, he saw it as a "challenge to the audience": "If . . . he really hopes someone jumps up and says, 'I know better! Let me tell you what you're doing wrong,' then " 'tis charity to show' makes perfect sense."

Another student reasoned similarly and persuasively about the fluctuations in Petruccio's character:

> Admittedly, everything Petruccio does [at his country home] is pretty harmless, but he still comes across like a big, bullying jerk. . . . The worst part is when Petruccio, Grumio and Hortensio all tease [Katherine] with food in 4.3. Watching them all gang up on her and taunt her with food when she is "giddy for lack of meat" is disgusting. And then, just when I start to feel like Kate and think that I cannot stand another minute of Petruccio, he relents. . . . Once Petruccio gets out of his taming mind-set . . . he calms down, and we see a fun-loving Petruccio. . . . Soon enough he and Kate are smooching in . . . the street.

Whether or not Petruccio's changes demonstrate his growth, thus adhering to one romantic-comic formula, his behavior is no more uniform than the tone of Katherine's final speech of submission is clear.

Still, through trial and error, the class found that allowing for the vicissitudes of character instead of ironing the text flat worked to characterize Petruccio. They had more trouble accommodating Katherine's character to her set piece in 5.2 because the speech can seem like such an extreme departure from her earlier character and, more to the point, from what today's audience wants to believe about her. I have learned over the years that, in general, to play a character involves suspending judgment about that character—that is, delivering the character's words wholeheartedly and straightforwardly, without attempting to manipulate the audience's reaction to the words. If the audience finds the words ironic, so be it, but, unless something in the dialogue or situation undeniably signals the character's irony, the actor should not try to represent the playwright by injecting irony into the speech. The limitation of this approach is manifest in the case of Katherine's speech because her tone is indeterminate. If the actor delivers the speech without irony, modern audiences balk. On the other hand, if she adopts an ironic view toward her words, even if she reserves that view for herself alone, then she may be perceived by audience members as interpreting the script for them. We tried the speech every which way, of course, and finally settled on the straightforward rendition: Katherine meant what she was saying. This choice put tremendous pressure on an amateur actor. During one performance, an audience member (a faculty member, no less) groaned audibly during the speech—presumably reacting to what he heard as its sexism—and many others objected to what they understood as Katherine's complete capitulation to Petruccio, try as we might not to reduce the lines to such a simplistic reading.[4]

Not all audiences responded the same way, though, and the actor playing Katherine learned enough flexibility, even during her limited run of six performances, to enact the role and that speech one performance at a time, one audience per day. "The best part of the performances," she wrote, "was having to adjust to the different audiences. You never knew what they would like or hate, what they would understand or appreciate. I'm so impressed by how deeply audience members thought about the play. . . . [I]ndividuals have approached me to ask questions about the play, the final speech, the language."[5] For students to figure out that *Shrew* is not just one play and that our production of it was far from singular is, for me, paramount. It is one angle on the prismatic quality of the play, which the students explored variously. "Perhaps by simply not choosing the farcical answer to many of our staging questions, we made moves toward creating a unified vision of the play," ventured one student, "although I don't think so. I think that we left enough of Katherine and Petruccio's actions ambiguous so that the audience could choose for itself." Another commented:

> Now, it is this very feeling of shock, realization, and vulnerability that I think the Davidson [College and community] audience would ideally feel at the end when Petruccio and Kate waltz off stage. They should think, "Oh my gosh, I liked Kate. I like Petruccio. I like them together, and I shouldn't have." I think that this reaction would stay true to Shakespeare's theme of the taming of the shrew, and it would be aware of the modern audience. Not only that, but we would make the audience laugh and enjoy the play as a romantic comedy only to discover in the end that it had elements of tragedy and farce.

In no instance was the play's inconsistency more felt than in its preoccupation with the subject of performance. To stage *Shrew* is to foreground that preoccupation. The play is filled with metatheatrical displays before internal audiences.[6] My Performing Shakespeare students understood the thematic weight of the play's pervasive interest in performativity, one of them writing, "there are many audiences in the play. People 'stand aside' to watch the action, inadvertently becoming part of the twentieth-century audience. I think this will enable the audience to bridge historical and theatrical distances." Other students remarked repeatedly on both Katherine's and Petruccio's role playing, a subject illuminated several years later by Amy L. Smith's fine analysis in "Performing Marriage with a Difference: Wooing, Wedding, and Bedding in *The Taming of the Shrew*." As one student wrote,

> To my mind, Kate's [final] speech is a performance. She speaks sincerely, but knowing all the time that it is for Petruccio's sake. . . . On one level she is telling Bianca and the Widow how to be good wives, and on another level, she is telling Petruccio, "See how much I love you that I will say all this? And in front of everyone?" Their private behavior is so different that I cannot believe Kate's speech is an indication of how Petruccio wants his marriage. . . . Kate's speech has plenty of advice for men, too. . . . She makes the speech that Petruccio wants to hear, but not without getting in a few points of her own.

This concept of a two-tiered performance on Katherine's part, suggested by one class member and enthusiastically endorsed by others, has its attractions and its limitations. While it may enhance the actor's rendition of the speech, as well as the ensemble's grasp of the play's conclusion, it is difficult to play, especially for amateurs, because it requires an actor to convey opposing meanings to two internal audiences. Moreover, the notion that Katherine and others will be happiest when conforming to social norms and expectations both permeates the play and runs directly counter to another of the play's clear implications: that happiness stems from flouting and subverting those norms and expectations.

In truth, on the matter of performance, *The Taming of the Shrew* talks out of both sides of its mouth. It repeatedly suggests that, for her own sake, Katherine would do well to stop binding and beating her sister and make nice to men. The crowning reward of falling in line and capitulating to her husband—of playing the submissive wife—is the tranquil marriage—tranquil, at least, for Petruccio, who envisions, when Lucentio and Hortensio ask him what Katherine's newfound obedience "bodes": "Marry, peace it bodes, and love, and quiet life; / An aweful rule and right supremacy, / And, to be short, what not that's sweet and happy" (5.2.112–14). If it does not bode so well for her, she will, in any case, be able to move on along the road to Padua by agreeing that the sun is the moon or vice versa (4.6).[7]

At the same time, Petruccio recommends to Katherine the same socially subversive behavior he displays when he arrives at their wedding dressed outrageously. "To me she's married," Petruccio boasts, "not unto my clothes," indicating that adherence to social norms is empty and artificial, a kind of self-betrayal (3.3.110). Later, when the couple returns to Padua in the midst of Bianca's own turn at misbehavior, Katherine and Petruccio become, for the first time, an internal audience, rather than a bewildering spectacle to others (5.1.51 sd). They have ceased performing. When Katherine demurs from kissing Petruccio in the street because it is socially unacceptable, he implies that they are not society's parrots but—like a king and another Shakespearean Kate—the "makers of manners" (*Henry V* 5.2.252). His suggestion that they will be fulfilled by pleasing themselves flatly contradicts the disapproval—from both the characters and the audience—of Katherine's frequent, express urge to "please [her]self" at the cost of alienating everyone around her (3.3.83).

The paradox in *Shrew* regarding performance—that it at once enables social belonging and strangles individuality—lies at the heart of romantic comedy, a genre that champions the individual over society and also the reintegration of the individual into a renewed society. It is an irreducible opposition, characteristic of Shakespeare. I cannot say that the nature of this opposition emerges clearly through performance, but I can say that postperformance reflection helps make it salient. The "issue of private vs. public behavior," recalled one student, "was bigger than we at first realized." I imagine Performing Shakespeare students have made many a latter-day realization about this issue, one adumbrated by their staging of a play that in many ways baffled their expectations.

NOTES

[1] The essays students read on Shrew in 1995 included those by Baumlin; Bean; Berek; Boose, "Scolding"; Burns; Coursen, *Shakespearean Performance* 49–73, 237–40; Garner; Hodgdon; Kahn, *Man's Estate*; Kehler; Novy, "Demythologizing"; Perret; Slights, "Raw"; and Wayne.

[2] For a fuller description and discussion of the Performing Shakespeare class at Davidson College, see Lewis, "'Performing Shakespeare': The Outward Bound of the English Department." The ensemble ethos is so important to the conception and success of the class that including one student's comment about it seems warranted: "We all relied on each other more than anyone realized, and yet everyone took everyone else for granted. It seemed inconceivable that someone could mess up, and yet the possibility was always there. What was amazing was that no one did mess up, and that if someone had, we knew we could have counted on someone else to fix it. . . . In performing a play, we learned that trusting your fellow cast members was a necessity. Without that trust—I would have been a nervous wreck the whole time. Instead, we took our leap of faith together, and we still feel the rewards of taking such a big risk."

[3] Although a full production is an ideal means of unveiling revelations about the entire play, it is not necessary. Many discoveries are available through more limited performance—for example, acting a single scene more than once, each time from the perspective of a different genre or character.

[4] Limited space prohibits my detailing the many steps the class took to complicate this speech and the ending of the play. Examples include Katherine's loving, rather than chiding, tone toward her sister and the Widow and the staging of the play's last line: just after Hortensio said, "thou has tamed a curst shrew," and as Lucentio added, "'Tis a wonder, by your leave, she will be tamed so," the Widow slapped Hortensio in the face, and all the characters on the stage froze.

[5] This sentiment, which found expression in numerous students' journals, derives partly from John Russell Brown's quirky little treatise *Free Shakespeare*, the first required reading in Performing Shakespeare. One student wrote, "What was most interesting . . . was . . . the unique personality of each audience. In addition, I loved to watch our cast adapt to each audience between the performances and even within one performance." Another concurred: "the audience, when allowed, contributes nearly as much to the shape of a Shakespearean performance as the actors themselves."

[6] One reason for the abundance of internal performances and audiences, I believe, is Shakespeare's less than adept way of moving characters on and off the stage in this early work. Rather than organically stream characters on and off as needed, he brings a large collection onstage at once (my cast elbowed one another as they passed through our two door-width entrances), only to leave most of them onstage with nothing to do but listen to and watch one or two others' shtick. This dramaturgical feature of *Shrew* could, of course, derive from, rather than cause, Shakespeare's interest in metadrama, but in view of how he handles entrances and exits more skillfully in subsequent plays, I incline to see the abundance of internal performances in this play as the effect of the playwright's less mature technique.

[7] That performance can quickly come to constitute reality is a fundamental tenet of the play from the very beginning: Christopher Sly begins to speak in verse once he is convinced that he is a lord (induction, sc. 2, line 66). Throughout the play, the language of the theater mingles with that of reality, so that when, for example, Tranio mentions "some show to welcome us to town," he blurs the boundary between the worlds inside and outside the theater (1.1.46).

What Does the Induction Do? Introducing Concepts of Action

Edward L. Rocklin

I teach an upper-division course devoted to the first half of Shakespeare's career. When the class begins discussing *The Taming of the Shrew*, I ask the students to share their responses, and I record them on the board. I do this to encourage students to ask the questions that seem most urgent to them and to initiate a discussion in which students share what excites, repels, or puzzles them about the play. In this opening dialogue, we begin to formulate some of the central issues that will guide our work. While it is impossible to predict all the questions that will arise, I discuss below some major issues that usually come up.

First, students are often puzzled by the framing story of Christopher Sly. Does Sly really fall asleep? Is he still onstage even if he isn't speaking? Why doesn't Sly reappear at the end? If Shakespeare wasn't going to bother with Sly at the end, why introduce him at the beginning? Second, many students find the Bianca-and-suitors plot confusing: it is hard to read because there are people in (literal) disguise and using other names, and you have to remember both names when you read their speeches. Third, since multiplot drama is new to most of them, they have questions about the relation between the two plots of the taming story and the relation of these plots to the induction. Fourth, students offer divergent responses to and interpretations of the ending: they wonder if Shakespeare's contemporaries did indeed "believe all that stuff about men being superior," and many ask if Katherine really does surrender to Petruccio and the cultural norms he invokes. (This response parallels the response to *Measure for Measure*, where students ask, Why does Isabella marry the Duke? That question provides a cue for introducing the concept of open silences—a concept that can also be useful for exploring the last scene of *The Taming of the Shrew*.) I ask students to write down their answers to these questions, and, when we finish exploring the play, I ask them to reread their original comments to see if they have been confirmed, modified, or radically revised by the classroom activities.

Since *The Taming of the Shrew* is the first play we study in this course, the class is also learning about the nature of the outdoor amphitheaters of London—a topic they read about in the text we are using (the second edition of *The Riverside Shakespeare*). I begin the next phase of our work by connecting the questions about the Sly plot to our discussion of the physical theater. The objective in this activity is for students to become further engaged with the play by using their new and still general knowledge of the Elizabethan stage. They will explore how the two scenes of what we call the induction were likely to be staged and, later, the question of where Sly, Sly's "lady," the Lord, and the servants are placed in relation to the actors performing the taming story. In exploring the induction, furthermore, they will discover how Shakespeare wrote cues for the performers in the dialogue he wrote for his characters.

In the model that I use for studying drama, the initiating question for each activity is some form of, What does X do? Thus I refocus our attention by asking, What does the first scene of the induction do? and note that we can begin to answer that question by performing the induction. I ask for two volunteers, who start by reading the opening exchanges between the Hostess and Sly. Then, we move into enacting this segment of the scene, usually in a very minimal fashion.

At this point, we pause so that the whole class can analyze the words of the scene for cues about context and action. What is the context? The dialogue makes it clear that Sly has been ordering drinks and has broken glasses, that he owes the Hostess for both items, and that she is running him out even as she demands payment. So, we are outside a tavern. How would the spectators come to know this? There might be a tavern sign over one of the stage doors, but probably costumes and behavior would be the primary signals. The Hostess would be dressed in clothes signifying her occupation, and Sly would be dressed poorly; his actions and his speech would indicate his drunkenness. I ask, What happens if we hear the sound of breaking glass just before this pair comes onstage? Not only would this hint at the action of the scene, it would also prefigure the role of noise in this play.

What about the action? The Hostess seems to be her own bouncer, and this raises the question of how physical the scene is. Is she a very strong woman? Or is she successful mainly because Sly is drunk? In particular, how much physical contact or violence might there be? What else do we discover about the Hostess? A typical answer might be, "She is unafraid and probably self-righteous because she believes she has the law on her side." What else do we discover about Sly? "That he is drunk and that he is ignorant but trying to sound educated and that he comes from a poor class." In fact, given the speech where he says he has been a "card-maker . . . a bear-herd, and . . . a tinker" (induction, sc. 2, lines 16–19), some students wonder if his drinking may explain the change of occupations. After a few minutes of discussion, the two students perform the scene again. The second time, they invent more action, so that the segment's potential to be farce begins to be realized. In one performance, the Hostess ended by shoving Sly hard enough to send him down, and Sly's final defiance, shouted from the ground, drew laughter for his surprising tumble, as did his imitation of a drunk trying to stay awake.

If we stop the performance here, we can ask, What has the play done so far? That is, if we imagine ourselves as first-time spectators who have only the title and these first few minutes of action, what are we thinking about this play? We will try to locate ourselves in relation to the action so far, which seems to have come to an odd pause, as the man who calls himself Sly sinks into a drunken stupor. One obvious move is to attempt to use the title to make sense of what we have seen so far. We will ask ourselves if the Hostess is the shrew. And we will think that if the Hostess *is* the shrew, it certainly does not look as if Sly will tame her. As members of a first-time audience, we have no idea that we are watching an induction. Shakespeare's opening grabs our attention while leaving us slightly off-balance.

As we come to the end of the rest of this scene—either through completing a performance or through a quick discussion—I introduce a concept of action and of how such action creates expectations. I tell students that we need to distinguish two senses of *action*—which I am going to call "action 1" and "action 2"—and then see how a scene can function as a unit of action in the second sense.

Action 1 includes everything we witness at a live performance or would witness in a transmission or recording of that performance. Action 2 focuses on motive and meaning. It is the purpose and intention that inform the outward action. To find this type of action, we ask what the actor, the character, or the dramatist is doing through the visible and audible action. Action 2 can be used to discuss what might be thought of as intermediate units of a scene or the scene as a whole. For example, in a later activity, when we explore Petruccio's first soliloquy (2.1.168–81), we can see that, given what he has learned about Katherine's nature (she broke the lute over the head of a man she thought was a tutor), he is working out a plan to woo her in a fashion designed to thwart the resistance he anticipates from her—and that his thought process moves systematically through imagining how Katherine might offer increasingly difficult challenges. This helps us understand what he is doing when he starts his wooing by imposing his own version of her name and calling her a liar, even as he also praises her in a variety of ways.

In the same way, we can focus on what the dramatist is doing through a scene as a whole event—the way the dramatist shapes the action of one scene to invite us to form expectations about the action of the next scene (or, in multiplot drama, a later scene concerning those actors). Here I point out that the first scene of the induction is designed to prompt us to anticipate the action of the second scene of the induction. Thus I ask the students to formulate as precisely as possible what this scene suggests will be the action of the next scene—keeping in mind that when we define the action of a scene, we need to use the verb that best captures the core meaning of this event.

The formulations students typically produce compose an array from less to more precise: the scene sets us up to watch whether or not the Lord succeeds in his plan; the scene prepares us to see how successful the Lord is in his attempt to transform Sly's preexisting identity; or the scene will present a struggle between the Lord's attempt to fool Sly and Sly's attempt to fool the Lord into thinking that Sly is fooled. At this point I formulate the prompt for rereading the second scene, to look for all the signals in the text that help guide the actors in re-creating the action 1—the physical, visible action—and, through their performance, to prompt audiences to understand the action.

Students do this exercise in small groups, working for about ten minutes. If they find it difficult to grasp the concept of action or look for cues, I suggest some specific questions: When does Sly stop resisting the new identity? What speech or action persuades him to accept a new identity? What are the different ways the Lord and his followers attempt to persuade Sly they are telling the truth?

Here are some of the key points students discover:

Sly resists until he asks, "Am I a Lord, and have I such a lady?" (induction, sc. 2, line 66), when he must either begin to accept the fiction or realize that accepting his new role can work to his advantage.

Up to line 23, Sly resists, and then for a long stretch he remains silent as the Lord and the servants speak (24–65). During these speeches, Sly presumably listens carefully. In viewing a performance, we may be able to infer something of his thought process by his facial expressions or body language. One question is how good the Lord is at disguising the fact that he is in charge. Some students argue that no matter what he does, the servants will still defer to the Lord—and of course the Lord does have the longest speeches, which may enable him to dominate the scene.

Another crucial signal is that when Sly performs the speech beginning "Am I a Lord?" (66), he shifts from prose to verse, the form of language that everyone around him speaks. Is Sly conscious of this shift? The answer is probably not, but you may want to clarify this point for students. Some of Shakespeare's characters are presented as aware of the difference between speaking in prose and verse. For example, in 4.1 of *As You Like It*, Rosalind and Celia (both still in disguise) have been talking with Jaques in prose. But when Orlando enters, he speaks one line of verse and thereby prompts Jaques to say, "Nay then God buy you, and you talk in blank verse" (31–32). Jaques, that is, not only is conscious of the two patterns but also calls the audience's attention to a shift that many of them might not hear—certainly not from Orlando's single line. There is also an interesting example in which Hamlet, told that the players are arriving in Elsinore, concludes his enthusiastic response by saying that "the lady shall say her mind freely, or the [blank] verse shall halt for't" (2.2.324–25). The introspective Hamlet, who is certainly much more self-aware than Sly, can be understood to be making a joke about the fact that he has been speaking prose throughout the scene. But what is similar in these cases is that the shift from prose to verse and the act of calling attention to the meter or lack of meter is a signal to the actor about the nature of his performance. Indeed, as suggested by Tiffany Stern's work in *Making Shakespeare: From Stage to Page* on "cue-scripts," or actor's parts, the actor playing Sly, like the actor playing Hamlet, would have seen instantly when his character

> shifted from prose to verse or verse to prose, since he would be looking at his own part, interrupted only by three- or four-word cues from another speaker (77–90; 123–36). So the shift from prose to verse here serves as a prompt to the actor that Sly is adopting the speech of those around him—and that the Lord's experiment seems to be succeeding.

This discussion thus offers me an opportunity to introduce students to the crucial fact that the dramatist must always write on two levels. Shakespeare is composing a scene centered on the social action by which this group seeks to reconstruct Sly's reality, and he builds in signals that show this transformation happening. At the same time, because he composes his dialogue for actors, he needs to offer implicit directions for how to perform key elements of the change. Two key elements are the business with drink and the element of sexuality introduced with the appearance of the page as Sly's "wife."

There is an array of options for how to produce comic moments in performing the exchanges about drinks. Does Sly get a drink when he first calls for it, or only when he repeats his request? Does he notice that the servant offers sack instead of ale and offers it in an aristocratic cup instead of a plebeian pot? Here or later, if he drinks the sack, does he have a physical reaction to a liquor he has never tasted before? It is one of the script's subtleties that Sly begins speaking in the verse appropriate for his new identity as a Lord but continues to drink like a poor man.

The entrance of the "lady" adds other comic possibilities. This is a moment when Sly can be become convinced of his new identity, so that his startlingly direct "Madam, undress you, and come now to bed" (sc. 2, line 113) can reveal him shedding the last vestiges of doubt as he starts to discard his clothes. But it can also be a moment when Sly uses a wink or a look to let the audience know that he is aware that he is being gulled, indicating he is thinking, Well, let's see how far you will go! There is even a complex option—namely, that Sly can be trying to fool those around him into thinking that he has accepted his new identity but then is fooled himself by the "lady," a point that can be emphasized when he says, "Ay, it stands so that I may hardly tarry so long" (121).

I summarize this exploration by noting that, according to the script, Sly changes how he speaks, how he does or does not acquire new tastes in liquor, how he attempts to master new forms of address, and how he attempts to make love to his "wife." In terms of food choices, modifications of language, alterations of class distinctions, and references to sexual relations, the transformation of Sly introduces some of the relationship changes that will occur between Petruccio and Katherine in the "taming" plot. This is a logical moment to introduce the analysis of how cultural codes shape behavior even as they operate in ways beyond the intentions and control of the individual.

As I do with many performance-centered activities, I ask students to do some writing in which they collect their thoughts and formulate guidelines for reading differently:

Prose-verse shifts. These can signal a variety of transitions: in this case, an ascent in class standing and the process by which a solitary figure seeks to join a group.

The functions of a character's questions. Asking questions can signal that a character is rethinking his or her situation or choices. What does asking a given question at a given moment prompt us to infer about a character's thought process?

Nonverbal response. When a character is listening to long speeches aimed at him or her, a key choice is to offer nonverbal cues as to what she or he is thinking or feeling.

Forms of address. Forms of address such as "Lord" can convey complex relations both by what term is used and how it is spoken. Changes in a form of address also can create powerful effects (bestowal or withdrawal of respect, for example).

Eating and drinking. Eating and drinking can create bonds between characters, and on the stage they usually have a much more direct effect than on the page. Food choices and table manners can also serve as markers of class.

Clothing. The clothes a character wears are crucial, especially in a society where sumptuary laws attempted to regulate who could wear what. A wardrobe of various costumes is a fundamental theatrical resource: from Christopher Sly to King Lear, characters indicate their movement up and down the social order by changing their dress.

Props. There are relatively few props in Shakespearean drama, but those that do appear often are charged with symbolic meaning—as is the case with the difference between the "pot" Sly calls for and the "cup" that is offered to him by the servant.

By means of this group of activities, students begin to become engaged not only with the rich details of the theatrical script but with the wider challenge of shifting from what we might call (using the language of computers) being "default readers" to becoming people who can read as experimenters and thus to become, like the actors, cocreators of the play in performance. I have also prepared them to ask, What does the second beginning of the play do?

NOTE

The concepts and practices presented in this essay are developed from chapter 3 of my *Performance Approaches to Teaching Shakespeare* 103–10. For a fuller development of how to transform the role on the page into the performance on stage, see the sections "Reading as an Actor: Transforming Role into Character" (130–40) and "Petruchio and Katherine: Working with Two Roles" (140–47) in the same chapter.

The Teaching of *A Shrew*: Exploring Textual Differences through Classroom Performance

Michael McClintock

The Taming of a Shrew, the 1594 quarto associated on its title page with the acting company Pembroke's Men, bears an uncertain relationship to Shakespeare's *The Taming of the Shrew*. Is *A Shrew* an early version of *The Shrew*? Is *A Shrew* a derivative "bad quarto" version of *The Shrew*? Are *A Shrew* and *The Shrew* related to a lost ur-*Shrew* play? The problematic textual status of both *Shrew* plays is hardly unique in Shakespeare studies. Still, the lack of critical attention that has been paid to *A Shrew* when contrasted with that paid to other Shakespearean multitext plays such as *Hamlet* or *King Lear* is striking. Up until the publication of the recent Arden edition of *The Taming of the Shrew*, edited by Barbara Hodgdon, and the anthology *Three Shrew Plays*, edited by Barry Gaines and Margaret Maurer, *The Taming of a Shrew* has been similarly missing in editions available for the classroom. *The Norton Shakespeare*, for example, provides both the quarto and folio texts of *King Lear* on facing pages along with a third conflated text of the play, while *A Shrew*, by contrast, is represented by five brief fragments, totaling some fifty lines, from the Christopher Sly episodes. Lack of easy access to the full text of *A Shrew* has been unfortunate, since, in my experience, *The Taming of a Shrew* is a highly teachable text that can be paired with *The Taming of the Shrew* in order to prompt useful insights in the classroom. When students are presented with the two texts and given the opportunity to appreciate the significant contrasts that emerge through their study and performance, they are able to ask questions and make judgments that, in the face of a single text by Shakespeare, they may feel less qualified to venture.

I regularly teach *The Taming of a Shrew* alongside *The Taming of the Shrew* in my undergraduate Shakespeare classes, which have enrollments of about twenty-five students each. Since there was no classroom edition of *A Shrew* available when I began teaching the play several years ago, I prepared my own basic edition, which I continue to use. I base much of my classroom discussion of the two plays on Leah Marcus's chapter "The Editor as Tamer: *A Shrew* and *The Shrew*" from her *Unediting the Renaissance*. The chapter is essential reading for any instructor teaching the two *Shrew* plays, but it could also be assigned as background reading for students. I typically put the two *Shrew* plays at the start of my course, since they help set up several of my larger goals. In practical terms, the plays provide the students with their first taste of classroom performance. Thematically, the two plays can introduce students to the competition between hierarchical and companionate models of marriage in early modern England (something to which they can return in their reading of later romantic comedies). Finally, the contrasts between the two plays compel students to begin making evaluations based on textual and performance evidence.

Our discussion of the two plays covers a number of the most significant contrasts, such as the more extensive role for the Sly frame in *A Shrew* and the markedly different speeches on obedience that Kate delivers at the end of each play. In this essay, however, I focus on two episodes that, in my experience, best demonstrate what can be achieved with a performance-based approach to teaching *A Shrew*. Much of our discussion of the two *Shrew* plays centers on the question of motivation for both Kate and Ferando/Petruccio. Marcus notes that editors have traditionally faulted *A Shrew* for not clarifying motivation (109). Ferando, for instance, has no lines equivalent to Petruccio's "I come to wive it wealthily in Padua; / If wealthily, then happily in Padua" (1.2.72–73). Yet, for Marcus, *A Shrew* does in fact offer motivation for Kate and Ferando, albeit of a different sort than that offered in *The Shrew*. This distinction, briefly discussed by Marcus, becomes the starting point for my more detailed comparison of the two plays.

In what follows, I focus first on my approach to teaching a brief episode in *A Shrew* involving Kate's and Aurelius's servant Valeria, who is disguised as a music instructor. This scene provides important insights into Kate's side of her relationship with Ferando. I then discuss an episode that appears in both *A Shrew* and *The Shrew*, in which Ferando/Petruccio convinces Kate that the sun is the moon and that an old man is a young woman. Having students perform the two versions of this episode in sequence provides a particularly sharp contrast between the two plays' representations of marriage, particularly in terms of the attitudes held by Ferando and Petruccio. Overall, my discussion should be taken as descriptive rather than prescriptive and as an amalgamation of my experiences teaching the *Shrew* plays rather than an account of a specific class.

A key moment in the presentation of Kate's character in *A Shrew* occurs at the end of her first exchange with Ferando, who (like Petruccio in *The Shrew*) uses their initial meeting unambiguously to announce his intentions: "I am the man / Must wed and bed and marry bonny Kate" (3.148–49).[1] After Kate's father, Alfonso, tells her that Ferando will be her husband, Kate publicly objects but then in an aside announces: "But yet I will consent and marry him, / For I methinks have lived too long a maid, / And match him too, or else his manhood's good" (3.169–71). Students who have read this often recognize *A Shrew*'s Kate's fear of being an old maid when it reappears in *The Shrew* (2.1.31–34), but they also show interest in *A Shrew*'s Kate's last line here. That line suggests that she sees in Ferando something of a challenge (what Kate means by "match him too" can generate a significant amount of discussion). This insight into Kate's motives informs a detailed examination of the opening of scene 4 in *A Shrew*, in which Valeria, disguised as a music instructor, attempts to teach Kate the lute. This episode, which is only reported by Hortensio in *The Shrew* (2.1.139sd–157), is one that helps me introduce performance in class and that benefits from a version of the method outlined by Michael Tolaydo in the Shakespeare Set Free series (41–46). By this method, students initially read through the scene one sentence at a time, focusing on questions of meaning. In a second reading, they proceed one speech at a time, discussing issues such as tone, emotion, and what the character hopes to accomplish in the episode. The final step is to have two students stand up and perform the episode for the class, with the rest of the students serving as "directors." My role as instructor for this final stage is mostly to raise questions for the student directors to consider, as well as to ensure that the student actors understand how to put the student directors' suggestions into action.

On the first reading, students often interpret the episode in essentially the same terms as Hortensio's report of the equivalent episode in *The Shrew*—a shrewish Kate loses her patience with the lesson and attacks her teacher with the lute. Interpretive difficulties with the episode in *A Shrew* are typically few. Valeria's allusion to the myth of Orpheus's moving trees and beasts with his music (4.1–4) may require a brief explanation, as may the socially derogatory connotations in Kate's "How now Jack Sauce, you're a jolly mate" remark (4.28). On the second reading, we recall Kate's aside in her first scene with Ferando, and particularly the sense that she saw Ferando as a worthwhile challenge, or "match." If Valeria is less than worthwhile, could Kate's reaction to him in this scene be something other than her "devilish spirit"? One part of Valeria and Kate's exchange stands out when we go over the scene again in this light:

VALERIA. Come lovely mistress, will you take your lute
And play the lesson that I taught you last?
KATE. It is no matter whether I do or no,
For, trust me, I take no great delight in it.
VALERIA. I would sweet mistress that it lay in me
To help you to that thing that's your delight.
KATE. In you with a pestilence, are you so kind!
Then make a night-cap of your fiddle's case
To warm your head and hide your filthy face.
VALERIA. If that sweet mistress were your heart's content,
You should command a greater thing than that
Although it were ten times to my disgrace.
KATE. You're so kind, 'twere pity you should be hanged,
And yet, methinks, the fool doth look asquint. (4.7–20)

When students consider Valeria's goals in the scene, they typically zero in on his "lovely mistress" and "sweet mistress" remarks and the suggestive "thing" that he promises would be Kate's delight and heart's content. What usually emerges from the second reading is a Valeria who is not an innocent victim of Kate's shrewish temper but a predatory figure trying unsuccessfully to seduce Kate. Kate, for her part, emerges from this reading as a sympathetic figure who initially tries to fend off Valeria with insults but eventually resorts to blows when Valeria's suggestions become too explicit.

When we move on to performance, the student directors attempt to put these insights into play. The student playing Kate is usually seated to play her lute while Valeria stands, and in the fifteen lines separating Valeria's "will you take your lute / And play the lesson that I taught you last?" (4.7–8) from Kate's "Ay, give me the lute" (4.24), directors will often have Valeria move closer to Kate with each of his speeches, ending up "in her face," as some of the directors put it. The student directors have had Valeria wink and bat his eyelashes once he has moved close to Kate, providing the action to provoke her "methinks, the fool doth look asquint" remark (4.20). In the exchange that follows, when Kate answers Valeria's "Why, mistress, do you mock me?" with "No, but I mean to move thee" (4.21–22), the student directors have Kate give Valeria a shove in order to reestablish some distance between the pair. Valeria is typically directed to move in again as Kate begins playing her "air lute" and to touch her hand as he corrects her: "That stop was false, play it again" (4.25). This physical contact provokes the exchange and violence that follows:

KATE. Then mend it thou, thou filthy ass.
VALERIA. What, do you bid me kiss your arse?
KATE. How now Jack Sauce, you're a jolly mate.
You're best be still, lest I cross your pate
And make your music fly about your ears.
I'll make it and your foolish coxcomb meet.
She offers to strike him with the lute.
VALERIA. Hold mistress, will you break my lute?
KATE. Ay, on thy head and if thou speak to me!
There; take it up and fiddle somewhere else.
She throws it down.
And see you come no more into this place
Lest that I clap your fiddle on your face. *Exit Kate.*
(4.26–36)

Student directors are sometimes divided over how Valeria should deliver his "do you bid me kiss your arse?" line. Some feel he feigns shock at what he supposedly heard, some think it is an attempt at the same kind of bawdy wit that Petruccio uses in his "What, with my tongue in your tail?" remark (2.1.214), and others argue that he is salaciously hopeful that she would in fact bid him to follow through on the suggestion. Directors normally have Kate stand up at this point and again "move" Valeria by approaching him threateningly with her air lute before throwing it to the ground on "There" (4.34).

This brief scene works well to show the class how a seemingly simple episode can in fact contain significant interpretive questions. The scene also provides a provocative contrast with the parallel moment in *The Shrew*. The decision to have Hortensio report the episode of Kate's hitting him with the lute after the fact rather than to stage it raises important questions of revision or adaptation. (If one of these plays is somehow based on the other one, why change from performance to reporting?) It also provides for different interpretations of Kate's character in each work. By performing the episode in *A Shrew*, students discover a level of motivation for Kate's actions that is simply not available in the reported episode from *The Shrew*, where the visual focus and interpretive authority remain solely with Hortensio as Kate's victim "*with his head broke*" (2.1.139 sd).

By the end of our examination of the *Shrew* plays, I ask groups of students to prepare scenes outside class to be presented in class, an assignment that will recur several times during the course of the semester. One of the first of these presentations involves a pair of scenes that provides one of the sharpest contrasts between the two shrew and tamer couples: the episode, appearing in both *Shrew* plays, in which Ferando/Petruccio convinces Kate to call the sun the moon and an old man a young woman as they travel back to Kate's father's house. By this point in our consideration of the plays, we will have noticed how Ferando, like Kate, clarifies his motives in a manner that contrasts significantly with his counterpart in *The Shrew*. For example, when Ferando arrives for his wedding "*basely attired and* [with] *a red cap on his head*" (4.107sd) and afterward insists that Kate leave with him immediately, forcing her to miss the wedding feast, he offers her an explanation that is also a challenge. His words constitute part of the match they are playing, which, as she has indicated in her aside, is exactly what she found attractive in Ferando in the first place: "Come Kate, stand not on terms, we will away. / This is my day, tomorrow thou shalt rule, / And I will do whatever thou commands" (5.78–80). The contrast with Petruccio in the equivalent episode is again striking, as Petruccio, instead of explaining himself to Kate, insists on exercising his property rights: "I will be master of what is mine own" (3.3.100).

In one group's production, the sun-moon scene from *A Shrew* began with a light tone, making the sun-versus-moon discussion less of a power struggle and more of a shared joke, a sense that was underscored by the actors' decision to deliver Ferando's and Kate's "Jesus save the glorious moon" (12.11–12) with a televangelist's fervor. The actors were able to sustain the amicable tone of the exchange when the scene went on to Ferando's explanation for the sun-moon test:

> I know it well thou knowest it is the sun,
> But I did try to see if thou wouldst speak
> And cross me now as thou hast done before.
> And trust me Kate, hadst thou not named the moon,
> We had gone back again as sure as death. (12.14–18)

As one student observed in the discussion after the scenes, although he gets his way, Ferando also credits Kate's intelligence here rather than trying to impose Orwellian doublethink on her, as Petruccio seems to do in *The Shrew*. The next group, performing the same episode from *The Shrew*, were not sympathetic to Petruccio, but instead presented him as petulant. Petruccio's insistence that the sun was the moon, for example, was delivered very loudly and punctuated with foot stomping, particularly in the final line:

> Now, by my mother's son—and that's myself—
> It shall be moon, or star, or what I list
> Or ere I journey to your father's house.
> Go on, and fetch our horses back again.
> Evermore crossed and crossed, nothing but crossed. (4.6.6–10)

Discussion after the scene brought out the fact that in *The Shrew*, there is no explanation of motives comparable to Ferando's in *A Shrew*. Instead, the dialogue in *The Shrew* emphasizes the power struggle. After Kate agrees to name the sun whatever Petruccio likes, Hortensio remarks, "The field is won." Petruccio then notes, "Thus the bowl should run, / And not unluckily against the bias" (4.6.24–26). Both men underline Petruccio's victory over Kate.

In the second part of the scene, both plays have Kate follow Ferando/Petruccio's lead and address the Duke of Sestos / Vincentio as a young woman. *The Shrew*, however, diverges from *A Shrew* when Petruccio breaks the shared joke with Kate and compels her to apologize to Vincentio for her "mad mistaking":

> Pardon, old father, my mistaking eyes
> That have been so bedazzled with the sun
> That everything I look on seemeth green.
> Now I perceive thou art a reverend father.
> Pardon, I pray thee, for my mad mistaking. (4.6.46–50)

Some groups performing this scene have Kate deliver the second and third lines of the speech to Petruccio with some annoyance for having been humiliated before she returns to a more polite tone for the end of the speech. Others inject the speech with sarcasm, momentarily offering Kate in *The Shrew* the chance to match her spouse. Productions of *A Shrew* often carry the sense of shared jokes from the first half of this scene into their treatment of the Duke, who in *A Shrew* is not given the comfort of being recognized as a man by either Ferando or Kate. In one production, the actors playing Ferando and Kate approached the Duke from both sides, each praising his maidenly beauty until the Duke was forced to flee in confusion:

> What, is she mad too? Or is my shape transformed,
> That both of them persuade me I am a woman?
> But they are mad, sure, and therefore I'll be gone,
> And leave their companies for fear of harm,
> And unto Athens haste to seek my son. *Exit Duke.* (12.44–48)

Where the scene from *The Shrew* ends with the men discussing marriage arrangements and excluding the silenced Kate (scene productions will sometimes physically separate Kate from the men at this point to visually highlight her exclusion), the scene in *A Shrew* ends with Ferando and Kate together and a speech by Ferando that can be seen as a statement of Ferando's desire for a companionate marriage:

> Why so, Kate, this was friendly done of thee,
> And kindly too. Why thus must we two live,
> One mind, one heart, and one content for both.
> This good old man does think that we are mad,
> And glad he is, I am sure, that he is gone.
> But come, sweet Kate, for we will after him,
> And now persuade him to his shape again. (12.49–55)

Discussion of the scene typically concludes with a consideration of the significance of how each scene ends. In *A Shrew*, Ferando and Kate leave together to undo their collective joke on the Duke, while in *The Shrew*, Hortensio is left to praise Petruccio's taming strategy and to anticipate trying it on his widow.

By the time we finish our comparison of the two *Shrew* plays, students are ready to continue their study of Shakespeare using literary and performance-based evidence to inform their readings and interpretations. While my Shakespeare course moves from the *Shrew* plays to three other comedies before turning to the history plays, after working with these plays one could take other possible directions. The performance-oriented study of the *Shrew* plays could lead into closer study of the two plays' editorial histories. Or comparing the two *Shrew* texts could be part of a course devoted to Shakespeare's multitext plays. Or one could move from the two *Shrew* plays to John Fletcher's *The Woman's Prize; or, The Tamer Tamed*, the 1611 sequel to *The Taming of the Shrew*. My hope is that whatever approach instructors take, more classes will enjoy some of the benefits that my students and I have attained by working with *The Taming of a Shrew*.

NOTES

I would like to thank my students at Bridgewater State College and McKendree College for their many contributions to this paper, as well as the participants in the "Teaching the 'Bad' Quartos" workshop at the 2006 Shakespeare Association of America conference for helpful feedback on this project.

[1] All quotations from *The Taming of a Shrew* refer to The Taming of a Shrew: *The 1594 Quarto*, ed. Miller.

The Harlequin *The Taming of the Shrew*

Bruce E. Brandt

Are audiences alienated by the misogyny in *The Taming of the Shrew*, or do they see it as part of the farcical romp that is the play? Students reading instead of watching the play and contemplating its underlying cultural assumptions can scarcely avoid confronting the play's misogyny. It is especially likely that my students will see misogyny in the play, since they are reading *The Taming of the Shrew* in a class that focuses on Shakespeare and early modern assumptions about gender and sexuality. At the beginning of the course, we take up *The Taming of the Shrew* as an introduction to Renaissance ideas about patriarchal roles and the nature of marriage. While reading the play, we begin reading Frances Dolan's edition of *The Taming of the Shrew*, which includes early modern treatises and homilies on marriage, a discussion of a woman's legal status after marriage and the differing authorities of husband and wife within the household, contemporary arguments for and against wife beating, and several early modern depictions of shrews and what might be done to them, including the notorious ballad "A Merry Jest of a Shrewd and Curst Wife Lapped in Morel's Skin, for Her Good Behavior," in which a husband wraps his wife in a salted horsehide and beats her until she bleeds. Given this context, it is easy for students to fail to see how amusing the play can be. What, they may ask, is funny about starving and tormenting one's wife, or training her as if she were a falcon? And indeed, I intend for students to think about these aspects of early modern life. However, I also intend to enrich the students' experience of Shakespeare, asking them to consider why, in performance, *The Taming of the Shrew* has the potential to be experienced as comic rather than cruel. Envisioning the performance possibilities of the printed text is always difficult for readers, and particularly so for those who, like many of my rural Midwestern students, have experienced little live theater. The difficulty is particularly great for a play such as *The Taming of the Shrew*, in which much of the comic effect derives from speed, timing, and delivery. Reading will not suffice. They must see the play performed.

Fortunately, a marvelous production of the play, one that is not only entertaining but highly serviceable for teaching and discussion, is available. The American Conservatory Theater (ACT) of San Francisco's energetic and acrobatic *The Taming of the Shrew* was televised on *Great Performances: Theatre in America* in 1976. This remarkable production was restored and released on VHS in Kultur's Broadway Theatre Archive series in 2000 and then on DVD in 2002. The fact that it is a televised stage production rather than a film based on Shakespeare's play is useful pedagogically. To understand Shakespeare, students need to imagine how his plays would have worked onstage, and seeing a long chase onscreen, as in Zeffirelli's film when Richard Burton and Elizabeth Taylor run over rooftops, may not help students visualize what happens on stage. The ACT production uses a bare stage with rails and scaffolding along the back and the sides, where the musicians sit and the actors often sit or stand when offstage. There is no proscenium arch, no curtain, and no set. As on the Elizabethan stage, the world of this play is created completely by language and action, which proceed at a rapid pace. While there are significant cuts, including the Christopher Sly scenes and Hortensio's visit to Petruccio after his failed romancing of Bianca, the performance is faithful to Shakespeare's language, and the cast proves fully capable of delivering the speeches "trippingly on the tongue."

The entire cast wears white commedia dell'arte–style costumes with colorful red accents. Most costumes are quite humorous, with odd hats and large buttons, although the costuming of the lead actors emphasizes their physical attractiveness. Petruccio, played by the muscular Marc Singer, is dressed in tights and a close-fitting vest worn without a shirt, when he isn't entirely bare-chested. Katherine, played by Fredi Olster, wears a dress with puffy sleeves; a fitted, low-cut, scooped-neck bodice; and a flowing skirt. All the costumes are designed to accommodate the production's emphasis on movement and physical comedy. The choice of the comedia dell'arte style may surprise students, who expect either modern dress or Elizabethan clothing in a performance of Shakespeare, and this choice can become a point of discussion in its own right. What are the potential gains or losses of the costuming decisions, or, more broadly, what are the consequences of setting Shakespeare in one period or another?

The commedia dell'arte costuming reflects and enhances the ACT's decision to play *Shrew* as farce. Much of the performance accords with Robert Heilman's mid-twentieth-century argument that characters in farce do not react to insults, injuries, and moral or ethical lapses as one would in real life: they "are not really hurt, do not think much, are not much troubled by scruples" (154). Operating according to these principles, the ACT production ensures that the sheer speed of the action keeps the violent interactions at the level of slapstick and free of realistic consequences. For example, Heilman suggests that "[w]hen Kate 'breaks the lute to' Hortensio, farce requires that he act terrified; but it does not permit him to be injured or really resentful or grieved by the loss of the lute, as a man in a non-farcical world might well be" (154). This is precisely the effect achieved by the ACT production. Hortensio enters with his head protruding through the body of the lute, with the fret board extending at a right angle to his neck. He indeed appears "terrified," or at least as if he is about to cry, but brightens immediately when Baptista suggests that he might give a lesson to his other daughter. The injury is already forgotten, and Baptista guides him off the stage, using the lute's neck as a leash. My students have invariably enjoyed the ACT's approach, but the decision and the nature of farce ought to become part of the subsequent class discussion. Peter Saccio, for example, agrees that *The Taming of the Shrew* is farcical but argues that Heilman overstates the genre's limitations (35), and Molly Easo Smith notes that "[r]ecent reevaluations of farce . . . have moved towards recognizing the genre's ability to subvert and criticize under cover of excessive play" (40). Students interested in the question of farcical and nonfarcical interpretations of *The Taming of the Shrew* might want to view Jonathan Miller's 1980 BBC production with John Cleese as Petruccio, a production that abstains from exaggerated physical comedy.

The ACT's comic performance interpolates a number of running gags. For example, each mention of Petruccio's deceased father during the opening scenes is punctuated with a musical chime by the percussion section, and all those onstage doff their hats. The characters come to expect the sound, and later Baptista, when he refers to his own death while discussing his daughter's dowry, pauses in anticipation of the same sound effect. He is rewarded instead with a harsh horn blast. Signor Gremio's bad breath, for which there is no textual warrant, is another such running joke. Whoever is unfortunate enough to be too close to him when he is speaking comes near to swooning. At one point Petruccio defensively claps a cap over Gremio's mouth, and Gremio is knocked over by his own breath, falling flat on his back with his legs pointing straight up. This absurd result is typical of the acrobatics and comically exaggerated postures that occur throughout the production. Entrances are made by strutting or tumbling, and characters comically move in unison. Much of this humor is extremely physical, as when Grumio is getting "rapped" and "knocked" by Petruccio for his failure to rap at Hortensio's gate (1.2.15–20). He is on his feet, flat on his back, up again, down again, all at great speed.

Katherine participates fully in the slapstick action. In the opening scene she kicks Signor Gremio's cane away every time she comes close to him, causing him to fall to his knees. For good measure, toward the end of the scene she hits Hortensio in the stomach, bringing him to his knees as well. The scene in which she ties Bianca's hands is similarly milked for its slapstick potential. Katherine has tied Bianca's wrists together with one end of a long rope that she uses as a leash to drag Bianca onto the stage. When Baptista attempts to intervene, his daughters run about him in opposite directions, and the rope coils around his neck. The most physical of these slapstick encounters is the initial meeting of Katherine and Petruccio. Because the class I am describing meets once a week for three hours, the students are able to view the video in its entirety at our first meeting. However, if time constraints allowed me to choose only one scene to show to a class, it would be this one. As the ACT plays it, the verbal interaction between Katherine and Petruccio is matched by their physical interaction. At one point their give-and-take becomes a wrestling match, in which Petruccio applies a leg lock to Katherine while he speaks and she in turn breaks the hold and applies it to Petruccio while she speaks. Whatever one's final interpretation of the play's lessons, the beginning of the ACT production suggests that the ensuing battle of the sexes will be between equals—between two people who can both dish it out and take it.

The ACT production's depiction of the initial meeting between Katherine and Petruccio also finds a way to suggest that this is in fact a love story. While Petruccio is awaiting his first meeting with Katherine, he prepares for battle, stripping off his vest and putting on his game face (so to speak) while rehearsing responses to her possible behaviors: "Say that she rail. . . . Say that she frown. . . . Say she be mute" (2.1.168–78). When she appears, he is facing away from her and turns toward her, saying "and now, Petruccio, speak" (2.1.179). With the very uttering of that "speak," he is struck into silence and immobility by his first sight of Katherine. He remains frozen in place while she slowly circles him and frankly appraises his body. From behind, where he cannot see her, her expression makes it clear that she likes what she sees, although she pointedly restores her haughty expression before moving back into his line of vision. In turn, he appears, by his facial expression, completely at sea, as though experiencing an unexpected emotion in her presence—in short, love at first sight. The production thus suggests from the beginning that this is the man Kate should marry, and not just the man that she will have to marry.

In Singer's portrayal, the fact that Petruccio's wooing plans did not prepare him for his first sight of Katherine provides an initial revelation of his character and modus operandi. He bullies his way into things and has a plan that he has not thoroughly thought out and does not fully understand. On hearing of Katherine, he had planned to marry her for her money and to tame the shrew who brought it. That he might fall for her had not entered his mind. We see this same tendency to "wing it" when he presents the disguised Hortensio to Baptista as tutor for his daughters. Singer delivers the line "[h]is name is Licio" (2.1.60) with a pause between "is" and "Licio." Clearly the two had not worked out a name in advance, and Petruccio must create one on the spur of the moment (getting a nice laugh from the audience as he does so).

That Petruccio does not fully understand his evolving feelings for Katherine is later evident in the ACT's interpretation of the scene where Katherine and Petruccio are returning to Padua and Petruccio insists that the sun is actually the moon. Prompted by Grumio to "[s]ay as he says or we shall never go," Katherine acquiesces (the line is Hortensio's, but the ACT has cut Hortensio from this scene and given the line to Grumio [4.6.11]). Her response is one of the cruxes for interpreting the play. She can be portrayed as being abjectly beaten down, as one who has learned to give in only superficially, or, as John Bean has argued, as one who suddenly realizes that playing word games with Petruccio can be mutually fulfilling (72–73). Overall, the ACT performance supports the third alternative. At first, though, Katherine agrees simply to agree.

> PETRUCCIO. I say it is the moon.
> KATHERINE. I know it is the moon.
> PETRUCCIO. Nay then you lie, it is the blesséd sun.
> KATHERINE. Then God be blessed, it is the blesséd sun.
> But sun it is not, when you say it is not,
> And the moon changes even as your mind.
> What you will have it named, even that it is,
> And so it shall be still for Katherine. (4.6.16–23)

Even as she concedes that the name will be whatever Petruccio wants, her tone belies her words, and she insults him in the emphasis she gives to "changes even as your mind." We continue to hear the stichomythic sparring of the opening. Moreover, Petruccio seems now to be unclear about what to do with his victory. He stops to think before saying that they should continue on their way, a pause that suggests he may not have expected her response or that he is grappling with the feelings created by her spirited acquiescence.

Katherine's enjoyment of the game is suggested ever more strongly as the scene continues. When Vincentio enters and Petruccio suggests to Katherine that she should greet this young gentlewoman, she does more than acquiesce. Her initial words, "Young budding virgin," are spoken slowly, a mere act of compliance, but then she brightens and begins speaking more rapidly and with more and more animation:

> fair, and fresh, and sweet,
> Whither away, or where is thy abode?
> Happy the parents of so fair a child,
> Happier the man whom favourable stars
> Allots thee for his lovely bedfellow. (4.6.38–42)

Her facial expression and tone reveal more than obedience. She is having fun. When Petruccio then says that Vincentio is actually an elderly man, Katherine's reference to her eyes being "bedazzled with the sun" (4.6.47), as it is spoken here, becomes a pointed but humorous jab at Petruccio's prior insistence that sun and moon are what he says they are. Petruccio mutely acquiesces to "sun."

Katherine's enthusiasm for her new role carries over to her delivery of her final forty-two-line monologue on wifely duty. Although Petruccio has made the wager on Katherine's obedience with his usual aggressive posturing, Singer's body language after she has been summoned suggests that Petruccio is anxious about the outcome. He is relieved and pleased when she appears, and the theatricality of her tossing her cap underfoot suggests that she is acting a role. The final lecture is over-the-top, and she enjoys it. Petruccio has told her to begin by addressing the Widow, and Katherine is glad to do so, for, as played here, Katherine had been deeply hurt by the "mean meaning" (5.2.32) of the Widow's insult just before the wager. In this performance, Katherine's lecture aims to prove the Widow wrong—to show that Petruccio is not "troubled with a shrew" (5.2.29). The speech concludes with Katherine thrusting her hand under Petruccio's foot, a move that he does not expect. His response is acted slowly in three parts. He first kneels, saying appreciatively, "Why, there's a wench!" He then says "Come on," and the couple stands. Finally, he says, "Kiss me, Kate" (5.2.184). This is the third time Petruccio has used this phrase. The first kiss, right after Petruccio announces their wedding day, takes Katherine by surprise and leaves her looking shell-shocked (2.1.316). The second is another test of her obedience, forcing her to overcome her shame at kissing publicly (5.1.124). This final kiss, in contrast, is the longest and most passionate of the play—it is the kiss of a woman who is glad to kiss her spouse. Katherine has come to care for Petruccio, and he for her. Then, the production introduces a final interpretive complication. When the kiss ends, Katherine turns her face to the audience and winks—a wink invisible to all onstage. This wink is, of course, a venerable way of closing the play on both stage and film, and many critics dislike it. Saccio, for example, finds winking at the audience to be a vulgar undercutting of the play's sense (39). Mary Pickford gave such a wink at the end of the first Shakespearean talkie, though her wink was directed to Bianca, who appeared to get the message. Since, in that film, Douglas Fairbanks is carrying Pickford offstage over his shoulder when she winks, the production makes no suggestion of mutuality—it's simply a question of who actually has the upper hand. She will get her way as long as he thinks that he is getting his. The effect of Olster's wink is different. The production suggests growth toward mutuality rather than mastery, and her wink does not undercut this interpretation. Nonetheless, it clearly affirms that Katherine does not see herself as the loser of this struggle, and students invariably like this ending.

In addition to its adoption of Katherine's wink, the ACT production of *The Taming of the Shrew* wittily engages other aspects of theater history, such as Petruccio's carrying a whip. My students will know this tradition from Dolan's anthology, if not from other performances. In this production, when Petruccio insists that they will not visit Padua until it is what time he says it is (4.3.189), he picks up a whip, gives it a loud crack, and then tosses it to Grumio, who uses it as a jump rope and skips off the stage. A traditional symbol of taming is tamed—the tradition is both presented and defused. This is, overall, what the entire production does through its use of the commedia dell'arte. The performance thereby facilitates discussion of the attitudes about gender and marriage that are embedded in *The Taming of the Shrew*, and it does so in a way that elicits a variety of readings and complicates students' reactions to the text.

NOTE

I first explored some of the ideas discussed here in a presentation given at the Fifteenth Annual Northern Plains Conference on Earlier British Literature, held at Minnesota State University, Moorhead, 20–21 April 2007.

Scenes from a Renaissance Marriage: *The Taming of the Shrew* on Film

James M. Welsh

Showcase Shrews for Celebrity Couples

Although *The Taming of the Shrew* offers an interesting view of the proper role of women in courtship and marriage in Shakespeare's day, it also affords the opportunity for broad comedy and knockabout farce. It is, in fact, a perfect vehicle for celebrity couples, as was demonstrated by the very first screen demonstration, which was Hollywood's first attempt to capture Shakespeare on film with the enhancement of sound and dialogue. This was the film directed by Sam Taylor in 1929 for United Artists, starring two of the original "united artists," Douglas Fairbanks and Mary Pickford, who were also united in marriage and as business partners at the time and were the most famous movie stars in Hollywood.

The second blockbuster filming of *The Taming of the Shrew* also featured a celebrity couple. Richard Burton starred as a churlish Petruccio, and Elizabeth Taylor played Kate. This film, released in 1967, also featured a celebrity director, the flamboyant Italian Franco Zeffirelli, best known at that time for his work in opera. Richard Burton and Elizabeth Taylor had already put their bickering on display on screen by playing the dysfunctional George and Martha in the film version of Edward Albee's *Who's Afraid of Virginia Woolf*, directed by Mike Nichols in 1966, which earned an Oscar for Taylor's performance and awards for both Burton and Taylor from the British Academy of Film and Television. Following the critical success of their first film together as a couple, one described by the biographer Paul Ferris as "the one solid triumph of the Burton-Taylor partnership" (148c), it hardly came as a surprise that they would be back playing Shakespeare's bickering couple the following year. However, *The Taming of the Shrew* is, indeed, a comedy, and thus the film was a great deal more enjoyable to watch than Albee's knock-down, drag-out drama of a marriage breaking apart. The Zeffirelli *Shrew* was far more verbal and complete than the earlier Fairbanks-Pickford adaptation, which was only just over an hour long at sixty-eight minutes. The Burton-Taylor adaptation was nearly twice as long, running for 122 minutes and shot in Italy rather than Hollywood. What these two adaptations, separated by nearly forty years, have in common is that they both use (or abuse) Shakespeare's original language. However, the differences between the films are enormous.

The Second Shall Be First: Zeffirelli Directing Burton and Taylor

If fidelity to the language is an issue, the Zeffirelli *Shrew* is by far closer to Shakespeare's play, even without the Christopher Sly induction. Ferris writes that, according to Burton, the film was made "in a commercial way, that is, it is a great mudpie-in-the-face romp" (131). The dialogue in the Zeffirelli version is certainly candid in a way that it could not have been in the 1929 version, and, to be sure, there is a whole lot more of it, given by a Petruccio who was trained for the London stage, capable of chewing up scenes with enormous gusto. Such formal training had not been given to Douglas Fairbanks and Mary Pickford, who had, until the making of this film, performed mute in front of the cameras. In what was meant for a stinging exchange at 2.1.212–22 in the Sam Taylor version, Pickford declares, "If I be waspish, best beware my sting!" And, since the exchange goes no further, the "sting" immediately fades. Burton's Petruccio, on the other hand, chuckling lecherously all the while, gives a full rendering of the exchange, ultimately challenging Kate with the bawdy line, "What? With my tongue in your tail?" But even though less of Shakespeare's language is cut in the Zeffirelli adaptation, much of the text is lacking.

The 1929 version is less than half as long as the 1967 version and might therefore serve as an effective introduction to the play in full, one that emphasizes its broadly comic physical movements. Lucentio is removed entirely (as are Tranio and Vincentio), and his lines are given to Hortensio. The minor characters are reduced to mere ciphers, and even some of the major ones' lines are cut. Bianca is a sweet but spineless, quivering nonentity. She is neither the schemer nor the flirt that she appears to be in the Zeffirelli production. In the earlier version she presents Pickford's Kate with little motivation for jealousy. Baptista Minola becomes a stereotyped, befuddled American father figure not far removed from the cartoonish Dagwood Bumstead, who can only clasp his hands in astonishment and look stupidly seraphic as trouble erupts around him. A visual epiphany reveals his almost effeminate character after Petruccio arrives at the church for the wedding, when Baptista attempts to start Kate on her march to the altar, clutching his daughter's bridal bouquet. Gremio here is no longer the pantaloon and rival suitor; he is simply a friend of the family and an interested observer. One valid criticism of the 1929 film is that it depends too heavily on exaggerated trivial action and violent slapstick—as witnessed by Petruccio's munching on an apple core at the wedding or Grumio's physically harsh treatment at his master's hand. The violent slapstick may be textually justified, but the exaggerated trivial action wears thin. When Grumio announces his master's arrival, for example, he has a coughing fit that may reveal something about the weather outside but is most certainly overdone.

But the Zeffirelli adaptation is in its own way overdone, too. The prettiness of the color cinematography, at first striking, eventually begins to cloy. Zeffirelli has attempted to capture more of the play—certainly more of the text is retained—and the Bianca subplot is nearly intact, the characters present and accounted for. But the Christopher Sly induction is gone, even though its spirit hangs like a pall over the film. The spirit of Sly lives in Burton's conception of Petruccio—a vulgar, boorish, drunken lout, whose mannerisms and apparel are curiously at odds with his diction and splendid verbal facility—usually punctuated in this adaptation by his lecherous chuckle. His awakening after a heavy night's drinking, lumbering about and dabbing his eyes with water, clearly recalls Sly's behavior in the induction. This Petruccio is a thoroughgoing materialist: we watch him gleefully inspecting the quality of Baptista's silver. In the contest wager of act 5, Burton's Petruccio ups the ante from Shakespeare's one hundred crowns to four thousand crowns. We can easily believe him when he declares earlier in the play that he comes "to wive it wealthily in Padua; / If wealthily, then happily in Padua" (1.2.72–73). He is not a very humane Petruccio. That he *may* love (rather than simply desire) Kate is perhaps suggested at one point as he observes her sleeping, almost touches her arm in a gesture of tenderness, then wakes her abruptly in order to continue the business of taming her, but such suggestions are few and far between. Overall, Burton's is not a very subtle interpretation of the character. In the earlier version Fairbanks (in close-up) hazards sidelong glances that function as visual asides, establishing something akin to dramatic irony. There is nothing like this in the Zeffirelli rendering. While these visual asides may not be exactly subtle, they at least suggest that there may be some measure of compassion behind Petruccio's rough exterior.

A Shrew That Bites or a Shrew That Devours?

By contrast, Burton's knockabout, boorish bumpkin is little better than he seems to be. There is always the suggestion of something absurdly chivalric and gentlemanly lurking fairly close to the surface of the Fairbanks Petruccio. Moreover, the sly facial expression of Pickford's Kate makes it obvious that she doesn't mean a word of her speech on obedience that the director somehow managed to salvage from the wreckage of the play. Elizabeth Taylor's Kate, however, is not being facetious in her delivery of the speech on obedience. She speaks with passion. This later Kate is sentimentalized in a way the earlier one is not. Her rancorous tone when she speaks to or about Bianca suggests that she hates her sneaking, sniveling sister. She wants a man and is aware of her handicap; her eyes linger on Petruccio as she views him surreptitiously through her house's stained-glass transom—and this after the most humiliating and outrageous experience of being chased and tumbled over the rooftops of Padua. Taylor's "wild Kate" is a wildcat in heat who apparently needs restraint—and so she is tamed, domesticated (as her housecleaning sequence demonstrates). There is one further point that needs to be stressed here, however. Taylor's fans had been prepared for the irascibility she brings to her interpretation of Kate after having seen her vigorous performance opposite Burton in *Who's Afraid of Virginia*

Woolf, whereas Pickford, "America's sweetheart," could only have played Kate in the same way—had she been so disposed—at the risk of alienating her adoring audience. On the other hand, Pickford's talent for mimicking her husband's swaggering gestures and braggadocio, although extraneous humor, to be sure, is unlike anything that can be found in the Zeffirelli version.

Shrinking the Shrew*: Shakespeare without Words; or, "With Additional Dialogue by Sam Taylor"*

One industry joke about the Fairbanks-Pickford *The Taming of the Shrew* had it that the credits noted that the play was by William Shakespeare, "with additional dialogue by Sam Taylor." Fidelity to Shakespeare aside, the sheer brevity of the Pickford-Fairbanks United Artists adaptation arguably creates a major problem in that the process of Kate's taming is unconvincingly brief. And within this restricted time, the process depends more on Petruccio's physical force than on his intelligence. Theirs is a battle of tantrums and fits rather than of banter and wits. The film compresses the play and makes it gimmicky. But the adaptation was originally intended as a silent film, and that in itself shifts the genre of the production toward one that emphasizes the visual rather than the verbal elements of the play, employing sight gags that distract from rather than support the dialogue.

The United Artists Shrew's *Antique Antics*

The 1929 *Taming of the Shrew* was made barely after the coming of sound for a naive mass audience not far removed from the era of vaudeville and burlesque and conditioned for "low" humor. When George Cukor directed Leslie Howard and Norma Shearer in the lavishly overproduced MGM adaptation of *Romeo and Juliet* a few years later, an academic consultant was brought in to protect the dignity of the Bard, but no such precautions were taken with *The Taming of the Shrew*. Fairbanks, who plays Petruccio, had been a matinee idol and a stage comedian before becoming a very popular film star, famous for his swashbuckling antics shaped by his costume films of the 1920s. Fairbanks was the original screen Zorro and had swaggered his way through such films as *Robin Hood*, *The Three Musketeers*, *The Iron Mask*, and *The Black Pirate.* There were, therefore, certain "signature" elements of his screen persona that almost *had* to be factored into any role that he would play. He was a "star," after all, and his fans could not be disappointed. Not surprisingly, he interprets Petruccio as a swaggering figure, who is self-parodied in the absurd costume he assumes for the wedding. As Señor Zorro and as Zorro's son, Don Q, and, later, as the eponymous main character in *The Gaucho*, Fairbanks was the master of the bullwhip, which becomes a prop in *The Taming of the Shrew*, placed in Kate's hands to make her seem more fearsome (and in that dimension, *this*

Kate needs all the help she can get!). However, in this film, Petruccio has the bigger whip. Of course, Pickford was a star, too—a truly major one, arguably even more popular than her husband—but the early screen persona of "Little Mary" was being transformed since the actress was growing older and since the persona had to be changed considerably for the role of Kate, a change that, one might argue, gave her more flexibility and freedom than her husband had, since he was constrained by the swashbuckling style of the costume films that had defined his popularity throughout the 1920s.

To better appreciate the achievement of what may at first glance seem merely a silly adaptation, one has to consider the 1929 *Taming of the Shrew* in the context of the other early Shakespeare films. In *Shakespeare on Silent Film*, Judith Buchanan notes that between 1899 (a year marking the "birth" of the cinema and the first Shakespeare adaptation) and 1927 (the coming of sound with Warner Bros. releasing *The Jazz Singer*, to be soon followed by the Pickford-Fairbanks *Shrew*) some three hundred silent films were adapted from Shakespearean materials (xvi). However, because of the archival problems of preserving those films and the instability of silver-nitrate film stock, which is susceptible to spontaneous combustion and to capricious disintegration in storage, only forty of those three hundred films were extant by the twenty-first century. The preservation of Shakespeare's filmed texts has been haphazard, with less than one-sixth of the materials surviving. By and large only archivists seem to be fully aware of the difficulties, frustrations, and expense of preserving these rare filmed texts.

Consequently, on first viewing, the 1929 *Taming of the Shrew* may appear to be an odd artifact, culturally coded to please movie audiences of the 1920s, whose expectations were far different and perhaps less sophisticated than those of audiences conditioned to movies with sound. And yet the Pickford-Fairbanks *Shrew* surely seems both entertaining and agreeable in comparison to Paul Czinner's *As You Like It* (1936), the first film to feature Laurence Olivier. Much of the text of that play was cut, and, as a consequence, characters such as Jaques and Touchstone were seriously slighted. Olivier's Orlando was the best-realized character from the play, but the casting of Elisabeth Bergner was a disaster, because she was too old and also unable to handle the lines, impeded as she was with a heavy German accent. She sounded like Marlene Dietrich with a cold. Moreover, a problem is created by Rosalind's remark to Celia as they enter the Forest of Arden, "Were it not better, / Because that I am more than common tall, / That I did suit me all points like a man?" (1.3.113–15), because in this production, Bergner is *not* the taller of the two actresses. In comparison, Pickford's squeaking shrew scurries onto the screen with a hilarity that is both unexpected and absurd. Her performance is akin to that of the "rude mechanicals" of the 1935 *A Midsummer Night's Dream*, involving a sly referential awareness of the absurdity and therefore of the comedy of the production. The early *Shrew* is a farcical romp, as must have been obvious to everyone involved in the production, but it touches the very heart of the play in an amusing and entertaining way, offering a simplified understanding of what the play might signify to a popular mass audience not necessarily immersed in Shakespeare. It invokes an earlier theatrical standard whereby the grand gestures of the nineteenth-century stage are somewhat grotesquely imposed on silent-cinema acting, where physical gestures were conventionally more naturalistic. But Fairbanks's and Pickford's *The Taming of the Shrew* can still inspire laughter, no less so because the text has been shorn. In this way the movie anticipates several other loopy filmed versions of Shakespeare's comedies, most notably the 1935 Warner Bros. *A Midsummer Night's Dream*, directed by Max Reinhardt and William Dieterle, which featured Jimmy Cagney, Joe E. Brown, and Hugh Herbert as the rude mechanicals and a yelping, boisterous, and hammy Mickey Rooney as Puck.

NOTE

Since the research standing behind this paper goes back over forty years, I should like to thank most especially Robert Hamilton Ball, who was kind enough to correspond with an eager beginner years ago, and Buddy Rogers, who married Mary Pickford after her separation from Douglas Fairbanks and whom I was able to meet on two occasions at the University of Kansas, Lawrence. I'd also like to thank Matty Kemp, the director of the Pickford Corporation, who made available for my use a print of the Sam Taylor film at a time when such materials were available only on 16mm film and not readily accessible to the public. Finally, I thank my friend and colleague John C. Tibbetts, of the University of Kansas, who interviewed Douglas Fairbanks, Jr., and originally introduced me to this body of cinema. Thanks also to the Kansas Humanities Council for supporting the Buster Keaton Celebration of 2007 in Iola, Kansas, where Fairbanks, Sr., was honored along with Keaton, and to my friend and colleague Richard Vela, who invited me to read and discuss parts of this essay at the Southwest/Texas Popular Culture and American Culture Association conference in Albuquerque, New Mexico, in early 2010. See also Ball; Buchanan; Ferris; Jorgens; Manvell; P. Morris, *Shakespeare on Film*; Rosenthal; Rothwell; Tibbetts and Welsh; Vance; and Welsh, Vela, and Tibbetts.

Whose Play Is It, Anyway? Viewing *The Taming of the Shrew* Pedagogically

Sheila T. Cavanagh

Videos of live performances and of productions staged exclusively for film or video (what I call here motion picture versions) have infiltrated classrooms where Shakespeare is taught, often to good effect. Since many students cannot attend live productions, videos provide instructors with diverse ways to incorporate theater into their courses. Using or assigning videos of motion picture versions of Shakespeare's plays can backfire, however, if students are not guided appropriately, since these versions frequently simplify the puzzles that make the plays most interesting pedagogically. Motion picture versions of *The Taming of the Shrew*, for instance, typically present the play as a conventional romantic comedy. Yet while a "happy ending" to the conflict between Kate and Petruccio may provide viewer contentment, it does not reflect the play's representation and prediction of a complex marital relationship. As Frances Dolan indicates, scholarly perspectives on Kate and Petruccio's marriage range broadly: "Critics have long disagreed about how to interpret the play, viewing it variously as a romantic comedy in which two spouses achieve mutual satisfaction ([Marianne] Novy), a rambunctious farce in which we should not take the violent taming too seriously ([Robert B.] Heilman), an embarrassment ([George Bernard] Shaw), even as a 'bad' play ([Shirley Nelson] Garner)" (1). The currently available motion picture versions suppress these varied possibilities. The relative conformity in interpretation means, therefore, that instructors need to use video with particular care. In the passages below, I describe instances of interpretive compression while detailing ways to take pedagogical advantage of this relative uniformity.

In most motion picture versions of *Shrew*, the love-story scenario prevents the audience from experiencing the discomfort sometimes prompted by portrayals of actual or implied spousal abuse in some stage versions. Presumably, directors believe general audiences want benign interpretations. Undergraduates also prefer romantic *Shrews*, if my students' horrified response to the harsh 2008 Royal Shakespeare Company stage presentation is representative. What the critic Charles Spencer called the "memorably grotesque" performance of Stephen Boxer as a drunken, crude, and slovenly Sly/Petruccio clearly violated their conceptualization of the play's proper tenor. Their shock at his behavior was intensified, since they were sitting right in front of him when he flashed his nude genitals toward the audience. This Petruccio remained gratuitously cruel, even toward the end of the play, where he tricks Kate into kissing another man. As Spencer remarks, in this production, where the "[d]irector Conall Morrisson pays Shakespeare the compliment of staging the play he actually wrote," the play becomes "an unflinching study of abuse" (*Daily Telegraph*).

In contrast, twentieth- and twenty-first-century motion picture versions avoid presenting *Shrew* as a distasteful drama. Instead, they offer a Kate who often seems happy with Petruccio as well as a Petruccio more appealing to audiences. In the 1950 live television version of *Shrew*, for example, Katherine (Lisa Kirk) flashes broad smiles and winks into the camera at two key moments in the production: first, when the dapper Petruccio (Charlton Heston) announces their engagement and, second, after he sweeps her into his arms at the end of her final speech. In each case, the message is clear. Despite verbal and physical assaults against Petruccio—this Katherine is prone to biting—Kirk's shrew is thrilled by her match. Similarly, Elizabeth Taylor's 1967 shrew sees Richard Burton's Petruccio as the answer to her ticking biological clock, as she looks pointedly—and lovingly—at her husband after gazing with affection on the group of children surrounding them during the final banquet scene. Fredi Olster's 1976 Katherine, in the American Conservatory Theater (ACT) of San Francisco production, offers wide grins and playful winks, delighted with the muscular Petruccio (Marc Singer). More recently, in the 2005 BBC *The Taming of the Shrew*, Katherine (Shirley Henderson) seems smitten with her volatile, cross-dressing Petruccio (Rufus Sewell), even showing disappointment when he abandons a threatened rape. Although Henderson's Katherine is deliciously vile in a way that far outstrips her celluloid predecessors, she still fits well within the pattern that encompasses all the motion picture shrews examined here. That is, she admits, when asked by Bianca's suitor "Harry," to loving her mercurial spouse and harbors no apparent ill will for his brutishness. Despite other variations in presentation, these versions of *Shrew* offer Shakespeare's play as a fairly unproblematic love story. Emphasizing humor, these versions limit moral ambiguity. Instead, whether the play is presented predominantly as a production of Shakespeare's drama (the 1980 version, originally aired by the BBC), an early entry into the world of cinema (the 1929 version directed by Taylor and starring Pickford and Fairbanks), a modernized variation on a theme (the 2005 BBC version or *Moonlighting*'s 1986 "Atomic Shakespeare" episode), or an abridgement for children (the 1994 animated Shakespeare), motion picture audiences are encouraged to accept Kate and Petruccio's drama simply as the representation of an enamored pair "madly mated" (3.2.233).

One way to address the dearth of nuanced motion picture versions of the play is to make students aware that there are multiple versions, however counterintuitive this might seem. Since most undergraduates will agree that the text can support a broader range of readings than these productions present, having them witness the uniformity of these performances generally piques their interest, and they eagerly comb through the text to see what can be justified. To expose students to different versions, instructors can show clips in class or lend DVDs to groups of students, who can watch them and report back to the class. Orchestrating group viewing has become particularly important, since students increasingly watch films and videos through instant-access mechanisms, such as *YouTube* and *Netflix* downloads. After students see key scenes or hear about a range of productions, they are prompted to discuss topics that reading alone is unlikely to spark, such as the common inclusion of wedding scenes in motion picture versions, despite the fact that none appears in the text. The wedding scenes tend to be funny: Bruce Willis's Petruccio in the *Moonlighting* episode "Atomic Shakespeare" rides into church on a horse wearing sunglasses, while Douglas Fairbanks comically enjoys a snack. They also confront a question the text has left unanswered: does Kate participate willingly? The *Moonlighting* episode's bound and gagged Cybill Shepherd provides a typically humorous response. Since the play could easily have included a wedding scene, students have the opportunity to discuss why it doesn't appear in the play, and why it is nevertheless included in these productions. Introducing the class to numerous videos of live performances and motion picture versions also enables considerations about current cultural expectations and other factors that influence production choices. As Spencer notes, "The tradition these days is to attempt to soften the piece's brutality" (*Daily Telegraph*). Familiarity with a single motion picture version often leaves students believing that whatever they watch is the "real" production rather than the interpretation of an individual director. Placing a number of motion picture versions of *Shrew* in the context of the more varied stage history gives students a greater opportunity to explore the range of directorial choices being made and to discuss various versions more knowledgeably.

While the "happy ending" *Shrew* may be justifiable textually, this narrowing of interpretive possibilities is accomplished by cutting scenes and avoiding the inventive characterizations that often enliven stage productions. Bianca, for example, frequently exhibits more questionable behavior in the theater than she does in motion picture versions. In the theater, for example, she frequently makes faces or other dismissive gestures behind her father's back, suggesting that she is not as virtuous as he believes. Stage productions are also more likely to make Petruccio's "taming" plans and the treatment of Christopher Sly harsher than they appear in motion pictures. Since motion picture productions regularly leave Sly out and provide a more appealing Petruccio, instructors can contrast them with recorded performances to raise students' awareness of the options that are being avoided and to discuss the possible reasons for textual changes and excisions, as well as the introduction of meaningful gestures, costumes, or movements that can sway an interpretation. A comfortable *Shrew* does not, for example, reflect aspects of the play that led John Fletcher to compose *The Tamer Tamed* only a few years after Shakespeare wrote *Shrew*. In *Tamer Tamed*, Petruccio's new wife, Maria, gathers together local women, who borrow tactics from Lysistrata in order to convince men to treat their wives better. By substituting public humiliation for sex, the women "tame" their husbands. As Gordon McMullan explains:

> *The Tamer Tamed*, by John Fletcher, is a remarkable, irreverent, and hugely entertaining response to *The Taming of the Shrew*, which parodies

> and inverts the earlier play's gender-politics, providing an eyebrow-raising alternative to traditional readings of Shakespeare's comedy. . . . This uncannily modern, even proto-feminist, play engages directly with the conduct-book mentality and negotiates a position of functional equality for women which, by the last act, thwarted and reduced as they are, the men are simply glad to endorse. (xiii)

Although the two plays are sometimes performed in tandem today, students generally are unfamiliar with *The Tamer Tamed*. Introducing it in class helps offset the common misconception that Shakespeare's audiences would not have balked at Petruccio's actions. While Fletcher's play does not offer proof about early modern reactions to *Shrew*, it provides evidence that Shakespeare's play might have prompted more varied responses than students initially consider. I have been able to incorporate this play into classes using a remaindered version available through the Royal Shakespeare Company. As of early 2010, however, instructors have been able to order Barry Gaines and Margaret Maurer's affordable combined edition of *The Taming of the Shrew*, *Tamer Tamed*, and *The Taming of a Shrew*, which is a welcome addition to the resources available for teaching *Shrew*. The subject matter of *The Tamer Tamed*, combined with its early composition date, helps students react more skeptically to the motion picture versions they view. In addition, despite its unclear authorial relationship to *The Taming of the Shrew*, *The Taming of a Shrew* helps contextualize discussions of the induction, a segment most video versions omit.

The 1980 BBC production of *The Taming of the Shrew*, part of the Complete Dramatic Works of William Shakespeare project, may be the most disappointing in this regard. Produced in historical costume, with few distinctive production choices, the DVD covers of these films indicate that they are presented "word for word as written by William Shakespeare." The BBC's claim is problematic for Shakespeare's *Shrew*, however, since the induction scenes are dropped in this particular production. While this excision may reduce audience confusion about a disappearing character, it eradicates one way that Kate's conversion can be "explained." That is, the players could be offering the drunken man a fantasy about a wife who would never question his authority. As the disguised servingman tells Sly in the text, the story of Kate and Petruccio is shown to him as a "pleasant comedy" (induction, sc. 2, line 121). Without Sly to anchor the "mirth and merriment" (126) as an elaborate trick, the interpretive possibilities shrink, and the audience does not see the play in the "original" manner implied by the BBC. As Dolan notes, "the Induction teaches viewers that characters form their identities by playing roles and that they can switch roles and thus identities; and that characters also form their identities in relation to other characters" (6). Without the induction, however, this structured inversion vanishes.

Nevertheless, only two of the widely available motion pictures of Shakespeare's *Shrew* present Sly, although neither actually includes the induction.

The 1994 animated version borrows from *The Taming of a Shrew* in order to complete Sly's story. It then presents the play lightheartedly, with the DVD jacket describing *Shrew* as

> [a] love story full of comical and unexpected twists which follows the courtship of Kate and Petruccio. Set in the days when a dowry was an essential part of any marriage settlement, the fiery Kate has no patience for such matters and she refuses to enter conventional arrangements. When she falls in love with Petruccio, her pride leads them both a merry dance with his refusal to give in to her wiles, but love wins the day even for this clashing couple!

Since this production is only thirty minutes long, it is relatively easy to show a representative selection of it in class as a prelude to discussions about Sly's role in the play and his regular omission from film. Doing this also facilitates considerations of how and why Shakespeare is being presented to children, which interpretations are considered age-appropriate, and how the production deviates from the text. Since many stage productions also include portions of *A Shrew*, this film offers a glimpse of what might be seen in a live show.

The Sly appearing in the 1988 Canadian Broadcasting Corporation (CBC) *Shrew* confuses student viewers but can still raise interesting interpretive questions. Here, Sly is played by the same actor (Colm Feore) who plays Petruccio. This Sly-like character deviates from the text of the induction when he merely collapses outside a tavern, in a scene filled with extratextual dialogue. In a drunken stupor, he dreams the story of Kate and Petruccio. At the end of the production, the camera returns to a silent, confused Sly as he awakens. Although one might wish that Shakespeare's text had been incorporated into Sly's appearances, the fact that Sly is present at all in this production fuels classroom discussions about the "real" Sly and what his presence accomplishes by means of the real induction scenes and his subsequent lines in Shakespeare's play. The CBC presentation of Sly underscores the possibility that the entire play could be the drunk's fantasy. It can also prompt consideration of what might be so "wrong" with the induction that it needs to be rewritten or dropped.

Despite changing the induction, this production of *Shrew* offers what may be the most interesting, though eccentric, adherence to the text of any of the performances discussed here. Here, Petruccio arrives home with his bride and utters the frequently omitted call for his cousin Ferdinand: "Sirrah, get you hence, / And bid my cousin Ferdinand come hither— / One, Kate, that you must kiss and be acquainted with" (4.1.119–21). This cousin rarely appears onstage in response to Petruccio's command—no stage direction calls for his appearance—so his presence in the production immediately draws the attention of those familiar with typical versions of the play. As Ralph Alan Cohen explains, Ferdinand tends to perplex those directing this drama. Following H. J. Oliver, who argues that Ferdinand does not actually exist except in Petruccio's twisted imagination, Cohen determines that "much in this scene suggests precisely this kind of absurd joke. From a production point of view, we found it impossible to take literally Petruccio's claims. . . . Is there a spaniel in the play? Cousin Ferdinand? Our solution [in production] was to make it clear by the servants' amusement and confusion that Petruccio is improvising as he goes along" (272). However, the CBC production brings Ferdinand onstage as a silent, watchful presence, dressed in oddly juvenile garb, suggesting that he may be a developmentally challenged ward of Petruccio's. Ferdinand often ogles Kate with ominous lasciviousness, which adds to the discomfort audiences may feel concerning Kate's stay at the house.[1] Eventually, Kate appears dressed in clothing similar to Ferdinand's, providing Ferdinand with an unsettling counterpart. While Ferdinand does not open great interpretive vistas, he offers a welcome and thought-provoking addition to the production. Students can discuss why he might be included, when so much else is excluded. By bringing their attention to textual idiosyncrasies they would otherwise overlook, such details can strengthen students' close reading skills and expand their investigation into the vexed relation between play texts and productions.

The CBC production also uses occasional commedia dell'arte devices, which further supports relevant class discussion. Only a few students arrive with any foreknowledge of commedia, so commedia performances support the incorporation of additional theatrical history into a course that contains *Shrew*. As the other commedia-based production, the 1976 version by the ACT, suggests, the slapstick associated with this theatrical style can temper Petruccio's abusive treatment of Kate. The commedia genre also facilitates an exaggerated emphasis on Petruccio's sexual attractiveness. Often wearing a costume that accentuates his crotch, this Petruccio sports chiseled muscles that are difficult for Kate—or the audience—to ignore. By emphasizing Petruccio's physical appeal, the production predictably implies that Kate's shrewishness will end when she can join with the right sexual partner. Thus, the audience is encouraged to believe that this physically exciting pairing represents a happy marriage.

The ACT's commedia production, like many of the other productions being considered here, uses Kate's obvious attraction toward Petruccio to soften potentially troubling scenes. Kate delivers her vexed final speech with her arms around her husband, playing with his hair as she speaks. She instructs the two listening wives (and those in the audience) to "[p]lace your hands below your husband's foot," and when she adds, "In token of which duty, if he please, / My hand is ready. May it do him ease" (5.2.181–83), she physically follows her own instruction. Her submissiveness, however, is answered with her husband's self-lowering, as he reaches down and kisses her hand. In general, this presentation includes little to suggest disharmony, even though in it Petruccio occasionally carries the character's traditional whip and Katherine slaps him quite forcefully when they first meet. By making fairly benign choices, the directors (William Ball and Kirk Browning) bring their stage production's depiction of Katherine's submission in line with motion picture versions of the play. Even the 1980 BBC version, which is generally harsher than other motion picture *Shrews*, concludes with Katherine putting her hand over Petruccio's hand instead of under his foot, as she smiles lovingly into his eyes. By highlighting gestures of love between Katherine and Petruccio, these versions of *Shrew* offer harmonious conclusions, no matter how tumultuous the journey.

Notably, however, a rare motion picture that questions both the humor and the efficacy of *Shrew*'s ending unexpectedly comes from a 1961 sitcom. The "Taming of Lucille" episode from the popular television comedy *Car 54, Where Are You?* challenges assumptions about the desirability of a tamed wife. Although the program begins with its main characters, two amiable policemen, expressing nervousness about Shakespeare, it ends with the character Gunther Toody (Joe E. Ross) wanting to punish Shakespeare for interfering with his marriage. Like the audience of *Moonlighting*'s version of *Shrew*, who knew the kinds of interactions to expect from Maddy (Cybill Shepherd) and David (Bruce Willis), regular viewers of *Car 54, Where Are You?* would be familiar with the stereotypically shrewish behavior of Gunther's wife, Lucille (Beatrice Ponz). Gunther portrays a henpecked husband, while Lucille dominates. In "The Taming of Lucille," however, this relationship is reversed after Gunther provides security for a Shakespeare in the Park *Shrew* at the same time that Lucille sees a movie where a bossy woman loses her husband. Lucille is chastened by this experience, just as Gunther is emboldened by Petruccio's triumph. Subsequently, Lucille caters to Gunther's every whim, while he mourns the loss of his feisty wife. At the end of the episode, equilibrium is restored, but only after Gunther expresses his anger at Shakespeare's really bad idea, fantasizing about punching the bard in the nose.

A typical sitcom from the 1950s and 1960s, *Car 54, Where Are You?* was not a particularly transgressive series, and "The Taming of Lucille" does not violate the comic boundaries established for this program. Thus, it is particularly noteworthy for its rejection of *Shrew*'s purportedly happy ending in favor of a celebration of unchecked female spirit. One might expect many adaptations to use such inversions as part of a carnivalesque reversal of familiar paradigms, but, as this essay indicates, motion picture versions of *Shrew* almost invariably avoid such possibilities.

Although I take my students to live productions whenever possible, I generally rely on video to provide classes with performance examples. As expected, my students' initial readings of the play provoke widely varying responses, similar to the varying critical reactions mentioned by Dolan. The use of motion picture versions gives students a broader frame of reference for their textual investigations, while viewing recorded live performances helps them develop an ear for Shakespeare's language and a way to see ambiguity and performance options. Since I began using video to prompt classroom discussion and frame writing assignments, my students demonstrate stronger critical skills. *The Taming of the Shrew* is a challenging play for twenty-first-century audiences. Despite their conformity, motion picture versions of the play help students develop appropriately complex responses.

NOTE

[1] See John Lacy's 1662 revision of the play, *Sauny the Scot*, for an interesting and pertinent variation on this theme.

Playing with the Meat of the Matter: A Props Exercise

Anne F. Gossage

There is more eating in *The Taming of the Shrew* than in any other Shakespeare comedy. Food, like other objects in the play, such as money, clothing, and indeed men and women themselves, has important symbolic and material significance. Therefore, the choice of object—that is, the prop—that is used to represent the food onstage is important. A performance exercise involving stage properties in *The Taming of the Shrew* has helped my students tease out some of this play's central conflicts. I ask students to perform a short food scene (4.3.36–60), during which Petruccio and Hortensio serve "meat" to a starving Katherine. The exercise works best with upper-level students in about a seventy-five-minute class period, but it can also work well over two shorter class periods. Playing with objects can help spur creative thinking about the language of the play, and getting students on their feet helps create an atmosphere in which they feel empowered to interpret the text by embodying it. It removes some of their fear of giving the "wrong answer."

To get students started, I talk with them about the scene, its significance in the play, and its performance history. As the scene begins, Katherine is already onstage. The servant, Grumio, has just been teasing her "with the very name of meat" (32), and she is hungry, tired, and frustrated. The Norton (following the Folio) stage direction reads, "Enter Petruccio and Hortensio, with meat" (35–36). I point out that "meat" can mean either "meat" as we know it or food in a more general sense (Dessen and Thomson 142). Petruccio brags proudly to Katherine about how "diligent" he has been to "dress the meat" himself (39–40).

Then there is an odd moment of silence from Katherine. Petruccio says, "What, not a word?" (42); he then threatens to take the food away again. I ask the students why Katherine says nothing at this point. Often someone will reply that Katherine must be eating, or trying to eat, at this point. However, I ask them to look a few lines down, to where Petruccio insists that Katherine must thank him before he will let her "touch the meat" (46). I explain that we will be trying an experiment in order to discover some possible explanations for Katherine's silence.

Then I cite an early modern stage direction in the earlier source play, *The Taming of a Shrew*, which reads, "Enter Ferando with a piece of meat upon his dagger's point" (Schafer, *Taming* 191). Students are generally quick to jump on the phallic implications of this image. We talk about other sexual suggestions in the Shakespeare version, about how Petruccio is possibly teasing Katherine not just with food but with himself. We discuss how "meat" or "flesh" is early modern slang for the male sex organ and that "stand" can mean "to have an erection." Students' eyes widen, and they start to pay closer attention to the language as they look again at Katherine's "I pray you, let it stand" (44) and at Petruccio's "dress thy meat myself and bring it thee" (40).

After this brief discussion, I break the students into groups of three or four. If a group has a fourth student, that student can act as "bookkeeper," calling out lines when performers lose their places in the text. I give each group a bag of eight or ten items from which they must choose a food prop to use as the "meat" that Petruccio offers Katherine. I then give each group fifteen to twenty minutes to work through how they will stage the scene with that prop. With particularly shy students, I give them the exercise as an assignment for the next class, thereby giving them a chance to prepare and possibly even to bring in their own objects. They may choose any prop or combination of props that they like, but they must be able to justify their choices to the class. I also recommend that they choose an item that will allow the characters to have as much physical interaction as possible.

The items vary according to what is available. (I often get odd looks at the checkout line of the student center on the day of this exercise.) Some of the things that I have included are

cooked hot dog, Slim Jim, or other long, edible meat
turkey or chicken leg, cooked
fast-food chicken nuggets or chicken tenders
ham slice or other sliced meat piece
can of Spam with pop-off lid
bagel or doughnut with hole
baguette
animal crackers
dried fruit strips
canned bean dip with pop-off lid

candy bar
banana
Jell-O
Rice Krispies treat
plastic dagger or sword
big, ugly dog bone, preferably with meat strips hanging on it (available in pet stores)
plastic chicken that squeaks loudly
dog biscuit
plastic dinner dish
dog dish
fast-food restaurant bag

I ask each group to perform the scene for the class (with texts in hand). I tell the students that they may do anything they like, as long as they don't hurt one another: I encourage them to be outrageous; to play with the props; to go for broad, physical comedy if possible; and not to be afraid to improvise as the scene progresses. I explain that this scene, like much of the play, is often performed "over the top" by actors onstage. The use of slapstick comedy in performances of domestic squabbles was also traditional in Shakespeare's time (Dolan 3). Alternatively, the play can become very dark in some modern productions, with Katherine a victim of domestic abuse.

After each group's performance, I ask them to explain why they made the choices that they did and how they think it went. Then the rest of the class gives feedback and analysis. In the feedback session, I encourage the other students to focus not on what they liked or disliked or on what was "good" or "bad" but on the payoffs or limitations of particular ways of doing the scene. I ask, "What did this performance suggest about the play that you didn't think of when you read the text?" After all the groups are finished, I ask the class to compare the versions. This discussion gets to the heart of how to interpret the play as a whole, and that is the point of the exercise. I never grade these performances.

Students, of course, tend to favor the most extreme, sexual, physical interpretations. Some of the best results come from groups in which the prop becomes the impetus for a physical struggle among the characters. For instance, one student playing Petruccio offered Katherine a plate of chicken nuggets (a student favorite), which she snatched at, but before she had a chance to take any, even with Hortensio's help, Petruccio proceeded to devour them hoggishly, leaving her none. Messy or disgusting props like Jell-O or Spam can have a slightly different effect. One group chose to place a pile of bean dip in the dog dish and to have Petruccio place it on the floor for Katherine, who was forced to kneel and to eat it without silverware. Another group hid their food prop in a bag that Petruccio threw around while Katherine and Hortensio tried to catch it. One Katherine had to catch animal crackers in her mouth as Petruccio threw them to her. These methods of teasing and frustrating a hungry Katherine effectively explain her silence before she finally thanks Petruccio for the food, in hopes of getting at least a little bit to eat.

The scenes in which student actors take their lines (and sometimes their food) to the audience also get high marks from their fellow students and contribute to our ongoing discussion of early modern performance practices and performance spaces.[1] Sometimes the student playing Katherine appeals to the audience with eye contact or gestures. Sometimes the student playing Petruccio will give food to an audience member in order to keep it away from Katherine. The audience member can then choose whether to let Katherine have any of the food. Sometimes there are outright food fights, with food flying all over the room (we have an understanding janitorial staff). Everyone in the audience likes to be in on the joke instead of passively watching.

Usually at least one group of students will put a bagel or doughnut on a dagger or sword, following the direction found in *A Shrew*. Not only is this sexually suggestive, which leads students to think about the nature of the physical relationship between the characters, but it also leads to good interaction as the bagel or doughnut gets torn apart, with Katherine grabbing for it, carefully avoiding the point of the blade. A group with two acting majors once gave a very phallic interpretation, with Petruccio holding a strategically placed hot dog in front of his body, and Katherine on her knees, eating the hot dog in a manner suggestive of fellatio. The classroom erupted with surprise and howling laughter, which intensified as Petruccio turned to his friend, with the hotdog still in place, saying, "Eat it up all, Hortensio, if thou lov'st me" (50), making this line a homoerotic joke. The correspondence between sexuality and material objects became clearly evident.

Students also enjoy the way that such performances bring out particular words of the text and make them stand out, like "stand" or "meat." They start noticing when those words come up again in other parts of the play. This helps them identify larger thematic, linguistic, and rhetorical patterns in the play as they encounter them. Sometimes students will cast against gender. If they don't, I often ask one group to try switching a female Katherine with a male student and to repeat their scene, in order to discuss the differing effects of having a male actor playing this particular female role.[2] I allow the students to take any leftover edibles away with them at the end, which always makes them inordinately happy. The nonedible items, like the squeaky plastic chicken or the dog bone, have also worked well by making a mockery of Katherine's hunger. Petruccios tend to clown around with these items, angering the Katherines. Katherine's "I thank you, sir" (47) is then said sarcastically, which can suggest a possible ironic reading of her final speech in the last act. Using obviously artificial props has also led to good discussion about Petruccio's taming strategy and how it involves making claims that directly oppose material reality in order to "kill" his wife "with kindness" (4.1.188). After all, if what Petruccio says to Katherine is often ironic, why would we assume that it is edible food that he offers her?

The exercise therefore explores some of the central debates about the play: Is Katherine "acting" or "really" tamed? Is the taming playful or domineering? Is it some sort of kinky dominance-and-submission sex game? Is Petruccio cruel or clever? Do they love each other or just use each other? What is "private" and "public" in the Renaissance? How can social interactions, marriage, or even gender be part of a game or a performance? The students' own performances illustrate these possibilities much more effectively than would a standard lecture. By the end of the exercise, students will have conceptualized, performed, and defended an interpretation of the scene, and they will have compared their vision with those of other students. Such exercises encourage students to see that there are multiple valid versions of the play and that their own ideas, bodies, and voices can contribute to the ongoing creative process of producing Shakespeare.

NOTES

[1] See Escolme on the importance of actor-audience interaction in Shakespeare performances.

[2] For guidelines on rehearsing and performing using original practices, see Tucker; Stern, *Rehearsal*; and Palfrey and Stern.

Using Performance to Teach Textual Skepticism in *The Taming of the Shrew*

M. G. Aune

Students reading the first thirty-seven lines of act 2, scene 1, of *The Taming of the Shrew* in *The Norton Shakespeare*, second edition, see its text developing Katherine's, Bianca's, and Baptista's characters by providing a glimpse into their domestic life. The two sisters enter in the midst of a sibling argument. Katherine seems to dominate her sister, having bound Bianca's hands and demanding that she reveal which of the suitors she prefers. Bianca is trying to pacify her sister and regain her freedom. Eventually Baptista enters and breaks up the fight, sending the weeping Bianca away and scolding Katherine. What the students reading the Norton edition do not know is that this is not the only way to interpret these lines.

In the source text for all later editions of *The Taming of the Shrew*, namely Shakespeare's First Folio, the scene offers many possibilities for stage action, but neither the stage directions nor the lines specify exactly what form that action must take.[1] The stage directions are as follows, at the beginning of the scene: "*Enter Katherina and Bianca*"; after Katherine's attack on Bianca at 2.1.23, we read: "*Strikes her*" and then "*Enter Baptiſa*." Katherine's direction, "*Flies after Bianca*," occurs immediately before Bianca's exit at 2.1.33. But the moments of the exits are ambiguous, and the folio's stage directions do not indicate whether Bianca's hands are tied or ever untied. Most modern editors attempt to clarify the action by adding explicit stage directions indicating that Bianca enters with her hands bound and specifying who leaves and when. Observing the differences between the First Folio and a modern edition of this scene creates an ideal opportunity to introduce and explore a critical thinking and reading strategy I call textual skepticism.

This approach has its roots in our awareness of how textual editing compromises authorial stability. It asks students to understand Shakespeare's plays and poems not only as literary objects but also as dynamic texts that gain and lose meaning through the processes of editing, reading, and performing. The approach also subverts the idea of Shakespeare as a lone literary genius. By the end of the semester, I want students to be critical about the Shakespearean text, to understand that it is a heavily mediated document that often differs substantially from the First Folio or, presumably, from what Shakespeare actually composed.

Textual skepticism can also have other advantages. It is a portable strategy. Students are able to use it not only for Shakespeare but also for texts in other literature and nonliterature classes. It can be particularly useful when applied to textbooks that present themselves as comprehensive and authoritative. Textual skepticism can also help students become more engaged in a course on

Shakespeare by leading them to perform parts of the plays and analyze the lines afterward, seeing how their performance choices were influenced by editorial decisions.

Before we read *The Taming of the Shrew*, so the students will not yet be familiar with the characters or the play, I assign an exercise. I begin by asking for two groups of three volunteers each. We step out of the classroom, and I give each group a transcription of 2.1.1–42 from the First Folio, which retains the original spelling, punctuation, and format (see the appendix). I ask each group to devise at least two different ways to perform the lines, but give them as little guidance as possible. If they ask for help, such as with the spelling or vocabulary of a phrase like "[f]or ſhame thou Hilding of a diuelliſh ſpirit" (2.1.28), I tell them that part of their challenge is to work with the text they have using only their own knowledge. I leave them to rehearse while I return to the class and the remaining students and I read the version of the scene in our textbook. We examine the lines and discuss the action that might be taking place onstage and how the editors of the Norton edition shape our understanding of the scene by adding stage directions, modernizing spelling, and clarifying speech prefixes. The Norton editors are especially intrusive, as a careful perusal of the appendix indicates. This form of editing, based on the Oxford edition, creates an ideal opportunity for textual analysis in the classroom.

When confronted with having to act the lines, the performers have numerous problems to solve. The first is learning to read the text with its irregular spelling, such as the long *s* in Bianca's first line, "Good ſiſter wrong me not" (2.1.1), and inconsistent speech prefixes such as Bianca's, which vary between "*Bian.*" and "*Bianca.*" Second are the decisions about performance. Although in the First Folio Bianca says, "Unbinde my hands," no stage directions are given as to whether Bianca has entered with her hands tied, so do we assume an implicit stage direction here, dictating that she has done so? If so, does Baptista untie them upon his entrance two lines later or allow her to run around with them still tied? Line twenty-six, "*Bianca* ſtand aſide, poore gyrle ſhe weepes," can be confusing. Bianca's name is in italics. Does that mean it is a speech prefix? If so, why would she say "stand aside, poor girl she weeps?" Line sixteen contains the nonword "bnt." Perhaps it should be "but," yet where did "bnt" come from?

Back in the classroom, I ask the students who are not rehearsing to imagine how this scene would appear onstage. They all are familiar with family squabbles, so I prompt them by asking some basic questions about character relationships and family dynamics: who does the text lead us to believe is to blame? When Katherine and her father first appear in the play, she scolds him for using her as a decoy to find a husband for Bianca: "I pray you, sir, is it your will / To make a stale of me amongst these mates?" (1.1.58). Bianca's address to her father is the model of obedience: "Sir, to your pleasure humbly I subscribe" (1.1.81). Who is the good sister here and who is the bad sister? Can we find the answers to these questions in the lines or the stage directions of the Norton text? (The editors have added a bracketed stage direction at the beginning of the scene, "*Enter* KATHERINE *and* BIANCA [*her hands bound*]," indicating that Katherine has literally tied her hands.) I ask them to make some notes about their thoughts and to circle any lines that seem particularly important to these questions. I point out to the students that whenever this play is staged, the performers have to decide the answers. I then tell them that they will see their classmates perform four versions of the scene and that their job is to take notes and ask questions based on our discussion, so as to understand the performers' decision-making process.

The first group returns, and the performers present the scene two different ways and answer their peers' questions to the best of their ability. I keep notes on the questions and answers to help facilitate the final discussion. The second group of performers is not allowed to watch the first. Once the questions are done, the first group leaves and the second enters. The process is repeated until all four performances are completed.

Once the performances are completed, the performers look up the scene as it appears in the Norton, while I give the audience the handout with the First Folio lines. Using our notes, we discuss the variations the performers presented and the textual factors that influenced their decisions. In the course of this discussion, I introduce relevant critical terminology (*copy text*, *control text*, *editorial emendation*, *folio*, *gloss*, *interpolation*, *modernization*, *speech prefix*, *stage directions*, and *silent emendation*) and guide the students to a sense of the means by and the extent to which the Norton editors have shaped our understanding of this scene. The editorial vocabulary helps the students articulate their own ideas about the text and understand the textual notes that I expect them to read and incorporate into their course work.

I have also used some variations on this approach to explore other reading strategies and to introduce general classroom procedures. I have found this exercise useful on the first day of classes to warm the students to one another and establish the importance of performance. I have added a gendered component, which asks the students to cross-cast the roles or switch the genders in varying combinations. Does our understanding of Katherine and Bianca change if men play them? if they are brothers rather than sisters? if Baptista is played by a woman? if Baptista is the mother? I have also used this exercise to introduce argumentation, asking groups to use the First Folio text to support contrary positions: for example, Bianca is the instigator, and Katherine is the victim; or, Baptista is the cause of the arguments either because he favors Bianca or because he favors Katherine.

Critical reading, especially of Shakespeare, emphasizes important skills including close reading, self-awareness, and attention to historical contexts. But the text is often neglected as an object of criticism. Using an approach derived from textual and performance criticism, such as the one described here, helps remind students that the text they read is heavily mediated, that this mediation often shapes their interpretation of the text, and that they are able to learn to read through that mediation to arrive at their interpretations.

NOTE

[1] See, for example, Shakespeare, *First Folio*, edited by Hinman.

APPENDIX

2.1 from F1

Enter Katherina and Bianca

Bian. Good ſiſ ter, wrong me not, nor wrong your ſ elſ ,
To make a bondmaide and a ſ lave of mee,
That I diſ daine: but for the ſe other goods,
ſnbinde my hands, Ile pull them off my ſ elfe,
Yea all my raiment, to my petticoate,
Or what you will command me, wil I do,
So well I know my dutie to my elders.
Kate. Of all thy ſutors heere I charge tel
Whom thou lou'ſ t be ſt: ſsee thou diſ ſemble not.
Bianca. Beleeue me ſuſter, of all the men aliue,
I neuer yet beheld that ſpeciall face,
Which I could fancie more then any other.
Kate. Minion thou lyeſt: Is't not *Horten ſio?*
Bian. If you affect him ſiſter, heere I ſweare
Ile plead for you my ſelfe, bnt you ſhal haue him.
Kate. O then belike you fancie riches more,
You wil haue Gremio to keepe you faire.
Bian. Is it for him you do enuie me ſo?
Nay then you ieſt, and now I wel perceiue
You haue but ieſted with me all this while:
I prethee, ſiſter Kate, vntie my hands.
Ka. If that be iest, then all the rest was ſo. *Strikes her*
Enter Baptiſta
Bap. Why, how now, Dame, whence growes this
inſolence?
Bianca ſtand a ſide, poore gyrl ſhe weepes:
Go ply thy Needle; meddle not with her.
For ſhame, thou Hilding of a deuilish ſpirit,
Why doſt thou wrong her, that did nere wrong thee
When did ſhe croſſe thee with a bitter word?
Kate. Her ſilence flouts me, and Ile be reuenge'd.
Flies after Bianca.
Bap. What, in my ſight? *Bianca* get thee in. *Exit.*
Kate. What will you not ſuffer me: Nay now I ſee

She is your treaſure, ſhe muſt haue a husband,
I muſt dance bare-foot on her wedding day,
And for your loue to her, lead Apes in hell.
Talke not to me, I will go ſit and weepe,
Till I can find occaſion of reuenge.
Bap. Was euer Gentleman thus greev'd as I?

2.1 from *The Norton Shakespeare*, 2nd ed.

Enter KATHERINE *and* BIANCA *[her hands bound]*

BIANCA. Good sister, wrong me not, nor wrong yourself,
To make a bondmaid and a slave of me.
That I disdaine; but for these other goods,
Unbind my hands, I'll pull them off myself,
Yea, all my raiment, to my petticoat,
Or what you will command me will I do,
So well I know my duty to my elders.
KATHERINE. Of all thy suitors, here I charge thee tell
Whom thou lov'st best. See thou dissemble not.
BIANCA. Believe me, sister, of all the men alive
I never yet beheld that special face
Which I could fancy more than any other.
KATHERINE. Minion, thou liest. Is't not Hortensio?
BIANCA. If you affect him, sister, here I swear
I'll plead for you myself, but you shall have him.
KATHERINE. O then, belike you fance riches more.
You will have Gremio to keep you fair.
BIANCA. Is it for him you do envy me so?
Nay, then, you jest, and now I well perceive
You have but jested with me all this while.
I prithee, sister Kate, untie my hands.
KATHERINE. If that be jest, then all the rest was so. *Strikes her.*
Enter BAPTISTA.
BAPTISTA. Why, how now, dame, whence grows this insolence?
Bianca, stand aside.—Poor girl, she weeps.—
[*To* KATHERINE] Go ply thy needle, meddle not with her.
For shame, thou hilding of a devilish spirit,
Why dost thou wronger that did ne'er wrong thee?
When did she cross thee with a bitter word?
KATHERINE. Her silence flouts me, and I'll be revenged.
[*She*] *flies after* BIANCA
BAPTISTA. What, in my sight? Bianca, get thee in. *Exit* [BIANCA]

KATHERINE. What, will not suffer me? Nay, now I see
She is your treasure, she must have a husband.
I must dance bare-foot on her wedding day,
And for your love ot her lead apes in hell.
Talk not to me. I will go sit and weep
Till I can find occasion of revenge. [*Exit*]
BAPTISTA. Was ever gentleman thus grieved as I?

Cross-Dressing, Comic Power Inversions, and "Supposes": Performing the Beginning and the End of *The Taming of the Shrew*

Laury Magnus

My teaching of *The Taming of the Shrew* to undergraduates in an introductory literature and composition class at the United States Merchant Marine Academy, a predominantly male federal service academy, starts out with a staged reading of the two induction scenes and culminates in two competing group performances of Katherine's final speech. Sandwiched between these performances is a straightforward discussion of the play within the play, with emphasis on scenes that stress playacting and dress up, especially those from the end of act 4 to the climactic finale of Katherine's speech. Focusing on the two induction scenes that are often omitted in production and having students perform them as well as the play's final speech highlights the metatheatricality of the play as a whole. Themes of playacting, gender conflict, and relations of power and subservience emerge in class performances involving cross-dressing. This is accomplished through the juxtaposition of the overt "dress-up" disguises and power inversions of the two induction scenes with the covert inversions implicit in Katherine's final speech. Through this approach, I hope to show students that, despite the lack of a closing frame, *The Taming of the Shrew*'s playacting motif, with its cross-gendered dynamics, is the factor that Shakespeare counts on to unify the induction and the action of the play within the play. [1]

I introduce the notion of "framed" action (citing *Alice's Adventures in Wonderland*, *The Canterbury Tales*, and *The Wonderful Wizard of Oz* as familiar analogues) and remind the class that the action inside the frame is contextualized by virtue of the frame itself. But, unlike some other examples, *The Taming of the Shrew* doesn't close its frame. Both Sly and the Lord disappear from the play by 1.1.247, and the play ends with the story of how Katherine wins Petruccio's wager and tops his victory off with her own, an emphatic, long speech on how wives should be silent, meek, and obedient.

Staging the Two Induction Scenes

To do a staged reading requires a rather large class, but it can be done with a small class by assigning double roles (which was original practice). Since my students are in regimental uniforms and have no personal effects, I bring in pieces of costumes (funnier when layered over their uniforms) and props (a bottle, hunting horns, kerchiefs, skirts, servants' vests, etc.). Though most of the induction's roles can be played by either gender, I cast the fight between male and female in scene 1 as a clash between two male players, one dressed up as a hostess, which is stressed by the fact that Sly's line 11, "I'll not budge an inch, *boy*," exposes the boy actor playing the Hostess, as Dusinberre brilliantly argues (67–69). A male volunteer should also be solicited to read the part of the Lord's Page, Barthol'mew, who will withdraw to dress up onstage as Sly's wife in scene 2 of the induction. If there is any time left at the end of this class, I rerun the lines of the Sly-Hostess conflict with a female student playing the Hostess and ask the class if this changes the dynamic of the induction. Students agree that having a male play the hostess immediately signals the tensions concerning gender dominance in the play and heightens the ridiculousness of Sly's assumption of lordship. After the induction performance, we discuss the following issues: Shakespeare's possible reasons for opening with Sly's drunken, disorderly behavior and confrontation with the Hostess; Sly's "swinish" sleep (sc. 1, line 30) as a motivation for the Lord's jest (which consists, basically, of elevating him from this swinishness through playacting); the Lord's imperious language of giving orders (with active verbs) in his instructions both for his huntsmen and for the players to perform their "practice;"[2] the way in which gender is deconstructed in Barthol'mew's performance as Sly's wife; and, finally, the way in which the absurd dynamics of delayed sexual gratification are woven into the entertainment factor of the play within the play.

The Play within the Play Leading to Kate's Speech

Moving from the induction to the play within the play, it is important to review the extremely confusing dramatis personae and explain who is playing which roles, stressing the separate casts for these two parts of the play and possibilities for doubling roles. In discussing the play within the play, we tackle passages that involve disguise, role playing, exchanges of clothing, and gender identity, as well as the rivalries between servants and masters. Here we keep track of discrepancies between the characters' appearances and their probable underlying motivations. Some noteworthy examples are Tranio and Lucentio's exchange of clothes and master-servant status, Biondello's playing along as Tranio/Lucentio's servant, Hortensio and Lucentio's tutor disguises, Petruccio's antic nuptial "disguise," and the Pedant's impersonation of Vincentio.

An important turning point concerning the motif of disguise is Petruccio's praise of "honest mean habiliments" (4.3.170) and disavowal of dress up. Here we see changes both in the tamer and the tamed, who have undergone nuptial deprivations (Petruccio, of course, to a lesser degree), and we begin to understand that outward show is less important than inner substance. This leads, in turn, to what might be called the "education" scene, wherein Katherine assents to call the sun the moon (4.6.13) and to call Vincentio a "budding virgin" (38). Kate's assent sends two different signals, one to the onstage and one to the play-going audience. The onstage audience is content to call a wife "obedient" when she has been *named* so and appears to be so. The play-going audience recognizes that Kate has chosen to cooperate with, to assimilate, and to use the jointly created fiction of man's commanding language for her own purposes. Kate's cooperation both creates and makes visible marital harmony. Masculine language may not in fact "command the sun" (4.3.190), but it highlights the efficacy of allowing men to think that they can do so.

The verbal catfight between the Widow and Katherine in 5.2 builds up to the internal closing frame of Petruccio's wager, one that harks back to, without reintroducing, the Lord's wager in the first scene of the induction ("Would not the drunkard then forget himself?" [line 37]). Through this final wager, Shakespeare achieves a resounding closure that awards a victory to both Petruccio and Katherine, since their marital concord (or its appearance) has won prestige, victory, and a goodly sum of money.

Studying, Rehearsing, Staging 5.2.66–193 and Interpreting the Performances

If possible, the class should be divided beforehand into two groups, one of them casting Katherine as a man and one as a woman. (If the class is too small to divide, the scene should be cross-cast and run twice with both a male and female Katherine.) I devote a whole class period for group discussion. I float between the two groups. Each group must cast the roles, assign props (especially the wager money) and the appropriate costumes for the performances of their Katherines, and come up with staging arrangements that place actors (seated or standing) at an improvised banquet table. Before this class, I distribute the talk-back questions and advise groups to decide exactly how they wish Katherine to deliver her speech to her audiences. Is Katherine's a speech about wifely obedience, about performing a socially approved role as obedient wife, or both? Or do her stage actions contradict everything she says? Based on their interpretation, groups will have to decide how to block line 66 ("Let's each one send unto his wife") to line 193 of 5.2, as well as what various characters will be doing as Kate delivers her speech. They will also need to appoint a director. Staging decisions should be justified from textual evidence given before this scene.

The group's blocking should also answer questions about where Kate directs certain lines and how specific characters (especially Petruccio) might react to these lines of her speech. Two questions are particularly important: How does Katherine deliver and Petruccio respond to "[a]nd place your hand beneath your husband's foot?" Do they finally "kiss" (or not), and what is the kiss like? (If this gets sticky, a puckered air kiss may be suggested.) They should also determine how the couple exits the "stage" and the impact of Hortensio's and then Lucentio's lines that close the play.

The final staged reading and talk back occurs in the next class, with a coin toss deciding which group goes first. The talk back should address the following questions (which can also be used for written analytic assignments): What feelings and responses to Katherine's submission speech was the audience (on-stage and off) aware of? How did the gender of the actor playing Katherine affect audience response? What "echoes," serious or absurd, of themes broached in the induction scenes did actors find? Who were the different auditors of Katherine's speech, and how did the performers engage various members of the stage audience at critical points—along with the off-stage audience? How did the other two couples respond, and what did this bode about their future marriages? Which paradoxes of the play came alive during the performance of this speech, especially as played by an actor of male as opposed to female gender? How did the class "audience" understand the meaning of the final speech as it was performed, and was this what the performing group tried to show in action? Was Katherine's "obedience" qualified by any of her gestures, especially her final gesture of hand placement; Petruccio's reactions; the kiss, nonkiss, or mock-kiss; the couple's manner of exit; or the closing two lines of editorial commentary—and if so, how?

The opening and closing frame of induction and wager should help students grasp that Katherine's speech has a great deal to do with how she playacts her role of obedient wife whose "public obedience" establishes Petruccio's reputation, her own reputation, and the social and financial profitability of their joint playacting. Shakespeare's metatheatricality allows him to stress the fractures between character and role playing (especially in the Bianca plot that deconstructs her apparent docility). Revealing these fractures is crucial to Shakespeare's dramatic exploration of the relation between tamer and tamed, master and servant, male and female, husband and wife. While the cross-gendered facets of playacting are not really available to contemporary audiences that approach the play through its film or television incarnations, they become readily comprehensible by students' dressing up, even in arbitrary ways, across gender lines, so as to stress possible conflicts among actor, dress, and gendered role.[3]

Having students make the connection between Katherine's final speech and the impersonations and the complex inversion, disguises, and pretenses of the induction scenes fosters an understanding of the play as a ludic celebration of role playing—its potential to create both a farcical send-up of social hypocrisy and a necessary fiction that can protect a privileged, private sphere between husband and wife. Moreover, in getting students to enter into the play's interpretative dynamics through staged readings that involve dress up and cross-dressing, they are primed to appreciate the thematic values of self-fashioning—the ways in which public role playing, both as a personal escape route from oppressive social conventions and as a means of developing true mutuality in interpersonal relationships, can be used in forging their own individual identities. At the United States Merchant Marine Academy, where men and women are encouraged to put aside their individuality and take on active, masculine roles as "strong" regimental leaders, students have an extra appreciation for this play—as well as an instinct for questions about "who's really in charge" underneath the roles and costumes of designated authority.

NOTES

[1] Students may wish to explore *The Taming of a Shrew*, with its disillusioning waking of Sly and his plans to return home and try "taming" his real wife. The different endings of the two plays are an excellent research topic, too.

[2] See Magnus, who shows how Kate's "language of command" mimics the Lord's language in the induction (104).

[3] I particularly recommend viewing the American Conservatory Theater of San Francisco's 1976 commedia dell'arte performance, with its lively acrobatics and stress on stock roles (though it omits the induction). I also recommend Peter Dews's 1986 televised version, starring Len Cariou and Sharry Flett (performed in Stratford, Ontario), a wonderful and hilarious staging of the two induction scenes and a marvelous performance of the play in general.

Dominating Humor in *The Taming of the Shrew*

Silver Damsen

The following lesson plan for *The Taming of the Shrew* calls for students first physically to stand and declare their philosophical positions on issues important to *The Taming of the Shrew* and then to compare different filmed versions of the play's text.

I have developed an exercise I call "Johnny Cash," or "Walking the Line," a great way to jump-start any undergraduate discussion of *The Taming of the Shrew*. This exercise involves a classroom's length of adhesive tape and ten to thirteen statements that articulate key propositions that are vital to exploring an interpretation of the play. These include the following:

No one is truly obedient.
Most people need to be or should be trained into obedience.
Many of those who appear to be obedient are pretending and making a game of it.
Men are naturally more obedient than women.
Obedience is a desirable trait.
A certain amount of obedience in a romantic partner is desirable.
It is highly entertaining to watch characters struggle for dominance.
It is natural to resist the dominance of another.
It is natural to enjoy dominating another.
Because of the nature of human society, some people should always dominate others.
If you act subordinate in order to humor or tease someone you think is actually inferior to you, then you are not really subordinate to that person.
The most satisfying subordination of another (either to watch or to participate in) involves mild force and mild resistance.

I ask students to stand on the left side of the line if they agree with the statement I read them, on the right side if they disagree, or directly on the line if they want to qualify and explain their responses in more detail. I then ask for volunteers and also call on students (standing on all positions in relation to the tape) to explain their decision making in further detail.

The most obvious benefit of this exercise is that it forces students literally to take a stand on an issue. Visual clues from students also help me select those who are most likely to want to respond to the question. Thus, taking a stand helps students who want to talk do so more easily and helps quieter students make solid contributions to class discussion. I have found that this exercise also helps beginning students appreciate and understand an early modern text, since it enables them to apply its key themes to their own experiences before they are asked to interpret either an early modern textual expression or performance of these same themes. Allowing students to voice their own values first also helps them differentiate between their values and those of others in a nonthreatening manner. In short, this format helps students move away from socially conditioned, nearly automatic responses to the sensitive issue of domination and subordination.

After doing this exercise, I have students compare film versions of the play, which is, as H. R. Coursen has convincingly argued in *Teaching Shakespeare with Film and Television*, the best way to make Shakespeare more accessible to undergraduates. Comparisons of several filmed versions of this play can be especially useful in helping beginning and intermediate students confront issues of domination and subordination. Before any class instruction of *Shrew* has taken place, even less critically sophisticated and well-read undergraduate students are generally aware that such issues permeate the play. Yet they also tend to perceive subordination and domination as either simply humorous and of no ideological significance or as blatantly misogynist, demonstrating by contrast the great leaps forward that women have made in their own era. This second response is more helpful than the first, yet both fail to carefully consider close readings of the text or interpretative cruxes of performance, either live or filmed.

Films useful for this type of classroom comparison should include (if possible) Jonathan Miller's 1980 BBC television production, because it is far darker than most productions (filmed or live), highlighting the seriousness of subordination. This version's darker nature undercuts the ideological naturalization of male domination and hence provides a very clear means of comparison to more lighthearted interpretations. For example, Miller does not use laugh tracks to cue the viewer to laugh at depictions of higher-status individuals dominating those of lower status. Instead, the closed and cramped sets motivate the viewer to crave greater freedom, and an almost deathly stillness prevails in Petruccio's wooing scene in 2.1. The characters move, but they are rarely playful and seem heavy and trapped. A sense of foreboding, instead of teasing humor, prevails in the courtship. Other useful filmed versions include Peter Dews's 1986 Canadian Broadcasting Corporation (CBC) film of a live Stratford, Ontario, production, a more conventionally comic rendering of the play that includes the rarely performed induction. Actors in both these productions wear traditional Elizabethan dress, which prevents costume and setting from being the most salient differences that students notice. However, while Dews's version includes the induction, which generally tends to support women's independent thought and action, the rest of the interpretation works against this reading. For example, the text of the induction frames the entire subordination of Katherine as part of a scheme to trick a poor tinker into believing that he is a lord. This can easily work to render any act of domination and subordination suspiciously inauthentic. However, because Dews's interpretation tends to play for audience laughter, it also tends to make light of all domination and subordination, especially gendered subordination. For example, Dews's interpretation invites and receives the live audience's approbation (loud laughter and applause) when Petruccio kicks Katherine immediately before he says, "Why does the world report that Kate doth limp?" (2.1.245). Because Petruccio is bigger than Katherine, the kick seems bullying, and some students will not join the filmed live audience in laughing at it (and may even enjoy pointing out the sexist bullying of Dews's version to their classmates).

Other useful films for this exercise include the readily available 1983 Bard Productions version, directed by John Allison (almost as accessible from any library as Miller's BBC version and also easily available online at very low prices). This American version also plays for laughs, especially those involving physical comedy. For example, central to Allison's interpretation of gendered relationships is a wrestling match between Katherine and Petruccio during their initial encounter. Viewers will probably see the humor when a petite but fiery Katherine pins Petruccio and attempts to pull his ears off. While Petruccio seemed bullying when he kicked Kate in the Dews's CBC production, Katherine seems funny when she attacks Petruccio here, since she is a smaller person physically dominating a larger one. Reversed physical humor makes this production of *Shrew* very accessible for students less well versed in reading Shakespeare. Though this production's pseudo-historical costuming and less skilled acting might prove annoying to students with more experience comparing Shakespeare performances, the two versions would be suitable for comparison, provided the instructor is able to perceive notable and important differences in interpretation between them.

My basic methodology for this lesson plan has included a general study of the play's text as a whole, viewings of scenes from Miller's and Dews's filmed versions and of scenes from Miller's and Allison's versions (centering on 2.1 and 5.2), analysis and discussion of the depictions of subordination and domination in each version, assigned written responses, and oral responses, in which each student described his or her ideal performance of Katherine's final speech (in 5.2).

The preferred film version varied, yet in each classroom experience the banter between Katherine and Petruccio in 2.1 was a highlight of the lesson. The teaching moment occurred when students acknowledged not only that their preferred version (whichever that was) explored domination and subordination but also that their enjoyment of this scene helped them explore their own attitudes toward domination and subordination, ideas about and practices of domination and subordination in the early modern period, and ways to look critically at this theme in other literary works and even in their own lives. Some students, especially female students, have expressed horror and disgust at how domination and subordination have functioned and continue to function importantly in gender relations. Other students have also commented that "subordination and domination" is a highly relevant topic for both the early modern period and contemporary society, so far-reaching that it includes status, class, and even interpersonal domination of one individual or group over another. Even the half-asleep student will have grasped the concept that literature, and especially plays, depends on interpretation: an interpretation of a director, of actors, and also of the audience. For example, students note that while they all agree that versions differ in important ways, they can still disagree on what these versions mean.

When I asked students to propose their own ideal performances of Katherine's speech, choices again varied. Yet all students who offered an ideal version offered one that highlighted the problems inherent in a strong female character agreeing to become subordinate to a male. Thus, one outcome of this exercise could be a student population that is more open to discussion of the issue of voluntary female subordination.

Written responses tended to follow one of several easily identifiable patterns. The patriarchal interpretation followed these lines: Katherine has come to understand herself as subordinate to men, and especially her husband, in a genuine sense at the close of the play. This subordination is the cost Katherine has to pay to be loved in a male-dominated society, yet it is still a choice that Katherine has made, seemingly guided by her attraction to Petruccio. This interpretation also argued for the substantial benefits Katherine derives from this choice, primarily the benefit of new domination of other women. While this was a "traditional" kind of interpretation, it was a subtly nuanced and thoughtful one. Less traditional interpretations included one that understood Katherine as having become the most manipulative character at the end of the play, so that she has, in this sense, changed places with Bianca. In the last scene Katherine receives the most male approval, and yet at her core she is still stubbornly independent. The last interpretation can be understood as an exaggeration of the version of the last scene in Miller's BBC production. Here students imagined a general reduction in all humor, especially slapstick, during the scene. Katherine's last speech was imagined as ideally delivered with a defeated and pathetic demeanor so as to emphasize the horrors of any kind of subjugation, but especially gender subjugation.

Oral responses did not show as much variety, perhaps because students tended to be swayed by one another's comments. The dominant preference in this instance was that Katherine's demeanor be mocking. Katherine is still performing subordination, but students understood this as a conscious performance, rather than as an expression of her heartfelt new knowledge of women's inferiority to men. One student, to the approval of the rest of the students present, suggested that Katherine should give a knowing wink to Petruccio (in the tradition of the first screen Katherine, Mary Pickford) *before* she begins this speech, as a clue to the audience that she doesn't mean what she's about to say.

The discussion of the ideal version was, then, both lively and unsettling. It also helped students understand the larger context of performance during the early modern period, an idea that Shakespeare explored in many of his plays. Students' conclusions about the difference between performance and "reality" has varied in my teaching exercises, but thinking about this difference has also worked to enrich student understanding of the idea of performance in early modern times. For example, in one of these classroom experiments students concluded that while performing subordination goes a long way toward making an individual subordinate, there is still more autonomy for the individual who sees his or her actions as performance and not as heartfelt truth.

Additional prompts to discussion in my classes have included the following:

How does the play-within-a-play structure qualify the performance of domination and subordination?

If Katherine is genuinely attracted to Petruccio, does this lessen or intensify the performances of subordination that he later makes her undergo?

In the induction, the Lord dominates the young male servant, forcing him into the role of Christopher Sly's wife. How is this similar to or different from Petruccio's forcing Katherine into the role of obedient wife?

What is the difference between an actor performing subordination on the stage and an individual performing subordination in everyday life?

Is Bianca still subordinate to her husband after they are married?

How important is the female-female competition in the play? See, for example, Katherine and Bianca in 2.2 and Katherine, Bianca, and the Widow in the final act.

Find examples of servants who take advantage of opportunities to lessen their subordination. See, for example, the suitors/tutors in Baptista's house and the tailor and servants of Petruccio.

Do you agree with the audience reactions to the Dews version of *The Taming of the Shrew*, such as audience members' roaring with laughter and clapping when Petruccio kicks Katherine during their initial meeting?

Can Katherine's initial avowed resistance to marriage be genuine when she displays such intense anger that Petruccio is late to the wedding? What has happened between their first encounter and the wedding to make her want him to appear?

Does Petruccio give Katherine what she really wants when he creates a context for her to humiliate her sister and the Widow and make her father proud of her?

How is the monetary reward that Petruccio hopes to gain from marrying Katherine similar to or different from the servant's wages or Baptista's asking for a good settlement for his younger daughter?

NOTE

This essay draws on my teaching of an introductory Shakespeare and drama class at the University of Illinois, Urbana; of a class session for Grace Tiffany's undergraduate Shakespeare class at Western Michigan University; and of a focus group for Sara Luttfring's Introductory Shakespeare course at the University of Illinois, Urbana. I would like to thank Tiffany and Luttfring for offering their time, their students, and also their own insights.

What's in a Word? Teaching *Play* with the *OED*

Grace Tiffany

When I teach, I forget my gender. My class, however, does not. The gender of the instructor is particularly important to students reading *The Taming of the Shrew*, a play that directly inspires debate about power relations between men and women. When presenting this play, I sense that students of both sexes feel obligated—partly because I am female—to disavow Petruccio's domestic politics. Rotely expressed disapprovals of the taming usually mask students' more nuanced and complicated opinions. One way I fight the predictable and lead students to consider (or admit that they already consider) the healthier aspects of Petruccio's treatment of Kate is to call attention to the gamesome aspects of the play.

To do this, I start by distributing a photocopied entry for the word *play* from the *Oxford English Dictionary* (*OED*). The accompanying instruction I give is simple: "Underline some definitions of *play* that seem to you to have relevance to the action of *The Taming of the Shrew*." Traditionally, I have made this a homework assignment and have deferred our discussion of the applicable definitions until the subsequent class meeting, during which students will offer observations while referring to their underlined or highlighted texts. However, two relatively new (at least at my institution) advances in classroom technology have expanded the means by which this classroom exercise can be administered and have, in my most recent experience, increased the level of class participation in the exercise. The first innovation is the online *OED*, now accessible through virtually all college or university libraries' home pages. The second is the recent fitting of many college and university classrooms with equipment for both computer and hard-copy data projection. By means of these "techno-carts," as I like to call them, a teacher can project the *OED* definitions of *play* on a screen in the front of the classroom so that even those who have lost their assignment sheet or simply not done the work can remain effectively part of the class, participating in the discussion instead of shrinking into their seats and hoping not to be called on. However, even in "low-tech" classrooms, these less-prepared members of the class can find strength to join the conversation if the instructor pauses to write each proffered definition of *play* on the board for general viewing.

How does the word *play* speak to—and from—the heart of this play? A brief look at the *OED*'s twenty-eight columns of definitions of this word will yield two answers. First, *play*'s numerous meanings indicate both the word's richness and its importance to Shakespeare's English. Many definitions of the noun *play*—such as "amusement, diversion" (def. II) and "sport, frolic" (II.6a)—date back to the medieval period and still obtained during Shakespeare's time (as most do in our own). The uses of *play* cited in the *OED* reveal this fact (and when students see how the *OED* records any word's stasis or progression, they are made familiar with the dictionary as a historical resource). Second, the word *play* has a phenomenal number of recorded meanings that have direct relevance to at least one part of *The Taming of the Shrew*. As an in-hand or on-the-board (or screen) resource, this simple list of *play*'s definitions—when artfully selected, since it would be impossible to cover or even show all twenty-eight columns—provides a clear and (of course) playful context for addressing *The Taming of the Shrew*. The ready and visible references to *play* enable both students and instructor to recall to memory, discuss, and observe the thematic links among any and all parts of the play.

For example, the definitions "amusement, diversion" and "sport, frolic," cited above, unleash a variety of observations regarding the activities the word *play* describes in *The Taming of the Shrew*. Students note that the bulk of Shakespeare's play is presented as an amusement for Christopher Sly, who is himself the butt of a prank played by the sportive Lord. Petruccio is entertained by the taming challenge, students find, and some notice that he uses the word "frolic" to signal his readiness to return Katherine to Padua for her sister's wedding (4.3.176). One definition of the noun *play*, "[d]ramatic performance, acting" (14a), has an obvious significance to the Sly induction, which features the Lord's household players, and to Lucentio's, Hortensio's, Tranio's, and the Pedant's respective performances of the roles of Cambio, Licio, Lucentio, and Vincentio in the play proper. Usually by the time I introduce the *OED play* exercise, the students have seen some scenes from *Shrew* on film, and my questions about how "Cambio" and "Licio" discharge their assumed roles usually leads to productive discussions of modern or early modern performance traditions. In the 1976 American Conservatory Theater production, for example, Lucentio's brilliant disguise consists of a pair of glasses. For students who note this, I recast what seems to them a lack of effort on Lucentio's part as a Shakespearean preference for symbolic (or synechdochic) rather than realistic disguise.

Invariably, some students will also tie the *OED* definition of play as "dramatic performance, acting," to Petruccio's exaggerated obnoxiousness as he tames Katherine and also to Katherine's final speech, when she may be feigning wifely submission. One definition of the verb *play*, "[p]erformance upon a musical instrument" (def. V), draws attention to the comic uses of actual and metaphoric music in the play, from the foul sounds of Hortensio's untuned lute (which is eventually broken over his head by Katherine) to the apparent harmony among characters in the play's final scene, when "jarring notes agree" (5.2.1). A definition of the noun *play*—namely, a "trifling with words; the use of words merely or mainly for the purpose of producing a rhetorical or fantastic effect" (II.7.b)—has relevance to Petruccio's dizzying dialogue during his first encounter with Kate, when, as Grumio puts it, he "throw[s] . . . figure[s]" in her face" (1.2.108). Another definition, "[a]morous disport; dalliance; sexual indulgence" (II.6.c), can lead to the question of whether Petruccio and Katherine actually consummate their marriage on their wedding night. Close readers observe that, despite all Petruccio's playful sexual language in his first interview with Kate, the pair doesn't celebrate their wedding night in the customary way (to say the least). This revelation may lead to interesting speculation regarding why Petruccio defers exercising his husbandly rights until the close of the play, when he delivers his last line to Kate: "we'll to bed" (5.2.188).

The more sinister meanings of *play* prompt some of the richest student commentary. Many observe that definition II.11 of the noun, "playing of a game or games for money or other valuable stakes; gaming, gambling," describes the three husbands' "laying" ("betting") on their wives' "duty" in the play's last scene (5.2.133). That observation usually leads to a discussion of whether Katherine is a full participant with Petruccio in this final game or has dwindled into her husband's pawn. (When this question comes up, I urge students to notice that a wife's right to reject the role of mere playing piece is wittily defended in this scene by Bianca, who calls her husband a "fool" for "laying on [her] duty" [5.2.133].) Another definition, "to do what one will with, to manage according to one's pleasure" (II.12), aptly defines Petruccio's desires regarding Katherine, according to some students, who can generally provide numerous examples of his thus "playing," or playing with, his wife.

The definitions of *play* in the *OED* are so numerous and, in parts, peculiar that students usually come up with surprises. One of my students called "the condition of being idle, or not at work"—cited by the *OED* (n., def. II.13) with a reference to Shakespeare's *All's Well That Ends Well*—the perfect description of all the "useless, lazy" men in the play, in ironic contradiction of Katherine's description of a husband as one who "commits his body / To painful labour" (5.2.152–53). Another student found an unfamiliar reference to a *play-bird*, defined by the *OED* as "a tame bird used as a decoy for catching wild birds in a net" (n., def. I.5.c). This student observed that the *play-bird* was Kate, the tamed falcon who, in the final scene, captures her unruly fellow wives and returns them to their husbands. But my favorite *OED* definition of *play*—sometimes remarked on by students, sometimes pointed out by me—has always been "opportunity . . . or room for action; scope for activity" (n., def. I.5.c). This reading of *play* yields a helpful interpretation of the paradoxical liberation Petruccio's taming grants Kate. By means of her reformation, she experiences a qualified freedom: an enhanced ability to express her wit and energies within the "room" of social constraint. And this is good. Sport is fun, and birds get to fly. Or is it good? Has a falcon been brainwashed and terrorized into serving its trainer or been taught to love and serve? Kate has learned to play a mere role, but why is it "mere"? Does role playing invalidate her authenticity? Don't we all have to learn to play something?

Considering the ludic metaphor, the students are now divided in their responses to this play. Their answers to questions become original. The discussion of "freedom within constraint" in *The Taming of the Shrew*, spurred by the *OED*, has laid the ground in many of my classes for a wider, cross-play discussion of freedom in Shakespeare. (I have found *The Tempest*, which returns to this theme, a good final play for a semester-long Shakespeare class that has begun with *The Taming of the Shrew.*)

Although one could base one's entire discussion of *The Taming of the Shrew* on *OED* dictionary definitions of the word *play*, I recommend that such a conversation be a true "short take" and that the teacher limit to about fifteen minutes the use of the *OED* as a prompt to discussion—or, at least, be prepared to move away from the *OED* text and back exclusively to the play text (or film) when student attention begins to flag. Instructors will find that fifteen minutes is enough time to create in the class a collective realization that *The Taming of the Shrew* is, in a host of ways, a play about play.

"She Strikes Him": Stage Work and *The Taming of the Shrew*

Meg F. Pearson

Though the usefulness of incorporating stage work into the Shakespeare classroom has been established for many years, we may sometimes lose sight of the goals of such work.[1] What are we trying to accomplish when we have our classes participate in dramaturgy, stage design, costuming, acting, and directing? In addition to helping students understand generally how dramatic literature functions, stage work obliges them to practice close reading, analysis, interpretation, and argumentation. Instead of being told what a particular play is about, students who create miniature productions of scenes necessarily work to persuade their classmates and their instructor that their visions fit best with what the text demands. In the case of *The Taming of the Shrew*, stage work allows students to argue the relative persuasiveness of several different readings.

The Assignment

The unit on the play begins with my lecture on Elizabethan scolding rituals, such as the practices of bridling and cucking, by which too-garrulous wives were forced to wear a metal bit or be dunked in a river until they learned to be silent.[2] I also discuss Elizabethan marriage practices and laws before assigning staging work as homework. The class is required to make concrete connections between textual cues in the play's dialogue and potential physical actions onstage. Specifically, I ask students to offer me notes and stage directions for one of several scenes. For *The Taming of the Shrew*, the four assignment options include the induction, Petruccio and Katherine's first meeting in 2.1, their ambiguous cooperation in 4.6, and Katherine's final speech in 5.2.[3] Students' work may be submitted in several formats: storyboards, lengthy stage directions, or narratives telling the story of what the audience would see in the scene. Each version must contain detailed instructions on what the actors are doing in their scene and an accompanying written rationale.

We discuss the four scenes over the course of two classes. The students gather in groups according to their scenes, compile their interpretations, and argue among themselves for a final version that attends to their scene's textual cues and remains reasonably consistent with the major themes and images in the play. The groups complete the unit by staging their scenes for their classmates. I have had groups perform their pieces in class and others film them outside class and then screen their work in class. The result is a lively exchange of ideas on the page and in discussion, an ideal situation for group work that can accommodate many different learning styles, and a decentered classroom experience that inevitably becomes one of the students' favorite parts of the course.

Below, I describe in more detail the processes and discoveries my classes have made in Kate and Petruccio's first and last scenes together.

Katherine and Petruccio's First Meeting (2.1.180–317)

The first encounter between Petruccio and Katherine contains only one stage direction apart from entrances and exits—"She strikes him" (2.1.215)—yet no other scene in the play so overflows with cues for action. The most obvious are the lines, "Come, sit on me" (197), "and so farewell" (212), "[i]n sooth, you scape not so" (233), and "[l]et me go" (234). The students are tempted to bolster their dialogue with overacting, forcing their Katherines and Petruccios to act out their *buzzards* and *wasps* and *cocks* with physical gestures. Once they begin discussing their options in groups, however, the participants soon begin to notice that the two are debating onstage and reblock their scenes accordingly. As John Basil has asserted in a guide to student acting, "It's the function of Shakespeare's characters to try to win the debate they're engaged in during a particular line, scene, or act; so you must be clear about your character's point of view and communicate his or her argument persuasively" (11).[4] Here, the students must first determine what the two combatants are talking about and then argue how either Kate or Petruccio might try to win.

One group started by seeking out action verbs and looking for movements that might be cued by "bear" and "burden" (2.1.198–200), "sting" and "pluck" (2.1.208–212), or "scape," "chafe," and "tarry" (2.1.233–34). Others tried to find punning language that could suggest movement, especially humorous movement, while another group found success when they focused on Petruccio alone. One student noted that Petruccio's questions were in fact threats, pointing especially to the "No, not a whit" speech, in which Petruccio tells Katherine what she can and "[can] not" do (2.1.235–49). Another student, outraged, pointed to the likelihood that Petruccio was using physical force, even making Katherine limp. From these discussions, the group discovered that their Petruccio's wit was backed up by force.

One clue was Petruccio's heavy-handed repetition within seconds of meeting his future bride. After Katherine assures him that "they call me Katherine that do talk of me" (2.1.182), Petruccio retorts,

> You lie, in faith, for you are called plain Kate,
> And bonny Kate, and sometimes Kate the curst,
> But Kate, the prettiest Kate in Christendom,
> Kate of Kate Hall, my super-dainty Kate—
> For dainties are all cates, and therefore Kate—
> Take this of me, Kate of my consolation. (2.1.183–88)

Many classroom stagings of this moment have shown Petruccio circling Katherine as he attempts to dizzy her both physically and mentally with his repetitions, but one of the more interesting scenes made Petruccio into a dog trainer teaching his not-yet-housebroken mutt her name. This Petruccio said "Kate" as though he were saying "girl" or "pooch" while pointing at her and using a condescending voice. Katherine's responses suddenly took on an entirely new tone of outrage. To defend this interpretation, the students argued that the dog allusions echoed the Lord's comments about his hounds in the first scene of the induction, linking Kate's taming to that of the earlier-mentioned animals.

Katherine and Petruccio's Final Scene

Students begin discussing 5.2 with hope in their hearts that after their play-long conflict, Petruccio and Katherine have reached some kind of agreement. They have "pranked" old Vincentio together, kissed in the street, and stopped fighting. However, all assurances fade when the class confronts Katherine's dozens of lines in support of husbands and obedience. Because so many students (and directors) desire to make this speech an inside joke between Katherine, Petruccio, and the audience, I require at least one group or handful of students to undertake a straight blocking and delivery, one that assumes that Katherine is speaking honestly or at least seriously.

The question students must now ask themselves is, Who is this person? One student observed that the words do not sound like those of Katherine or Kate, pointing to the strange formality of the speech and, in particular, the words *meet* and *amiable*.[5] Interestingly, *amiable* appears only in this speech, and the only other character to use *meet* as an adjective is working in the induction to fool Sly into thinking himself a just-awakened lord.[6]

Katherine proceeds apace with her strange new diction, and students attempt to make sense of how to stage it. Their responses range across the spectrum, even for those students who wish to allow Katherine to be in on the joke. Since most of this speech does not dictate physical gestures, students become more inventive in their interpretations of Kate's actions. Some Kates roam across the stage as they move through various metaphors, striding among troubled fountains (146), debts owed (58), and women's bodies (169). Others have her pointing at the other women's "threat'ning, unkind brow[s]" or shoving them, thus demonstrating that their bodies are indeed "soft, and weak" (140, 169). In both these scenarios, the result is a Katherine who improvises a speech using well-worn truisms about wives. She seems to be playing a role, and doing so on the fly. Alternatively, some students playing Katherine have formed "scare quotes" with their hands to point out the senselessness of what she is saying. In such a staging we find Katherine indicating that she knows how pat her references are—"thy lord, thy king, thy governor" and "to serve, love, and obey" (142, 168)—and using lists in a way that indicates how long this debate has been raging. Her use of examples makes her political, argumentative, even lawyerly. They note the politically charged references to sovereignty and treason. She speaks as would a male character in the play. Is this a role, or is this how it looks to be tamed?

The most chilling staging from a recent class placed Katherine in the middle of the floor facing the audience and had her deliver the speech in a dejected monotone. This group found her language so rote and lifeless that they believed Katherine must deliver the speech as though she had no spirit left, as if she were on Prozac. The speech's reasoning is riddled with clichés, these students argued, and Katherine was never "so boring" before. The three couplets that complete the speech turned into a toxic nursery rhyme in this version, leading one student in the audience to liken Katherine to a Stepford wife.[7]

The students often finish the play having created several major inconsistencies in their productions. The character of Katherine that most of them argue for in act 2 has changed in the final scene. Like many scholars and directors before them, they feel helpless and frustrated by this recalcitrant ending and believe that the play must be changed to be "effective." We discuss their mental gymnastics and consider seriously what we must do, what we must think, if the text is so resistant to an enjoyable comic ending. To indicate the insights and emotional responses that stage work can create, I close with one student's troubled reflection: to tame an animal is to kill it in some way, but we nonetheless do it to make life less burdensome. Humans, this student concluded, are loathsome.

NOTES

1 A quick glance at only the teaching issues of *Shakespeare Quarterly* from 1984, 1990, and 1996 reveals many articles arguing for performance and workshops as "the 'right way' to teach Shakespeare." See especially Thompson, "*King Lear.*"

2 For useful illustrations and information about the punishments for scolds, see Ingram; Boose ("Scolding"). For Elizabethan marriages, I often refer students to "A Homily of the State of Matrimony," which may be found in Dolan's edition of *Shrew* (169–84). Dolan's book includes illustrations of a cucking stool and of a metal bit.

3 If the class is particularly large, I may also give the students a choice of 4.3, a taming scene at Petruccio's house.

4 My thanks to my colleagues in the Department of Theater at the University of West Georgia for their help with theater pedagogy. Special thanks to Amy Cuomo and Shelly Elman.

5 I often point the groups to searchable online texts of the play here, to determine whether this language is indeed new or whether it is out of place. I rely on MIT's *Complete Works of William Shakespeare* (http://shakespeare.mit.edu) for this purpose; it allows users to search an entire play on one page.

6 "Your honour's players, hearing your amendment, / Are come to play a pleasant comedy, / For so your doctors hold it very meet, / Seeing too much sadness hath congealed your blood, / And melancholy is the nurse of frenzy" (induction, sc. 2, lines 124–28).

7 The reference is to the automatons used to replace the actual wives in the quaint town of Stepford, Connecticut, in Ira Levin's book *The Stepford Wives* (1972) and the two film adaptations of the novel.

Performance DVD: From the Stage to the Page (and Back Again)

Wesley Kisting

The benefits of teaching Shakespeare in performance are well-known. Performance significantly improves student comprehension of a play's structure, pacing, and language and shows students that lines can be delivered differently to promote different meanings. Performance also replaces typical early-semester complaints about "old" or "difficult" diction with appreciative remarks about Shakespeare's wit and enduring appeal. For these reasons, at least some exposure to Shakespeare through film is now common in college and high school classrooms, a trend that will continue to grow now that services such as *Netflix*, *Amazon Prime*, and *YouTube* offer instant and affordable or free access to filmed performances. Few approaches invigorate discussion in the Shakespeare classroom more effectively than the thoughtful inclusion of film.

On the other hand, few approaches can sabotage close reading more quickly—especially among students of the digital generation, who generally perceive film to be more accessible and engaging than print. This misperception stems from their discomfort with close reading. Close reading is essential to any stimulating encounter with texts, and thus it is a vital focus of any responsible literary pedagogy. But there is the rub. Once film is permitted to enter, class discussion easily drifts away from the text to general aesthetic considerations, making it difficult for the instructor to require the students to attend closely to language. Many students regard the inclusion of film as tacit permission to stop reading as they start watching the plays. Swayed by a director's vision, they gravitate toward homogeneous understandings of character and theme, not the rich, varied interpretations that emerge when they read and perceive the text through the theaters of their individual minds. Consequently, the quality of class discussion suffers.

These problems can be eliminated, and the course greatly enhanced, by encouraging students to treat performance as a natural extension of their other research and writing activities. This strategy, which is extremely effective at translating students' enthusiasm for film into a sincere proclivity for close reading, is implemented by assigning an involved film project called the performance DVD, in which students are asked to collaborate in small groups to direct, perform, and film a brief scene from one of Shakespeare's plays and then to explain and defend their directorial vision to the rest of the class. The assignment sheet reads as follows:

1. In a group of two to four students, select a continuous five- to ten-minute portion of a play in which performance significantly shapes our understanding of character and theme. You need not adhere to the existing act and scene divisions, but the portion you choose must run five to ten minutes and

contain significant speaking parts for all group members. Minor roles may be cut, combined, or performed by nonclassmates, but no group member should dominate, or disappear from, the scene.

2. Discuss the major themes of the play and the particular importance of the scene you have chosen. Arrive at a consensus about which issues, speeches, and actions in this scene are most significant for shaping our perceptions of the characters and the play as a whole. What is "at stake" in this scene? What does this scene contribute to our knowledge of the characters' relationships or motives that other scenes do not?
3. Formulate a directorial vision. Decide how the scene should be staged and performed to convey the insights you wish to contribute. The following questions will help you begin:

   Which speeches, words, or gestures carry greatest significance and deserve special emphasis? How will you convey this to the audience?
   How might setting, costume, music, sound, lighting, props, et cetera help clarify the mood or create nuance in the meaning of the scene?
   How might the characters' postures, movements, and proximity to others convey their feelings and relationships?
   How might simple camera or editing techniques help guide the audience's focus and clarify your vision?

4. Bring your directorial vision to life by rehearsing and filming your performance.
5. Film a four-to-six-minute commentary in which you explain your directorial vision and your specific performance decisions. Every member of the group must contribute. Please address all of the following questions, in order:

   Describe your directorial vision concisely. What insights and themes did you want to convey, and why?
   What were the most important performance decisions you made to convey this vision successfully? Describe four, discussing each briefly.
   What were the greatest challenges you faced in attempting to convey your vision? Describe three, discussing each briefly.

6. Edit the footage into a polished final product. When you finish, burn your performance and commentary to DVD.
7. Turn in your finished DVD. Each group member should also submit a typed paragraph evaluating the cooperation of the group. Describe anything about your peers' involvement, positive or negative, that warrants consideration during grading.

Understandably, trepidation abounds when I distribute this sheet on the first day of class. Many students are intimidated by the thought of performing on camera or in front of their peers. Others are deeply concerned about being evaluated on acting ability, and a few are uncomfortable with the idea of working with a group to earn a shared grade. All these reactions are useful opportunities to begin building rapport through reassurance. I tell them that the performance DVD involves the same skills that underlie written analysis, with two exceptions: groups must reach a consensus about the most productive way to interpret a scene, and they must illustrate and defend that vision by performing, instead of quoting, the text. I also clarify that their grade will depend equally on the thoughtfulness of their directorial vision and the success with which that vision comes across clearly in performance—not on their acting ability per se. These remarks usually suffice to calm their first-day anxieties. To ensure that the performance DVD actually leads to rich, rewarding engagement with Shakespeare's plays throughout the semester, the next class period must be used to give careful, sustained attention to issues of performance and interpretation.

Enter *The Taming of the Shrew*, which I always include first on the syllabus because it is immediately accessible and engaging to most students. Other plays can launch a semester just as effectively, but none requires less guidance or fewer introductory remarks from me. Beginning with a play that need not be elaborately explained by the instructor is important because it allows students to confront their initial discomfort with Shakespearean diction without feeling discouraged by their inability to understand. Students still experience useful confusion about specific, debatable details, such as Petruccio's motives for wooing Katherine or the purpose of the Christopher Sly induction, but their confidence is bolstered by a reasonably solid grasp of the play's central issues and events. Most are immediately willing to answer questions about gender, societal expectations, and the ethics of Petruccio's taming strategies, while the rest can usually be coaxed to contribute at least one comment—an important icebreaker that encourages more involved participation later.

Another reason I begin with *The Taming of the Shrew* is because it builds enthusiasm quickly for the performance DVD by impressing students with the value and pleasure of attending to performance issues—not only obvious concerns such as casting, costuming, lighting, spatial positioning, and verbal delivery, but also subtler elements, such as calculated pauses and extended silences, which can significantly alter the interpretation of a scene. This is best accomplished by including brief excerpts from multiple filmed performances. I use those directed by Samuel Taylor (1929), Franco Zeffirelli (1967), and Peter Dews (1982). Depending on time constraints and the natural flow of class discussion, I focus on one of three scenes: Katherine's initial introduction to Petruccio (2.1), the sun-moon debate (4.6), or the wedding banquet (5.2). Contrasting different performances of one of these scenes never fails to excite discussion about the dynamics of the relationship between Katherine and Petruccio. One vital caveat, however, is to exclude film from the first hour of discussion. If I do not, students fall into a passive "viewer" mind-set that is difficult to change.

I always begin the discussion of the play by asking what qualities make Katherine a shrew. As students respond to this disarmingly simple question, their answers reveal how differently they each perceive her: violent, rude, jealous, wounded, misunderstood, mistreated, confident, courageous—the list goes on. Next, I ask which of these descriptions is most plausible in the context of later developments and themes in the play. Although they are aware that there is no correct answer, my students enjoy the challenge of building plausibility for their views, and discussion thrives on the ensuing disagreement. My task is to guide this scrutiny toward productive material. When, for example, questions arise about Petruccio's motives for wooing Katherine, I point them toward 1.2.47–102, 193–205, and 2.1.112–60, passages that often elicit strong opinions that Petruccio is preoccupied with wealth and bravado. These ideas then can be challenged productively by asking about performance: How does Petruccio react when he first sees Katherine at 2.1.179? How sincere is he at 2.1.235–49, when he describes her as gentle, pleasant, courteous, soft, and affable? Students quickly realize that the answers to these questions depend on how Katherine looks, talks, and moves.

Another productive approach is to query the logic of Petruccio's tactics and how they work on Katherine. Here, we examine his explanations at 2.1.128–35 and 166–78, which suggest that he intends to match her peremptory nature with his own and to employ reverse psychology, respectively. We also consider Katherine's reactions to Petruccio's flattery at 2.1.235–49 or during the wedding events reported in 3.2. When these avenues have been exhausted, I pose another question: is Katherine necessarily the main focus of Petruccio's tactics? This question is always met with silence until I point out that some characters express unexpected sympathy for Katherine in response to Petruccio's behavior. Gremio says, "Tut, she's a lamb, a dove, a fool to him" (3.3.30); Curtis elsewhere remarks, "By this reckoning he is more shrew than she" (4.1.71). Such comments elicit the question, Does Petruccio intend to change Katherine by direct coercion or by freeing her from the confining stigmas others have forced upon her? If the latter view is correct, Katherine may choose to change herself.

This is an excellent time to examine the relation between Petruccio's tactics and the Lord's treatment of Sly in the induction. Does the Lord successfully convince Sly to forget he is a beggar? Most students assume he does, but there are very good reasons a beggar might willingly play along with a farce that finds him "conveyed to bed, / Wrapped in sweet clothes, rings put upon his fingers, / A most delicious banquet by his bed, / And brave attendants near him" (induction, sc. 1, lines 33–36). If so, perhaps Katherine's transformation is also not without rewards for her. Arguably, shrewish conduct is not so much eliminated as redirected when Petruccio authorizes Katherine to "swinge" and scold Bianca and the Widow (5.2.108). Likewise, Katherine's speech on wifely duty may be a clever attempt to negotiate an attractive marital bargain, in which husbands are committed "[t]o painful labour both by sea and land" while wives are sanctioned to lie "warm at home, secure and safe" (5.2.153, 155).

By now, students begin to believe that they have considered every possibility the text can offer. This is when I propose that the play may not be about Katherine's motives, transformation, or gender at all, because she is obviously not a woman and not real. This comment usually stuns my students, who always forget that all of the "women" in the play are initially presented as deliberate male fictions—disguises adopted by Bartholomew and the players to reinforce the facade that Sly is a wealthy, powerful lord. Perhaps the whole point is that this play has no women in it. If so, *The Taming of the Shrew* is not about relationships between men and women but about the fictions men construct and associate with women to reinforce their own self-image. In these terms, the entire play warrants reexamination.

Ultimately, the value of this approach to teaching the play—constantly forcing students to reconsider and defend their positions—is that it creates a powerful impetus to read closely, which, in turn, enhances class discussion and students' comprehension of the play. The value of the performance DVD is to encourage students to continue this habit of close engagement throughout the semester. Ironically, students' enthusiastic and precise responses to each play prove that they possess the ability to engage rewardingly with the text, but for whatever reason they will not sustain this level of involvement unless there is the promise of releasing that energy back into a medium they instinctively consider more exciting—namely film. This is why, although it can be successfully completed in as few as four weeks, the performance DVD works best if it is due at the end of the semester. Since my classes range from twelve to twenty-one students, I usually reserve the last three class periods for these screenings. This tactic also provides students with an excellent opportunity to review what they have learned. We watch only the performance, not the commentary. Then I ask students to share their reactions to that performance before allowing the group to explain the directorial vision. On average, this takes twenty minutes per group: ten to watch the performance and ten to discuss it. I also distribute a simple feedback form that asks class members to rate their reactions to each performance anonymously, on a scale of 1 to 10. These response sheets are not shared with the groups, but they provide me with useful input when grading the projects later.

NOTES ON CONTRIBUTORS

M. G. Aune is an associate professor of English at California University of Pennsylvania. He has published "Shakespearean Biography, Celebrity, and the Popular Culture/Academic Culture Divide" in *Borrowers and Lenders: The Journal of Shakespeare and Appropriation*, among other articles and book chapters.

Bruce E. Brandt is a professor of English at South Dakota State University. He is the author of *Christopher Marlowe in the Eighties: An Annotated Bibliography of Marlowe Criticism from 1978 through 1989* and articles on subjects ranging from Shakespeare to Ursula Le Guin. He teaches Marlowe and other English Renaissance playwrights.

Douglas Bruster is a professor in the English department of the University of Texas, Austin. He has edited *Everyman* and *Mankind* for the Arden Early Modern Drama series and is the author of *Shakespeare and the Question of Culture* and *To Be or Not to Be*, among other books.

Sheila T. Cavanagh is NEH Distinguished Teaching Scholar of English at Emory University and directs the Emory Women Writers Resource Project (http://womenwriters.library.emory.edu/ewwrp/) and codirects the World Shakespeare Project (www.worldshakespeareproject.org). She is the author of *Cherished Torment: The Emotional Geography of Lady Mary Wroth's* Urania, *Wanton Eyes and Chaste Desires: Female Sexuality in* The Faerie Queene, and numerous articles on pedagogy and on early modern literature.

Alice Dailey is associate professor of English at Villanova University. She is author of *The English Martyr from Reformation to Revolution* and has published articles in *Shakespeare Survey*, *Religion and Literature*, *Borrowers and Lenders*, and *Prose Studies*. She is currently working on a book on Shakespeare's history plays.

Silver Damsen is a graduate of the University of Illinois's doctoral program in literature. She has published numerous theater reviews in *The Upstart Crow* and *Shakespeare Bulletin*.

Margaret Dupuis is a tenured member of the English faculty at Western Michigan University and teaches undergraduate and graduate courses on early modern drama and poetry. She has published articles on Thomas Wyatt and John Marston.

Laurie Ellinghausen is an associate professor of English at the University of Missouri, Kansas City. She's the author of *Labor and Writing in Early Modern England, 1567–1667* and has published articles on Thomas Nashe, Thomas Dekker, and Isabella Whitney. She is presently developing a program for high school teachers of Shakespeare.

Laura Grace Godwin is an assistant professor of theater history and arts administration at Christopher Newport University. She has published theatrical reviews for *Shakespeare Bulletin* and *Theatre Journal*. In 2008 she directed *The Taming of the Shrew* for the American Southwest Theatre Company at New Mexico State Theatre Arts.

Anne F. Gossage is an assistant professor of English at Eastern Kentucky University, where she teaches early modern literature, science fiction, and Shakespeare. She has published articles in *Kentucky Philological Review*, *Seventeenth-Century News*, and *The Dictionary of Literary Biography* as well as a book chapter on the use of Shakespeare in the cartoon series *South Park*. She regularly leads students and faculty members on study trips overseas, often with a focus on Shakespeare in performance. Her current interests include actor training and questions of outdoor settings of performances of early modern plays.

Peter H. Greenfield is professor emeritus at the University of Puget Sound. Among his publications are (with Jane Cowling) *Monks, Minstrels, and Players: Drama in Hampshire before 1642*, as well as essays on local dramatic activity and traveling players and, mostly recently, "Touring," in *The Oxford Handbook of Early Modern Theatre*. He is the former editor of *Research Opportunities in Medieval and Renaissance Drama* and a long-time contributor to the Records of Early English Drama project.

Jay L. Halio is professor emeritus of English at the University of Delaware. He has taught numerous classes in Shakespeare and Renaissance literature, has edited *Macbeth* and *King Lear* (among other plays), and has authored many books, including *Shakespeare in Performance: A Midsummer Night's Dream*.

Peter C. Herman is a professor in the English department at San Diego State University. His latest books are *Royal Poetrie: Monarchic Verse and the Political Imaginary of Early Modern England* and *Destabilizing Milton:* Paradise Lost *and the Poetics of Incertitude.* He has edited numerous anthologies, including *Approaches to Teaching Milton's Shorter Poetry and Prose* and the second edition of *Approaches to Teaching* Paradise Lost.

James Hirsh is a professor of English at Georgia State University. He is the author of *The Structure of Shakespearean Scenes*; *Shakespeare and the History of Soliloquies* (winner of the South Atlantic Modern Language Association Book Award); and articles and book chapters. He has received the GSU Distinguished Honors Professor Award for Teaching Excellence.

Shawn Kairschner is an assistant professor in the Department of Theatre at Villanova University. He has published articles in *Modern Drama* and *Performance Research* and has considerable experience as a director in the United States and Europe, including a three-year stint as the artistic director of the Sideway Theater Company in Berkeley, California. Kairschner was in the first cast of American actors to appear onstage at the rebuilt Globe Theatre in London.

Wesley Kisting is an associate professor of English at Georgia Regents University and directs the Knowledge Integrated (KNIT) program, an initiative to improve student learning and engagement throughout the undergraduate curriculum. He has published in *Clio*, *Philological Quarterly*, and the *Upstart Crow*. He is at work on a book about the political and aesthetic impact of casuistry (discourse of conscience) on early modern English literature.

Cynthia Lewis is Charles A. Dana Professor of English at Davidson College. Her publications include *Particular Saints: Shakespeare's Four Antonios, Their Contexts, and Their Plays* and articles in such journals as *Shakespeare Quarterly*, *Studies in English*

Literature, *Comparative Drama*, and *Renaissance Drama*, as well as in collections. She is the recipient of several teaching awards.

Todd M. Lidh is an assistant professor of English and director of the first-year-experience program at the Catholic University of America. His work has appeared in *Ben Jonson Journal* and *Shakespeare Bulletin*, as well as in the *Journal of the Wooden O Symposium*, on whose editorial board he is a member. He is also on the advisory board for *SHAKSPER*. He has developed a map and walking tour of contemporary London, which locates early modern theater sites, and is currently at work on a book-length treatment of Shakespearean misdirection.

Laury Magnus is a professor of humanities at the U.S. Merchant Marine Academy in New York. Her books include *Who Hears in Shakespeare: Auditory Worlds on Stage and Screen* (edited with Walter Cannon) and performance editions of Shakespeare's *The Taming of the Shrew*, *Romeo and Juliet*, *The Comedy of Errors*, *and Measure for Measure*. She has written "Shakespeare in Television and Film" for *The Oxford Handbook to Shakespeare* and a performance chapter on *Macbeth* for the Bloomsbury Arden Macbeth: *A Critical Reader.*

Robert Matz is senior associate dean in the College of Humanities and Social Sciences and a professor of English at George Mason University. He has authored the books *The World of Shakespeare's Sonnets: An Introduction* and *Defending Literature in Early Modern England: Renaissance Literary Theory in Social Context*. His teaching focuses on Shakespeare, early modern poetry and poetics, and gender and sexuality. He is now at work on a modern edition of two early modern marriage sermons.

Margaret Maurer is William Henry Crawshaw Professor of Literature at Colgate University. She has published essays on Donne, Samuel Daniel, Ben Jonson, and Shakespeare, including "The Rowe Editions of 1709/1714 and 3.1 of *The Taming of the Shrew*" and "Constering Bianca: *The Taming of the Shrew* and *The Woman's Prize, or the Tamer Tamed.*" With Barry Gaines she has edited an edition of *The Taming of a Shrew*, *The Taming of the Shrew*, and *The Woman's Prize; or, The Tamer Tamed.* She has served many times as a resident scholar in the NEH-sponsored Teaching Shakespeare Institute for secondary-school teachers at the Folger Shakespeare Library.

Michael McClintock is an assistant professor of English at Bridgewater State University. He teaches Shakespeare, early English drama, and early British literature. His current projects include an examination of the clown roles in *The Taming of a Shrew* and *The Taming of the Shrew.*

Joseph M. Ortiz is an associate professor of English at the University of Texas, El Paso, and the author of *Broken Harmony: Shakespeare and the Politics of Music*, as well as of articles in *Shakespeare* and *Milton Studies*, among other journals. He teaches Renaissance literature and music as well as classical literature.

Meg F. Pearson is an associate professor in the Department of English and Philosophy at the University of West Georgia. Her most recent publications have addressed the function of infamy in Marlowe's *Edward II* and argued for a pedagogy of revenge in *Titus Andronicus*. Her current project, entitled "Behold and See," examines spectating as a social competence, one acquired through the interaction with visual expressions of a culture, particularly early modern theater.

Joseph Ricke is professor of English at Taylor University in Upland, Indiana. He teaches courses in expository writing, world literature, medieval literature, Renaissance literature, and Shakespeare.He has directed *Romeo and Juliet*, *A Midsummer Night's Dream*, *As You Like It*, *The Winter's Tale*, *Love's Labour's Lost*, *Fulgens and Lucrece*, and *Antigone*. He performs and records for the Chaucer Studio.

Edward L. Rocklin is a professor of English at California State Polytechnic University, Pomona. He has published essays in *Shakespeare Quarterly*, *Shakespeare Survey*, *Shakespeare Yearbook*, *Shakespeare Bulletin*, the *Journal of Dramatic Theory and Criticism*, *College English*, *English Journal*, and *California English*. He is the author of *Performance Approaches to Teaching Shakespeare* and *The Shakespeare Handbooks: Romeo and Juliet*.

Grace Tiffany is a professor of English at Western Michigan University and a 2010 recipient of that institution's Distinguished Teaching Award. She is the author of *Erotic Beasts and Social Monsters: Shakespeare, Jonson, and Comic Androgyny*, as well as five works of historical fiction based on Shakespeare's comedies and maintains a Shakespeare blog at www.shakespearefiction.com. She teaches Shakespeare and early modern British literature.

James M. Welsh is professor emeritus of English at Salisbury University in Salisbury, Maryland. He studied Shakespeare and textual criticism with Charlton Hinman and Paul Murray Kendall and earlier studied rhetoric and composition with Kenneth Rothwell at the University of Kansas. Now emeritus cofounding editor of *Literature/Film Quarterly*, he has edited, written, and published over twenty books dealing with literature, drama, and film. He teaches courses on Shakespeare, drama and film, history and film, and French, British, and American film directors.

CONTRIBUTORS AND SURVEY RESPONDENTS[†]

The editors thank the following teachers and scholars, who made this book possible.

Corinne S. Abate, *Morristown-Beard School*
Philip V. Allingham, *Lakehead University*
M. G. Aune, *California University of Pennsylvania*
Ann McCauley Basso, *University of South Florida*
Lisbeth Em Benkert, *Northern State University*
Mary E. Benson, *Avila University*
Sean Benson, *Malone College*
Bruce E. Brandt, *South Dakota State University*
Douglas A. Brooks, *Texas A&M University*
Douglas Bruster, *University of Texas, Austin*
Mary Ann Bushman, *Illinois Wesleyan University*
Annalisa Castaldo, *Widener University*
Thomas M. Catania, *Molloy College*
Sheila T. Cavanagh, *Emory University*
Michael J. Collins, *Georgetown University*
Karen Cunningham, *University of California, Los Angeles*
Alice Dailey, *Villanova University*
Silver Damsen, *University of Illinois*
Emily Detmer-Goebel, *Northern Kentucky University*
Martha Kalnin Diede, *Northwestern University*
Maryann Diedwardo, *Lehigh University*
Leslie Dunn, *Vassar College*
Laurie Ellinghausen, *University of Missouri, Kansas City*
Anthony Ellis, *Western Michigan University*
Stacy Erickson, *Manchester College*
Lois Feuer, *California State University*
Patrick Finn, *St. Mary's University College*
Michael Flachmann, *California State University, Bakersfield*
Brett Foster, *Wheaton College*
Alan Galey, *University of Toronto*
Brenna Ginger, *South Jefferson High School*
Paul Gleed, *Binghamton University, State University of New York*
Laura Grace Godwin, *New Mexico State University*
Anne F. Gossage, *Eastern Kentucky University*
Hugh Grady, *Arcadia University*
Peter H. Greenfield, *University of Puget Sound*
David G. Hale, *State University College of New York, Brockport*

[†]We regret the passing of Douglas A. Brooks, who was to have been a contributor to this volume.

Jay L. Halio, *University of Delaware*
Donna J. Hart, *Greenville College*
Chris Hassel, *Vanderbilt University*
Erica Hately, *Kansas State University*
Robert W. Haynes, *Texas A&M International University*
Donald Hedrick, *Kansas State University*
Peter C. Herman, *San Diego State University*
Rachel E. Hile, *Indiana University–Purdue University*
James Hirsh, *Georgia State University*
Susan E. Hrach, *Columbus State University*
Janelle Jenstad, *University of Victoria*
Edward Trostle Jones, *York College of Pennsylvania*
Shawn Kairschner, *Villanova University*
Kathleen Kalpin, *University of South Carolina, Aiken*
Harry Keyishian, *Fairleigh Dickinson University*
Ros King, *University of Southampton*
Wesley Kisting, *Georgia Regents University*
Bernice Kliman, *Nassau Community College*
Matt Kozusko, *Ursinus College*
David L. Kranz, *Dickinson College*
Constance Brown Kuriyama, *Texas Tech University*
Denis Lagae-Devoldere, *Paris-Sorbonne University*
Unhae Langis, *University of Southern California*
Douglas M. Lanier, *University of New Hampshire*
Cynthia Lewis, *Davidson College*
Todd M. Lidh, *Catholic University*
Joseph Linzmeier, *Ming Chuan University*
Catherine Loomis, *University of North Carolina, Greensboro*
JoJo Magno, *Warren County Community College*
Laury Magnus, *U.S. Merchant Marine Academy*
Robert Matz, *George Mason University*
Margaret Maurer, *Colgate University*
Michael McClintock, *Bridgewater State College*
Patricia Mezzacappa, *William A. Morris Intermediate School 61*
Sharon C. Mitchell, *Ohio State University*
Michael Neill, *Vanderbilt University*
Karen Newman, *New York University*
James N. Ortego II, *Troy University*
Joseph M. Ortiz, *University of Texas, El Paso*
Peter Paolucci, *York University*
Vimala Pasupathi, *Hofstra University*
Meg F. Pearson, *University of West Georgia*
Dee Anna Phares, *Northern Illinois University*
Robert B. Pierce, *Oberlin College*
Joseph A. Porter, *Duke University*
Kendrick Prewitt, *University of the Ozarks*
Richard Rambuss, *Emory University*
William Rampone, *South Carolina State University*

David Richman, *University of New Hampshire*
Hugh Macrae Richmond, *University of California, Berkeley*
Joseph Ricke, *Taylor University*
Fiona Ritchie, *McGill University*
Kelly A. Rivers, *University of Tennessee*
Edward L. Rocklin, *California State Polytechnic University, Pomona*
Sharon Eve Sarthou, *University of Mississippi*
LaRue Love Sloan, *University of Lousiana, Monroe*
Dorothy Stephens, *University of Arkansas*
Miles Taylor, *LeMoyne College*
Rana Tekcan, *Istanbul Bilgi University*
Sabine Thuerwaechter, *University of California, Riverside*
Christopher Turner, *College of Charleston*
Virginia Vaughan, *Clark University*
Bente Videbaek, *Stony Brook University, State University of New York*
Valerie Wayne, *University of Hawai'i, Manoa*
Barry Weller, *University of Utah*
James Wells, *Belmont University*
James M. Welsh, *Salisbury University*
Matthew Wikander, *University of Toledo*
Carolyn D. Williams, *University of Reading*
David Wood, *Northern Michigan University*

WORKS CITED

Adamson, Sylvia, et al., eds. *Reading Shakespeare's Dramatic Language: A Guide*. London: Thomson, 2001. Print.

Altick, Richard D. "Symphonic Imagery in *Richard II*." *PMLA* 62.2 (1947): 339–65. Print.

Andresen-Thom, Martha. "Shrew-Taming and Other Rituals of Aggression: Baiting and Bonding on the Stage and in the Wild." *Women's Studies* 9.2 (1982): 121–43. Print.

Ardolino, Frank. "The Induction of Sly: The Influence of *The Spanish Tragedy* on the Two Shrews." *Explorations in Renaissance Culture* 31.2 (2005): 165–87. Print.

As You Like It. By William Shakespeare. Dir. Paul Czinner. Screenplay adapt. Robert J. Cullen and Carl Mayer, from a treatment suggested by James M. Barrie. Inter-Allied Film, 1936. DVD.

"Atomic Shakespeare." *Moonlighting*. Dir. Glenn Gordon Caron. 25 Nov. 1986. VHS.

Austin, J. L. *How to Do Things with Words*. Oxford: Clarendon, 1962. Print.

Baldwin, Robert. "A Note on John Fletcher." *Modern Language Notes* 38.6 (1923): 377–78. Print.

Baldwin, T. W. *William Shakspere's Small Latine and Lesse Greeke.* 2 vols. Urbana: U of Illinois P, 1944. Print.

Ball, Robert Hamilton. *Shakespeare on Silent Film*. New York: Theatre Arts, 1968. Print.

Barton, Anne. Introduction. Shakespeare, *Riverside Shakespeare* 138–41.

Barton, John. *Playing Shakespeare: An Actor's Guide*. New York: Anchor, 1984. Print.

Basil, John. With Stephanie Gunning. *Will Power: How to Act Shakespeare in Twenty-One Days.* New York: Applause, 2006. Print.

Bate, Jonathan. *Shakespeare and Ovid*. Oxford: Clarendon, 1993. Print.

Bate, Jonathan, and Russell Jackson. *Shakespeare: An Illustrated Stage History*. New York: Oxford UP, 1996. Print.

Baumlin, Tina French. "Petruchio the Sophist and Language as Creation in *The Taming of the Shrew*." *SEL* 29 (1989): 237–57. Print.

Beadle, Richard, and Pam King, eds. *York Mystery Plays: A Selection in Modern Spelling*. 1984. New York: Oxford UP, 1999. Print.

Bean, John C. "Comic Structure and the Humanizing of Kate in *The Taming of the Shrew*." *The Woman's Part: Feminist Criticism of Shakespeare*. Ed. Carolyn Ruth Swift Lenz, Gayle Greene, and Carol Thomas Neely. Urbana: U of Illinois P, 1980. 65–78. Print.

Beck, Ervin. "Shakespeare's *The Taming of the Shrew*." *Explicator* 57.1 (1998): 8–11. Print.

Benson, Sean. "'If I Do Prove Her Haggard': Shakespeare's Application of Hawking Tropes to Marriage." *Studies in Philology* 103.2 (2006): 186–207. Print.

Berek, Peter. "Text, Gender, and Genre in *The Taming of the Shrew*." *Bad Shakespeare*. Ed. Maurice Charney. Rutherford: Fairleigh Dickinson UP, 1988. 91–104. Print.

Bergeron, David. "The Wife of Bath and Shakespeare's *The Taming of the Shrew*." *University Review* 35 (1969): 279–86. Print.

Bersuire, Pierre. *Metamorphosis Ovidiana Moraliter . . . Explanata.* Paris, 1509. Ed. Stephen Orgel. New York: Garland, 1979. Print.

Bevington, David. *English Renaissance Drama.* New York: Norton, 2002. Print.

———. Introduction. Shakespeare, *Necessary Shakespeare* 2–4.

Bevington, David, Anne Marie Welsh, and Michael L. Greenwald, eds. *Shakespeare: Script, Stage, Screen.* New York: Pearson-Longman, 2006. Print.

Bicks, Caroline. *Midwiving Subjects in Shakespeare's England.* London: Ashgate, 2003. Print.

Boose, Lynda E. "Scolding Brides and Bridling Scolds: Taming the Woman's Unruly Member." *Shakespeare Quarterly* 42.2 (1991): 179–213. Print.

———. "*The Taming of the Shrew*, Good Husbandry, and Enclosure." *Shakespeare Reread: The Texts in New Contexts.* Ed. Russ McDonald. Ithaca: Cornell UP, 1994. 193–225. Print.

Boose, Lynda, and Richard Burt. *Shakespeare, the Movie: Popularizing the Plays on Film, TV, and Video.* London: Routledge, 1997. Print.

———. *Shakespeare, the Movie II: Popularizing the Plays on Film, TV, Video and DVD.* London: Routledge, 2003. Print.

Brown, John Russell. *Free Shakespeare.* New York: Applause, 1997. Print.

Brown, Pamela Allen. *Better a Shrew Than a Sheep: Women, Drama, and the Culture of Jest in Early Modern England.* Ithaca: Cornell UP, 2003. Print.

Brunvand, Jan Harold. "The Folktale Origin of *The Taming of the Shrew*." *Shakespeare Quarterly* 17.4 (1966): 345–59. Print.

Bruster, Douglas. "The Politics of Shakespeare's Prose." *Rematerializing Shakespeare: Authority and Representation on the Early Modern English Stage.* Ed. Bryan Reynolds and William N. West. Basingstoke: Palgrave, 2005. 95–114. Print.

Buchanan, Judith. *Shakespeare on Silent Film: An Excellent Dumb Discourse.* Cambridge: Cambridge UP, 2009. Print.

Bullough, Geoffrey. *Narrative and Dramatic Sources of Shakespeare.* London: Routledge, 1957–75. 8 vols. Print.

Burns, Margie. "The Ending of *The Shrew*." *Shakespeare Studies* 18 (1986): 41–64. Print.

Callaghan, Dympna. Preface. Shakespeare, Taming of the Shrew: *An Authoritative Text* vii–xvi.

Capp, Bernard. *When Gossips Meet: Women, Family, and Neighbourhood in Early Modern England.* Oxford: Oxford UP, 2003. Print.

Carlin, Martha. "'What Say You to a Piece of Beef and Mustard?': The Evolution of Public Dining in Medieval and Tudor London." *Huntington Library Quarterly* 71.1 (2008): 199–217. Print.

Chambers, E. K. *William Shakespeare: A Study of Facts and Problems.* 1930. Oxford: Clarendon, 1988. Print.

Cohen, Ralph Alan. "Looking for Cousin Ferdinand: The Value of F1 Stage Directions for a Production of *The Taming of the Shrew*." *Textual Formations and Reforma-*

tions. Ed. Laurie E. Maguire and Thomas L. Berger. Newark: U of Delaware P, 1998. 264–80. Print.

Cohen, Walter. "The Sonnets and 'A Lover's Complaint.'" Shakespeare, *Norton Shakespeare* 1915–22.

Coletti, Theresa. "A Feminist Approach to the Corpus Christi Cycles." *Approaches to Teaching Medieval English Drama*. Ed. Richard K. Emmerson. New York: MLA, 1990. 79–89. Print.

Cone, Mary. *Fletcher without Beaumont: A Study of the Independent Plays of John Fletcher.* Salzburg: Institut für Englische Sprache und Literatur, 1976. Print.

Coursen, H. R. *Shakespearean Performance as Interpretation.* Newark: U of Delaware P, 1992. Print.

———. *Teaching Shakespeare with Film and Television.* Westport: Greenwood, 1997. Print.

Cressy, David. *Birth, Marriage, and Death: Ritual, Religion, and the Life-Cycle in Tudor and Stuart England*. Oxford: Oxford UP, 1999. Print.

———. *Education in Tudor and Stuart England*. New York: St. Martin's, 1976. Print.

Crystal, David, and Ben Crystal. *Shakespeare's Words: A Glossary and Language Companion*. London: Penguin, 2002. Print.

Davies, Stevie. *The Taming of the Shrew*. London: Penguin, 1995. Print. Penguin Critical Studies.

Davis, Natalie Zemon. *Society and Culture in Early Modern France*. Stanford: Stanford UP, 1975. Print.

de Grazia, Margreta, and Stanley Wells, eds. *The New Cambridge Companion to Shakespeare.* New York: Cambridge UP, 2010. Print.

Dekker, Thomas. *Satiro-mastix; or, The Untrussing of the Humorous Poet.* London, 1602. Print.

Dessen, Alan C., and Leslie Thomson. *A Dictionary of Stage Directions in English Drama, 1580–1642.* Cambridge: Cambridge UP, 1999. Print.

Dobson, Michael, and Stanley Wells, gen. eds. *The Oxford Companion to Shakespeare*. New York: Oxford UP, 2008. Print.

Dolan, Frances E. Introduction. Shakespeare, *Taming of the Shrew* [1996] 1–38.

———. Preface. Shakespeare, *Taming of the Shrew* [1996] vii–xi.

Donawerth, Jane. *Shakespeare and the Sixteenth-Century Study of Language*. Urbana: U of Illinois P, 1984. Print.

Duffin, Ross W. *Shakespeare's Songbook.* New York: Norton, 2004. Print.

Dusinberre, Juliet. *Shakespeare and the Nature of Women.* London: Palgrave, 2003. Print.

Elam, Keir. *Shakespeare's Universe of Discourse: Language-Games in the Comedies*. Cambridge: Cambridge UP, 1984. Print.

The English Renaissance in Context. Schoenberg Center for Electronic Text and Image. U of Pennsylvania Libs., n.d. Web. 21 Jan. 2010.

Erne, Lukas. *Shakespeare's Modern Collaborators.* London: Continuum, 2008. Print.

Escolme, Bridget. *Talking to the Audience: Shakespeare, Performance, Self*. New York: Routledge, 2005. Print.

Evenden, Doreen. *The Midwives of Seventeenth-Century London.* Cambridge: Cambridge UP, 2000. Print.

Fabliaux, Fair and Foul. Trans. John DuVal. Binghamton: Medieval and Renaissance Texts and Studies, 1992. Print.

Ferguson, Margaret, Maureen Quilligan, and Nancy Vickers, eds. *Rewriting the Renaissance: The Discourses of Sexual Difference in Early Modern Europe*. Chicago: U of Chicago P, 1986. Print.

Ferris, Paul. *Richard Burton*. London: Weidenfeld, 1981. Print.

Fletcher, John. *The Tamer Tamed*. Introd. Gordon McMullan. London: Hern, 2004. Print.

———. *The Tamer Tamed; or, The Woman's Prize*. Ed. Celia R. Daileader and Gary Taylor. Manchester: Manchester UP, 2007. Print.

———. *The Woman's Prize; or, The Tamer Tamed*. Bevington, *English Renaissance Drama* 1215–96.

Flight into Egypt. Beadle and King 79–87.

Fraser, Russell. *Young Shakespeare*. New York: Columbia UP, 1988. Print.

Freedman, Penelope. *Power and Passion in Shakespeare's Pronouns: Interrogating "You" and "Thou."* Aldershot: Ashgate, 2007. Print.

Fynes-Clinton, Michael, and Perry Mills. "What Is the Play About?" *The Taming of the Shrew*. By William Shakespeare. Ed. Fynes-Clinton and Mills. 2nd ed. Cambridge: Cambridge UP, 2000. 178–79. Print.

Gaines, Barry, and Margaret Maurer, eds. *Three Shrew Plays:* The Taming of a Shrew, *Shakespeare's* Taming of the Shrew, *and Fletcher's* The Woman's Prize; or, The Tamer Tamed. Indianapolis: Hackett, 2010. Print.

Garber, Marjorie. *Coming of Age in Shakespeare*. New York: Routledge, 1997. Print.

———. *Shakespeare after All*. New York: Pantheon, 2004. Print.

Garner, Shirley Nelson. "*The Taming of the Shrew*: Inside or Outside of the Joke?" *Bad Shakespeare*. Ed. Maurice Charney. Rutherford: Fairleigh Dickinson UP, 1988. 105–19. Print.

Garrick, David. *Catharine and Petruchio*. London, 1756. Print.

Gay, Penny. *As She Likes It: Shakespeare's Unruly Women*. London: Routledge, 1994. Print.

Gayley, Charles Mills. *Beaumont, the Dramatist.* New York: Century, 1914. Print.

The Geneva Bible: A Facsimile of the 1599 Edition with Undated Sternhold and Hopkins Psalms. Ozark: Brown, 1990. Print.

Gillespie, Stuart. *Shakespeare's Books: A Dictionary of Shakespeare's Sources.* London: Athlone, 2004. Print.

"Glossary." *Treasures in Full: Shakespeare in Quarto*. British Lib., n.d. Web. 24 May 2012.

Gosson, Stephen. *The Schoole of Abuse*. 1579. Ed. Arthur Freeman. New York: Garland, 1973. Print.

Gowing, Laura. *Domestic Dangers: Women, Words, and Sex in Early Modern London.* Oxford: Clarendon, 1996. Print.

Greenblatt, Stephen. "The Dream of the Master Text." Shakespeare, *Norton Shakespeare* 67–78.

———. "Fiction and Friction." *Shakespearean Negotiations.* Berkeley: U of California P, 1988. 66–93. Print.

———. *Renaissance Self-Fashioning: From More to Shakespeare*. Chicago: U of Chicago P, 1980. Print.

Gurr, Andrew. *Playgoing in Shakespeare's London*. Cambridge: Cambridge UP, 1987. Print.

———. *The Shakespearean Stage, 1574–1642.* Cambridge: Cambridge UP, 1970. Print.

Gurr, Andrew, and Mariko Ichikawa. *Staging in Shakespeare's Theatres.* Oxford: Oxford UP, 2000. Print.

Halio, Jay L. "The Induction as Clue in *The Taming of the Shrew.*" *"A Certain Text": Essays in Honor of Thomas Clayton.* Ed. Linda Anderson and Janis Lull. Newark: U of Delaware P, 2002. 94–106. Print.

Haller, William, and Malleville Haller. "The Puritan Art of Love." *Huntington Library Quarterly* 5.2 (1942): 235–72. Print.

Haring-Smith, Tori. *From Farce to Metadrama: A Stage History of* The Taming of the Shrew, *1594–1983*. Westport: Greenwood, 1985. Print.

Harner, James, ed. *World Shakespeare Bibliography Online.* Folger Shakespeare Lib.–Johns Hopkins UP, 2012. Web. 27 Feb. 2013.

Harris, Jonathan Gil. "'Look Not Big, nor Stamp, nor Stare': Acting Up in *The Taming of the Shrew* and the Coventry Herod Plays." *Comparative Drama* 34.4 (2000–01): 365–98. Print.

Heilman, Robert B. "The *Taming* Untamed; or, The Return of the Shrew." *Modern Language Quarterly* 27.2 (1966): 147–61. Print.

Henderson, Katherine Usher, and Barbara F. McManus. *Half Humankind: Contexts and Texts of the Controversy about Women in England, 1540–1640*. Chicago: U of Illinois P, 1985. Print.

Henslowe, Philip. *Henslowe's Diary*. Ed. R. A. Foakes. 2nd ed. Cambridge: Cambridge UP, 2002. Print.

Heywood, John. *The Plays of John Heywood*. Ed. Richard Axton and Peter Happé. Cambridge: Brewer, 1994. Print. Tudor Interludes 6.

Hodgdon, Barbara. "Who Is Performing 'in' These Text(s)? or, *Shrew*-ing Around." *In Arden: Editing Shakespeare*. Ed. Ann Thompson and Gordon McMullan. London: Arden Shakespeare, 2003. 95–108. Print.

Holderness, Graham. *Shakespeare in Performance: The Taming of the Shrew*. Manchester: Manchester UP, 1989. Print.

———. "Text and Performance: *The Taming of the Shrew.*" *Shakespeare in Performance: Contemporary Critical Essays*. Ed. Robert Shaughnessy. New York: St. Martin's, 2000. 123–41. Print. New Casebooks.

Holderness, Graham, and Bryan Loughrey. "General Introduction." Holderness and Loughrey, *Pleasant Conceited Historie* 1–12.

———. Introduction. Holderness and Loughrey, *Pleasant Conceited Historie* 13–36.

———, eds. *A Pleasant Conceited Historie, Called* The Taming of a Shrew. New York: Harvester, 1992. Print. Shakespearean Originals: First Eds.

Holland, Peter, ed. *Shakespeare Survey Fifty-Nine: Editing Shakespeare.* Cambridge: Cambridge UP, 2006. Print.

"A Homily of the State of Matrimony." Shakespeare, *Taming of the Shrew* [1996] 169–83.

"A Homily of the State of Matrimony." 1563. Klein 13–25.

Hope, Jonathan. *Shakespeare's Grammar.* London: Thomson, 2003. Print.

Hopkins, Matthew. *The Discovery of Witches.* 1647. *Early English Books Online.* EEBO, n.d. Web. 15 Apr. 2013.

Howard, Jean E. "Additional Passages." Shakespeare, *Norton Shakespeare* 227–28.

———. "Crossdressing, the Theatre, and Gender Struggle." *Shakespeare Quarterly* 39.4 (1988): 418–40. Print.

———. "The Difficulties of Closure: An Approach to the Problematic in Shakespearean Comedy." *Comedy from Shakespeare to Sheridan: Change and Continuity in the English and European Dramatic Tradition.* Ed. A. R. Braunmuller and J. C. Bulman. Newark: U of Delaware P, 1986. 113–30. Print.

Howell, Wilbur Samuel. *Logic and Rhetoric in England, 1500–1700.* New York: Russell, 1961. Print.

Hull, Suzanne W. *Chaste, Silent, and Obedient: English Books for Women, 1475–1640.* San Marino: Huntington, 1982. Print.

Hutson, Lorna London. *The Usurer's Daughter: Male Friendship and Fictions of Women in Sixteenth-Century England.* London: Routledge, 1994. Print.

Ingram, Martin. "'Scolding Women Cucked or Washed': A Crisis in Gender Relations in Early Modern England?" *Women, Crime, and the Courts in Early Modern England.* Ed. Jenny Kermode and Garthine Walker. [London]: UCLP, 1994. 48–80. Print.

James, Heather. "Shakespeare's Learned Heroines in Ovid's Schoolroom." *Shakespeare and the Classics*. Ed. Charles Martindale and A. B. Taylor. Cambridge: Cambridge UP, 2004. 66–85. Print.

Jardine, Lisa. *Still Harping on Daughters: Women and Drama in the Age of Shakespeare.* Sussex: Harvester, 1983. Print.

Jonson, Ben. *Epicene; or, The Silent Woman*. Bevington, *English Renaissance Drama* 775–860.

Jordan, Constance. "The Household and the State: Transformations in the Representation of an Analogy from Aristotle to James I." *Modern Language Quarterly* 54.3 (1993): 307–26. Print.

Jorgens, Jack J. *Shakespeare on Film*. Bloomington: Indiana UP, 1977. Print.

Joseph, Miriam. *Rhetoric in Shakespeare's Time.* New York: Harcourt, 1962. Print.

Joseph's Trouble about Mary. Beadle and King 48–58.

Kahn, Coppélia. *Man's Estate: Masculine Identity in Shakespeare*. Berkeley: U of California P, 1981. Print.

———. "*The Taming of the Shrew*: Shakespeare's Mirror of Marriage." *Modern Language Studies* 5.1 (1975): 88–102. Print.

Kastan, David Scott, ed. *A Companion to Shakespeare.* Oxford: Blackwell, 1999. Print.

Kehler, Dorothea. "Echoes of the Induction in *The Taming of the Shrew*." *Renaissance Papers* (1986): 31–42. Print.

Klein, Joan Larsen. *Daughters, Wives, and Widows: Writings by Men about Women and Marriage in Early Modern England, 1500–1640.* Urbana: U of Illinois P, 1992. Print.

Knutson, Roslyn Lander. *Playing Companies and Commerce in Shakespeare's Time.* Cambridge: Cambridge UP, 2001. Print.

Korda, Natasha. "Household Kates: Domesticating Commodities in *The Taming of the Shrew.*" The Taming of the Shrew*: Critical Essays*. Ed. Dana Aspinall. New York: Routledge, 2002. 277–304. Print.

Lacy, John. *Sauny the Scot; or, The Taming of the Shrew. Literature Online*. Chadwyck-Healey, 1996. Web. 4 Apr. 2013.

Latham, Simon. *Latham's Falconry, or, The Faulcons lure, and cure*. London, 1633. *Early English Books Online*. Web. 15 Apr. 2013.

Levin, Ira. *The Stepford Wives.* New York: Joseph, 1972. Print.

Lewis, Cynthia. "'Performing Shakespeare': The Outward Bound of the English Department." Riggio 295–306.

Linklater, Kristen. *Freeing Shakespeare's Voice: The Author's Guide to Talking the Text.* New York: Theatre Communications Group, 1992. Print.

MacCary, W. Thomas. *Friends and Lovers: The Phenomenology of Desire in Shakespearean Comedy*. New York: Columbia UP, 1985. Print.

Magnus, Laury. "How to Read *The Taming of the Shrew* as Performance." *The Taming of the Shrew*. Ed. Magnus. Newburyport: Focus, 2009. 101–04. Print.

Maguire, Laurie. "The Naming of the Shrew." Shakespeare, Taming of the Shrew*: An Authoritative Text* 123–37.

Manvell, Roger. *Shakespeare and the Film*. New York: Praeger, 1971. Print.

Marcus, Leah S. "The Editor as Tamer: *A Shrew* and *The Shrew*." Marcus, *Unediting* 101–31.

———. *Unediting the Renaissance: Shakespeare, Marlowe, Milton*. London: Routledge, 1996. Print.

McDonald, Russ. *The Bedford Companion to Shakespeare: An Introduction with Documents*. 2nd ed. Boston: Bedford, 2001. Print.

———. *Shakespeare and the Arts of Language*. Oxford: Oxford UP, 2001. Print.

McKeithan, Daniel Morley. *The Debt to Shakespeare in the Beaumont-and-Fletcher Plays.* Austin: N.p., 1938. Print.

McMullan, Gordon. Introduction. Fletcher, *Tamer* [2004] xiii–xvii.

Mendelson, Sara, and Patricia Crawford. *Women in Early Modern England, 1550–1720*. Oxford: Oxford UP, 1998. Print.

"A Merry Jest of a Shrewd and Curst Wife Lapped in Morel's Skin, for Her Good Behavior." Shakespeare, *Taming* [1996] 257–88.

Middleton, Thomas, and Thomas Dekker. *The Roaring Girl*. Bevington, *English Renaissance Drama* 1371–451.

A Midsummer Night's Dream. By William Shakespeare. Dir. Max Reinhardt and William Dieterle. Screenplay by Charles Kenyon and Mary McCall, Jr. Warner Bros., 1935. DVD.

Miller, Stephen. Introduction. Miller, *Taming* [Cambridge ed.] 1–55.

———. *The Taming of a Shrew*. Ed. Miller. Oxford: Oxford UP, 1998. Print. Malone Soc. Rpts.

———. "*The Taming of a Shrew* and the Theories; or, 'Though This Be Badness, Yet There Is Method In't.'" *Textual Formations and Reformations*. Ed. Laurie E. Maguire and Thomas L. Berger. Newark: U of Delaware P, 1998. 251–63. Print.

———. The Taming of a Shrew: *The 1594 Quarto*. Ed. Stephen Roy Miller. Cambridge: Cambridge UP, 1998. Print. New Cambridge Shakespeare: The Early Quartos.

Morley, Thomas. *A Plaine and Easie Introduction to Practicall Musicke*. London, 1597. Print.

Morris, Brian. Introduction. Shakespeare, *Taming* [1981, Arden ed.] 1–149.

Morris, Peter. "Shakespeare on Film." *Films in Review* 24.3 (1973): 132–63. Print.

———. *Shakespeare on Film*. Ottawa: Canadian Film Inst., 1972. Print.

Muir, Kenneth. *The Sources of Shakespeare's Plays*. New Haven: Yale UP, 1978. Print.

Munro, John. *The Shakspere Allusion-Book*. Freeport: Books for Libs., 1970. Print.

Murphy, Andrew. *Shakespeare in Print: A History and Chronology of Shakespeare Publishing*. Cambridge: Cambridge UP, 2003. Print.

Neufeld, Christine Marie. *Xanthippe's Sisters: Orality and Femininity in the Later Middle Ages*. Diss. McGill U, 2001. Print.

Newman, Karen. "Renaissance Family Politics and Shakespeare's *The Taming of the Shrew*." *English Literary Renaissance* 16.1 (1986): 86–100. Print.

———. *Shakespeare's Rhetoric of Comic Characters: Dramatic Convention in Classical and Renaissance Comedy*. New York: Methuen, 1985. Print.

Noah and His Sons. Stevens and Cawley 25–48.

Novy, Marianne. "Demythologizing Shakespeare." *Women's Studies* 9.1 (1981–82): 17–27. Print.

———. "Patriarchy and Play in *The Taming of the Shrew*." *English Literary Renaissance* 9 (1979): 264–80. Print.

O'Brian, Peggy, et al., eds. *Shakespeare Set Free: Teaching* A Midsummer Night's Dream, Romeo and Juliet, *and* Macbeth. New York: Washington Square, 2006. Print.

O'Connor, John, and Katharine Goodland. *A Directory of Shakespeare in Performance*. New York: Palgrave, 2007–11. 3 vols. Print.

O'Connor, Kelly N. "Fine Array and Mean Habiliments: Costuming the Shrew." *Shakespeare Newsletter* 57.1 (2007): 19+. Print.

Onions, C. T. *A Shakespeare Glossary*. 1911. Rev ed. Robert Eagleson. Oxford: Clarendon, 1986. Print.

Orgel, Stephen. *The Authentic Shakespeare*. London: Routledge, 2002. Print.

———. Introduction. Shakespeare, *Complete Pelican* 143–46.

———. "Shakespeare and the Kinds of Drama." *Critical Inquiry* 6.1 (1979): 107–23. Print.

Ovid. Heroides *and* Amores. Trans. Grant Showerman. 1914. Ed. and trans. G. P. Goold. 2nd rev. ed. Cambridge: Harvard UP, 2002. Print. Loeb Classical Lib. 41.

"Pageant of the Shearmen and Taylors." *Two Coventry Corpus Christi Plays*. Ed. Hardin Craig. 2nd ed. London: Oxford UP, 1957. 1–31. Early English Text Soc. Extra Ser. 7.

Palfrey, Simon, and Tiffany Stern. *Shakespeare in Parts*. Oxford: Oxford UP, 2007. Print.

Parker, Patricia A. *Literary Fat Ladies: Rhetoric, Gender, Property*. New York: Routledge, 1988. Print.

———. *Shakespeare from the Margins: Language, Culture, Context*. Chicago: U of Chicago P, 1996. Print.

Partridge, Eric. *Shakespeare's Bawdy: A Literary and Psychological Essay and a Comprehensive Glossary*. New York: Dutton, 1969. Print.

Paster, Gail Kern. *The Body Embarrassed: Drama and the Disciplines of Shame in Early Modern England*. Ithaca: Cornell UP, 1993. Print.

Peele, George. *The Old Wife's Tale*. Ed. Charles Whitworth. 2nd ed. New York: Norton, 1996. Print. New Mermaids.

Perkins, William. *The Arte of Prophecying; or, A Treatise Concerning the Sacred and Onely True Manner and Method of Preaching*. London, 1607. *Early English Books Online*. Web. 20 Dec. 2009.

Perret, Marion D. "Petruchio: The Model Wife." *Studies in English Literature* 23.2 (1983): 223–35. Print.

"Play." *The Compact Oxford English Dictionary*. 2nd ed. 1993. Print.

Plett, Heinrich F. *Rhetoric and Renaissance Culture*. Berlin: Gruyter, 2004. Print.

Porter, Cole. *Kiss Me, Kate: A Musical Comedy*. New York: Harms, 1951. Print.

Powell, Chilton L. *English Domestic Relations, 1487–1653*. New York: Columbia UP, 1917. Print.

Priest, Dale G. "Induction, Theatricality, and Power in *The Taming of the Shrew*." *Shakespeare Bulletin: A Journal of Performance Criticism and Scholarship* 17.2 (1999): 29–31. Print.

Rackin, Phyllis. *Shakespeare and Women*. Oxford: Oxford UP, 2005. Print. Oxford Shakespeare Topics.

Ramsey-Kurz, Helga. "Rising above the Bait: Kate's Transformation from Bear to Falcon." *English Studies: A Journal of English Language and Literature* 88.3 (2007): 262–81. Print.

Rebhorn, Wayne A. "Petruchio's 'Rope Tricks': *The Taming of the Shrew* and the Renaissance Discourse of Rhetoric." *Modern Philology* 92.3 (1995): 294–327. Print.

Rich, Frank. "Shakespeare in the Wild West, in the Park." *The New York Times*. New York Times, 13 July 1990. Web. 12 Dec. 2009.

Richards, Kenneth, and Laura Richards. *The Commedia dell'Arte: A Documentary History*. London: Blackwell, 1990. Print.

Riggio, Milla Cozart. *Teaching Shakespeare through Performance*. New York: MLA, 1999. Print.

Roberts, Jeanne Addison. "Horses and Hermaphrodites: Metamorphoses in *The Taming of the Shrew*." *Shakespeare Quarterly* 34.2 (1983): 159–71. Print.

Rocklin, Edward L. *Performance Approaches to Teaching Shakespeare*. Urbana: NCTE, 2005. Print.

Rosenthal, Daniel. *One Hundred Shakespeare Films: BFI Screen Guides*. London: British Film Inst., 2007. Print.

Rothwell, Kenneth S. *A History of Shakespeare on Screen: A Century of Film and Television*. Cambridge: Cambridge UP, 1999. Print.

Rudlin, John. *Commedia dell'Arte: An Actor's Handbook*. London: Routledge, 1994. Print.

Rutter, Carol. *Clamorous Voices: Shakespeare's Women Today*. New York: Routledge, 1989. Print.

———. *Clamorous Voices: Shakespeare's Women Today*. London: Women's, 1988. Print.

Saccio, Peter. "Shrewd and Kindly Farce." *Shakespeare Survey* 37 (1994): 33–40. Print.

Salisbury, Eve, ed. *The Trials and Joys of Marriage*. Kalamazoo: Medieval Inst. Pubs., 2002. Print; Web. TEAMS ed.

Schafer, Elizabeth. "*A Shrew* and *The Shrew*." *Treasures in Full: Shakespeare in Quarto*. British Lib., n.d. Web. 21 Jan. 2010.

———, ed. *The Taming of the Shrew*. By William Shakespeare. Cambridge: Cambridge UP, 2002. Print. Shakespeare in Production Ser.

Schaus, Margaret C., ed. *Women and Gender in Medieval Europe: An Encyclopedia*. New York: Routledge, 2006. Print.

Schoenbaum, Samuel. *Shakespeare's Lives*. Oxford: Clarendon, 1970. Print.

———. *William Shakespeare: A Documentary Life*. New York: Oxford UP, 1975. Print.

Seronsy, C. C. "'Supposes' as the Unifying Theme in *The Taming of the Shrew*." *Shakespeare Quarterly* 14.1 (1963): 15–36. Print.

Shakespeare, William. *Applause First Folio of Shakespeare in Modern Type: Comedies, Histories, and Tragedies*. Ed. Neil Freeman. New York: Applause, 2001. Print.

———. *The Arden Shakespeare Complete Works*. Ed. Richard Proudfoot, Ann Thompson, and David Scott Kastan. Walton-on-Thames: Nelson, 1998. Print.

———. *The Complete Pelican Shakespeare*. Gen. ed. Stephen Orgel and A. R. Braunmuller. New York: Penguin, 2002. Print.

———. *The Complete Works of Shakespeare*. Ed. David Bevington. 6th ed. New York: Pearson-Longman, 2008. Print.

———. *The Complete Works of William Shakespeare*. Massachusetts Inst. of Technology, 1993. Web. Jan. 2010.

———. *The First Folio of Shakespeare: The Norton Facsimile*. Ed. Charlton Hinman. Introd. Peter Blaney. New York: Norton, 1996. Print.

———. *Four Great Comedies*. New York: Signet, 1998. Print.

———. *Mr. William Shakespeares Comedies, Histories and Tragedies, Published according to the True Originall Copies*. London, 1623. First Folio. *Internet Shakespeare Editions*. U of Victoria, 24 Dec. 2011. Web. 6 Feb. 2012.

———. *The Necessary Shakespeare*. Ed. David Bevington. 3rd ed. Boston: Pearson, 2008. Print.

———. *The Norton Shakespeare*. Ed. Stephen Greenblatt, Walter Cohen, Jean E. Howard, and Katharine Eisaman Maus. 2nd ed. New York: Norton, 2008. Print.

———. *The Norton Shakespeare: Essential Plays / The Sonnets*. Ed. Stephen Greenblatt, Walter Cohen, Jean E. Howard, and Katharine Eisaman Maus. Abr. 2nd ed. New York: Norton, 2009. Print.

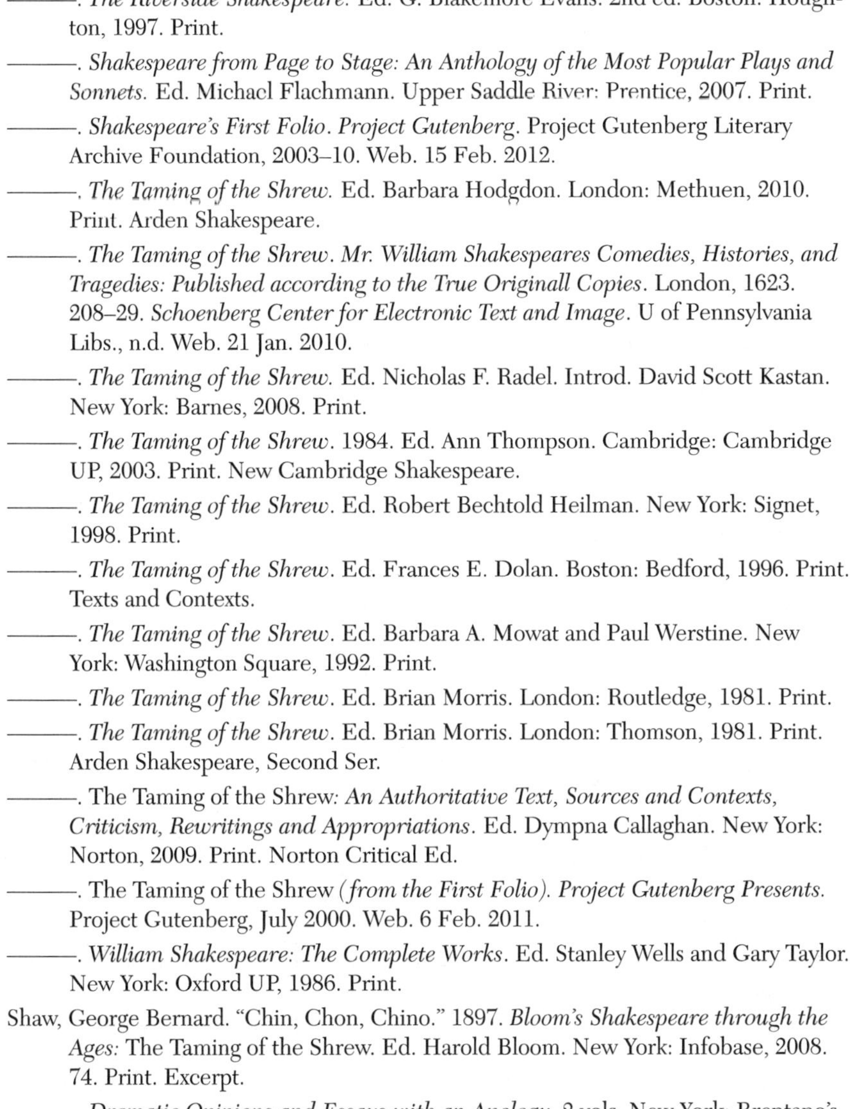

———. *The Riverside Shakespeare.* Ed. G. Blakemore Evans. 2nd ed. Boston: Houghton, 1997. Print.

———. *Shakespeare from Page to Stage: An Anthology of the Most Popular Plays and Sonnets.* Ed. Michael Flachmann. Upper Saddle River: Prentice, 2007. Print.

———. *Shakespeare's First Folio*. *Project Gutenberg*. Project Gutenberg Literary Archive Foundation, 2003–10. Web. 15 Feb. 2012.

———. *The Taming of the Shrew.* Ed. Barbara Hodgdon. London: Methuen, 2010. Print. Arden Shakespeare.

———. *The Taming of the Shrew*. *Mr. William Shakespeares Comedies, Histories, and Tragedies: Published according to the True Originall Copies*. London, 1623. 208–29. *Schoenberg Center for Electronic Text and Image*. U of Pennsylvania Libs., n.d. Web. 21 Jan. 2010.

———. *The Taming of the Shrew.* Ed. Nicholas F. Radel. Introd. David Scott Kastan. New York: Barnes, 2008. Print.

———. *The Taming of the Shrew*. 1984. Ed. Ann Thompson. Cambridge: Cambridge UP, 2003. Print. New Cambridge Shakespeare.

———. *The Taming of the Shrew*. Ed. Robert Bechtold Heilman. New York: Signet, 1998. Print.

———. *The Taming of the Shrew*. Ed. Frances E. Dolan. Boston: Bedford, 1996. Print. Texts and Contexts.

———. *The Taming of the Shrew*. Ed. Barbara A. Mowat and Paul Werstine. New York: Washington Square, 1992. Print.

———. *The Taming of the Shrew*. Ed. Brian Morris. London: Routledge, 1981. Print.

———. *The Taming of the Shrew*. Ed. Brian Morris. London: Thomson, 1981. Print. Arden Shakespeare, Second Ser.

———. The Taming of the Shrew*: An Authoritative Text, Sources and Contexts, Criticism, Rewritings and Appropriations*. Ed. Dympna Callaghan. New York: Norton, 2009. Print. Norton Critical Ed.

———. The Taming of the Shrew *(from the First Folio)*. *Project Gutenberg Presents*. Project Gutenberg, July 2000. Web. 6 Feb. 2011.

———. *William Shakespeare: The Complete Works*. Ed. Stanley Wells and Gary Taylor. New York: Oxford UP, 1986. Print.

Shaw, George Bernard. "Chin, Chon, Chino." 1897. *Bloom's Shakespeare through the Ages:* The Taming of the Shrew. Ed. Harold Bloom. New York: Infobase, 2008. 74. Print. Excerpt.

———. *Dramatic Opinions and Essays with an Apology*. 2 vols. New York: Brentano's, 1928. Print.

Shepard, Alexandra. *Meanings of Manhood in Early Modern England.* Oxford: Oxford UP, 2003. Print. Oxford Studies in Social History.

"Shrew." Def. 1. *The Oxford English Dictionary*. 2nd ed. 1989. Print.

Slights, Camille Wells. "The Raw and the Cooked in *The Taming of the Shrew*." *Journal of English and Germanic Philology* 88.2 (1989): 168–89. Print.

———. *Shakespeare's Comic Commonwealths.* Toronto: U of Toronto P, 1993. Print.

Smith, Amy. "Performing Marriage with a Difference: Wooing, Wedding, and Bedding in *The Taming of the Shrew*." *Comparative Drama* 36.3-4 (2002–03): 289–320. Print.

Smith, Henry. *A Preparative to Marriage.* London, 1591. *Early English Books Online.* Web. 22 Jan. 2010. STC 22686.

Smith, Molly Easo. "John Fletcher's Response to the Gender Debate: *The Woman's Prize* and *The Taming of the Shrew.*" *Papers on Language and Literature: A Journal for Scholars and Critics of Language and Literature* 31.1 (1995): 38–60. Print.

Smith, Thomas. *De Republica Anglorum.* Ed. Mary Dewar. Cambridge: Cambridge UP, 1982. Print.

Sokol, B. J., and Mary Sokol. *Shakespeare, Law, and Marriage.* Cambridge: Cambridge UP, 2003. Print.

Somebody, Avarice, and Minister (Somebody and Others; or, The Spoiling of Lady Verity). London, [1550?]. Print.

Speaking Shakespearean Verse. Perf. Royal Shakespeare Company. Films for the Humanities, 1990. DVD.

Spencer, Charles. "*The Taming of the Shrew*: Lure of Cruelty." *The Telegraph.* Telegraph Media Group, 6 May 2008. Web. 28 Aug. 2013.

Spevack, Marvin. *A Complete and Systematic Concordance to the Works of Shakespeare.* 9 vols. Hildesheim: Olms, 1968–80. Print.

Squier, Charles L. *John Fletcher.* Boston: Twayne, 1986. Print.

Stearne, John. *A Confirmation and Discovery of Witchcraft.* London, 1648. *Early English Books Online.* Web. 15 Apr. 2013.

Stern, Tiffany. *Making Shakespeare: From Stage to Page.* London: Routledge, 2004. Print. Accents on Shakespeare.

———. *Rehearsal from Shakespeare to Sheridan.* Oxford: Clarendon, 2000. Print.

Stevens, Martin, and A. C. Cawley, eds. *The Towneley Plays.* 2 vols. Oxford: Oxford UP, 1994. Print. Early English Text Soc. Supplementary Ser. 13 and 14.

Swetnam the Woman-Hater: *The Controversy and the Play.* Ed. Coryl Crandall. Lafayette: Purdue U Studies, 1969. Print.

"The Taming of Lucille." *Car 54, Where Are You?* Republic Pictures Home Video, 1990. VHS.

The Taming of the Shrew. By William Shakespeare. Dir. Edward Hall. Propeller Shakespeare Company, Ann Arbor. 23 Feb. 2013. Performance.

The Taming of the Shrew. By William Shakespeare. Dir. Josie Rourke, with Neil LaBute. Chicago Shakespeare Theater, Chicago. 2010. Performance.

The Taming of the Shrew. By William Shakespeare. Dir. David Richards. British Broadcasting Company, 2005. DVD.

"The Taming of the Shrew." Dir. Sally Wainwright. *Shakespeare Retold.* British Broadcasting Company, 21 Nov. 2005. Television.

The Taming of the Shrew. By William Shakespeare. Dir. Aida Ziablikova. Christmas Films with HBO, 2004. VHS.

The Taming of the Shrew. By William Shakespeare. Dir. Gregory Doran. Perf. Jasper Britton. Royal Shakespeare Company, London. 11 Jan. 2003. Performance.

The Taming of the Shrew. By William Shakespeare. Dir. Kenneth Albers. Perf. Jonathan Adams and Robynn Rodriguez. Oregon Shakespeare Festival, Ashland. 2000. Performance.

The Taming of the Shrew *(Shakespeare Animated Tales Series)*. British Broadcasting Company, 1994. VHS.

The Taming of the Shrew. By William Shakespeare. Dir. A. J. Antoon. Perf. Morgan Freeman and Tracey Ullman. New York Public Theater. Central Park, New York. 1990. Performance.

The Taming of the Shrew. By William Shakespeare. Dir. Richard Monette. Canadian Broadcasting Company, 1988. DVD.

The Taming of the Shrew. By William Shakespeare. Dir. Peter Dews. Canadian Broadcasting Company, 1986. DVD.

The Taming of the Shrew. By William Shakespeare. Dir. John Allison. Bard Productions, 1983. DVD.

The Taming of the Shrew. By William Shakespeare. Dir. Jonathan Miller. Perf. John Cleese. British Broadcasting Company, 1980. Ambrose, 2000. DVD.

The Taming of the Shrew. By William Shakespeare. Dir. William Ball and Kirk Browning. Perf. Fredi Olster and Marc Sanger. American Conservatory Theater of San Francisco. 1976. Kulture, 2002. DVD.

The Taming of the Shrew. By William Shakespeare. Dir. Franco Zeffirelli. Perf. Richard Burton and Elizabeth Taylor. Columbia, 1967. DVD.

The Taming of the Shrew. By William Shakespeare. 1950. Video Yesteryear, 1999. VHS.

The Taming of the Shrew. By William Shakespeare. 1929. Dir. Sam Taylor. Perf. Douglas Fairbanks and Mary Pickford. Telavista, 2007. DVD.

The Taming of the Shrew. By William Shakespeare. Dir. D. W. Griffith. Perf. Florence Lawrence and Arthur V. Johnson. American Mutoscope and Biograph, 1908. Film.

Taverner, John. Gresham College music lectures. 1610. British Lib., London. Sloane MS 2329. N. pag.

Ten Things I Hate about You. Screenplay by Karen McCullah Lutz and Kirsten Smith. Dir. Gil Junger. Perf. Heath Ledger, Julia Stiles, and Joseph Gordon-Levitt. Touchstone, 1999. DVD.

Thompson, Ann. Introduction. Shakespeare, *Taming* [2003] 1–49.

———. "King Lear and the Politics of Teaching Shakespeare." *Shakespeare Quarterly* 41.2 (1990): 139–46. Print.

Tibbetts, John C., and J. M. Welsh. *His Majesty the American: The Cinema of Douglas Fairbanks, Sr.* South Brunswick: Barnes; London: Yoseloff, 1977. Print.

Tiffany, Grace. *Erotic Beasts and Social Monsters: Shakespeare, Jonson, and Comic Androgyny.* Newark: U of Delaware P, 1995. Print.

———. "Reinterpreting Marriage in *The Taming of the Shrew.*" *Shakespeare Newsletter* 54.4 (2004–05): 98. Print.

"Title Page." *Mr. William Shakespeares Comedies, Histories, and Tragedies: Published according to the True Originall Copies*. 1623. *Schoenberg Center for Electronic Text and Image*. U of Pennsylvania Libs., n.d. Web. 21 Jan. 2010.

Todd, Margo. *Christian Humanism and the Puritan Social Order.* Cambridge: Cambridge UP, 1987. Print.

Tolaydo, Michael. "Up on Your Feet with Shakespeare: The Wrong Way and the Right." *Shakespeare Set Free: Teaching* Twelfth Night *and* Othello. Ed. Peggy O'Brian et al. New York: Washington Square, 1995. 41–49. Print.

Tucker, Patrick. *Secrets of Acting Shakespeare: The Original Approach*. New York: Routledge, 2002. Print.

Underdown, David. "The Taming of the Scold: The Enforcement of Patriarchal Authority in Early Modern England." *Order and Disorder in Early Modern England*. Ed. Anthony Fletcher and John Stevenson. Cambridge: Cambridge UP, 1985. 116–36. Print.

Vance, Jeffrey. *Douglas Fairbanks*. Berkeley: U of California P, 2009. Print.

van den Berg, Sara. "The Shakespeare in the Park." *SHAKSPER Digest* 11.0500. 13 Mar. 2000. Online posting.

Vanita, Ruth. "'Proper' Men and 'Fallen' Women: The Unprotectedness of Wives in *Othello*." *Studies in English Literature, 1500–1900* 34.2 (1994): 341–56. Print.

Vickers, Brian. *In Defence of Rhetoric*. Oxford: Clarendon, 1989. Print.

Vitry, Jacques de. "The Devil Marries a Quarrelsome Woman." *Sermones: Putnams's Dark and Middle Ages Reader*. Ed. Harry E. Wedeck. New York: Capricorn, 1962. 117. Print.

Wayne, Valerie. "Refashioning the Shrew." *Shakespeare Studies* 17 (1985): 159–87. Print.

Weller, Barry. "Induction and Inference: Theater, Transformation, and the Construction of Identity in *The Taming of the Shrew*." *Creative Imitation: New Essays on Renaissance Literature in Honor of Thomas M. Greene*. Binghamton: Medieval and Renaissance Texts and Studies, 1992. 297–329. Print.

Wells, Stanley, ed. *Shakespeare: A Bibliographical Guide*. Oxford: Clarendon, 1990. Print.

Welsh, James M., Richard Vela, and John C. Tibbetts. *Shakespeare into Film*. New York: Checkmark, 2002. Print.

Werstine, Paul. "Narratives about Printed Shakespeare Texts: 'Foul Papers' and 'Bad Quartos.'" *Shakespeare: An Anthology of Criticism and Theory, 1945–2000*. Ed. Russ McDonald. Malden: Blackwell, 2004. 296–318. Print.

Whately, William. *A Bride-Bush*. London, 1623. *Early English Books Online*. Web. 22 Jan. 2010. STC 25298.

William Shakespeare's The Taming of the Shrew. Dir. William Ball and Kirk Browning. American Conservatory Theater of San Francisco. 1976. Educational Broadcasting Company, 2002. DVD.

Wilson, Thomas. *The Arte of Rhetorique, 1560*. Ed. G. H. Mair. Oxford: Clarendon, 1909. Print.

Winstead, Karen A. *Virgin Martyrs: Legends of Sainthood in Late Medieval England*. Ithaca: Cornell UP, 1997. Print.

Woodbridge, Linda, ed. *Shakespeare, a Selective Bibliography of Modern Criticism*. West Cornwall: Locust, 1988. Print.

———. *Women and the English Renaissance: Literature and the Nature of Womankind, 1540–1620*. Urbana: U of Illinois P, 1984. Print.

Wright, Louis B. *Middle-Class Culture in Elizabethan England*. 1935. Ithaca: Cornell UP, 1958. Print.

INDEX

Modern Language Association of America

Approaches to Teaching World Literature

Achebe's Things Fall Apart. Ed. Bernth Lindfors. 1991.
Arthurian Tradition. Ed. Maureen Fries and Jeanie Watson. 1992.
Atwood's The Handmaid's Tale *and Other Works*. Ed. Sharon R. Wilson, Thomas B. Friedman, and Shannon Hengen. 1996.
Austen's Emma. Ed. Marcia McClintock Folsom. 2004.
Austen's Pride and Prejudice. Ed. Marcia McClintock Folsom. 1993.
Balzac's Old Goriot. Ed. Michal Peled Ginsburg. 2000.
Baudelaire's Flowers of Evil. Ed. Laurence M. Porter. 2000.
Beckett's Waiting for Godot. Ed. June Schlueter and Enoch Brater. 1991.
Behn's Oroonoko. Ed. Cynthia Richards and Mary Ann O'Donnell. 2014.
Beowulf. Ed. Jess B. Bessinger, Jr., and Robert F. Yeager. 1984.
Blake's Songs of Innocence and of Experience. Ed. Robert F. Gleckner and Mark L. Greenberg. 1989.
Boccaccio's Decameron. Ed. James H. McGregor. 2000.
British Women Poets of the Romantic Period. Ed. Stephen C. Behrendt and Harriet Kramer Linkin. 1997.
Charlotte Brontë's Jane Eyre. Ed. Diane Long Hoeveler and Beth Lau. 1993.
Emily Brontë's Wuthering Heights. Ed. Sue Lonoff and Terri A. Hasseler. 2006.
Byron's Poetry. Ed. Frederick W. Shilstone. 1991.
Works of Italo Calvino. Ed. Franco Ricci. 2013.
Camus's The Plague. Ed. Steven G. Kellman. 1985.
Writings of Bartolomé de Las Casas. Ed. Santa Arias and Eyda M. Merediz. 2008.
Cather's My Ántonia. Ed. Susan J. Rosowski. 1989.
Cervantes' Don Quixote. Ed. Richard Bjornson. 1984.
Chaucer's Canterbury Tales. Ed. Joseph Gibaldi. 1980.
Chaucer's Troilus and Criseyde *and the Shorter Poems*. Ed. Tison Pugh and Angela Jane Weisl. 2006.
Chopin's The Awakening. Ed. Bernard Koloski. 1988.
Coleridge's Poetry and Prose. Ed. Richard E. Matlak. 1991.
Collodi's Pinocchio *and Its Adaptations*. Ed. Michael Sherberg. 2006.
Conrad's "Heart of Darkness" and "The Secret Sharer." Ed. Hunt Hawkins and Brian W. Shaffer. 2002.
Dante's Divine Comedy. Ed. Carole Slade. 1982.
Defoe's Robinson Crusoe. Ed. Maximillian E. Novak and Carl Fisher. 2005.
DeLillo's White Noise. Ed. Tim Engles and John N. Duvall. 2006.
Dickens's Bleak House. Ed. John O. Jordan and Gordon Bigelow. 2009.
Dickens's David Copperfield. Ed. Richard J. Dunn. 1984.
Dickinson's Poetry. Ed. Robin Riley Fast and Christine Mack Gordon. 1989.
Narrative of the Life of Frederick Douglass. Ed. James C. Hall. 1999.

Works of John Dryden. Ed. Jayne Lewis and Lisa Zunshine. 2013.
Duras's Ourika. Ed. Mary Ellen Birkett and Christopher Rivers. 2009.
Early Modern Spanish Drama. Ed. Laura R. Bass and Margaret R. Greer. 2006.
Eliot's Middlemarch. Ed. Kathleen Blake. 1990.
Eliot's Poetry and Plays. Ed. Jewel Spears Brooker. 1988.
Shorter Elizabethan Poetry. Ed. Patrick Cheney and Anne Lake Prescott. 2000.
Ellison's Invisible Man. Ed. Susan Resneck Parr and Pancho Savery. 1989.
English Renaissance Drama. Ed. Karen Bamford and Alexander Leggatt. 2002.
Works of Louise Erdrich. Ed. Gregg Sarris, Connie A. Jacobs, and James R. Giles. 2004.
Dramas of Euripides. Ed. Robin Mitchell-Boyask. 2002.
Faulkner's As I Lay Dying. Ed. Patrick O'Donnell and Lynda Zwinger. 2011.
Faulkner's The Sound and the Fury. Ed. Stephen Hahn and Arthur F. Kinney. 1996.
Fitzgerald's The Great Gatsby. Ed. Jackson R. Bryer and Nancy P. VanArsdale. 2009.
Flaubert's Madame Bovary. Ed. Laurence M. Porter and Eugene F. Gray. 1995.
García Márquez's One Hundred Years of Solitude. Ed. María Elena de Valdés and Mario J. Valdés. 1990.
Gilman's "The Yellow Wall-Paper" and Herland. Ed. Denise D. Knight and Cynthia J. Davis. 2003.
Goethe's Faust. Ed. Douglas J. McMillan. 1987.
Gothic Fiction: The British and American Traditions. Ed. Diane Long Hoeveler and Tamar Heller. 2003.
Poetry of John Gower. Ed. R. F. Yeager and Brian W. Gastle. 2011.
Grass's The Tin Drum. Ed. Monika Shafi. 2008.
H.D.'s Poetry and Prose. Ed. Annette Debo and Lara Vetter. 2011.
Hebrew Bible as Literature in Translation. Ed. Barry N. Olshen and Yael S. Feldman. 1989.
Homer's Iliad *and* Odyssey. Ed. Kostas Myrsiades. 1987.
Hurston's Their Eyes Were Watching God *and Other Works*. Ed. John Lowe. 2009.
Ibsen's A Doll House. Ed. Yvonne Shafer. 1985.
Henry James's Daisy Miller *and* The Turn of the Screw. Ed. Kimberly C. Reed and Peter G. Beidler. 2005.
Works of Samuel Johnson. Ed. David R. Anderson and Gwin J. Kolb. 1993.
Joyce's Ulysses. Ed. Kathleen McCormick and Erwin R. Steinberg. 1993.
Works of Sor Juana Inés de la Cruz. Ed. Emilie L. Bergmann and Stacey Schlau. 2007.
Kafka's Short Fiction. Ed. Richard T. Gray. 1995.
Keats's Poetry. Ed. Walter H. Evert and Jack W. Rhodes. 1991.
Kingston's The Woman Warrior. Ed. Shirley Geok-lin Lim. 1991.
Lafayette's The Princess of Clèves. Ed. Faith E. Beasley and Katharine Ann Jensen. 1998.
Works of D. H. Lawrence. Ed. M. Elizabeth Sargent and Garry Watson. 2001.
Lazarillo de Tormes *and the Picaresque Tradition*. Ed. Anne J. Cruz. 2009.

Lessing's The Golden Notebook. Ed. Carey Kaplan and Ellen Cronan Rose. 1989.
Works of Naguib Mahfouz. Ed. Waïl S. Hassan and Susan Muaddi Darraj. 2011.
Mann's Death in Venice *and Other Short Fiction*. Ed. Jeffrey B. Berlin. 1992.
Marguerite de Navarre's Heptameron. Ed. Colette H. Winn. 2007.
Works of Carmen Martín Gaite. Ed. Joan L. Brown. 2013.
Medieval English Drama. Ed. Richard K. Emmerson. 1990.
Melville's Moby-Dick. Ed. Martin Bickman. 1985.
Metaphysical Poets. Ed. Sidney Gottlieb. 1990.
Miller's Death of a Salesman. Ed. Matthew C. Roudané. 1995.
Milton's Paradise Lost. First edition. Ed. Galbraith M. Crump. 1986.
Milton's Paradise Lost. Second edition. Ed. Peter C. Herman. 2012.
Milton's Shorter Poetry and Prose. Ed. Peter C. Herman. 2007.
Molière's Tartuffe *and Other Plays*. Ed. James F. Gaines and Michael S. Koppisch. 1995.
Momaday's The Way to Rainy Mountain. Ed. Kenneth M. Roemer. 1988.
Montaigne's Essays. Ed. Patrick Henry. 1994.
Novels of Toni Morrison. Ed. Nellie Y. McKay and Kathryn Earle. 1997.
Murasaki Shikibu's The Tale of Genji. Ed. Edward Kamens. 1993.
Nabokov's Lolita. Ed. Zoran Kuzmanovich and Galya Diment. 2008.
Works of Ngũgĩ wa Thiong'o. Ed. Oliver Lovesey. 2012.
Works of Tim O'Brien. Ed. Alex Vernon and Catherine Calloway. 2010.
Works of Ovid and the Ovidian Tradition. Ed. Barbara Weiden Boyd and Cora Fox. 2010.
Poe's Prose and Poetry. Ed. Jeffrey Andrew Weinstock and Tony Magistrale. 2008.
Pope's Poetry. Ed. Wallace Jackson and R. Paul Yoder. 1993.
Proust's Fiction and Criticism. Ed. Elyane Dezon-Jones and Inge Crosman Wimmers. 2003.
Puig's Kiss of the Spider Woman. Ed. Daniel Balderston and Francine Masiello. 2007.
Pynchon's The Crying of Lot 49 *and Other Works.* Ed. Thomas H. Schaub. 2008.
Works of François Rabelais. Ed. Todd W. Reeser and Floyd Gray. 2011.
Novels of Samuel Richardson. Ed. Lisa Zunshine and Jocelyn Harris. 2006.
Rousseau's Confessions *and* Reveries of the Solitary Walker. Ed. John C. O'Neal and Ourida Mostefai. 2003.
Scott's Waverley Novels. Ed. Evan Gottlieb and Ian Duncan. 2009.
Shakespeare's Hamlet. Ed. Bernice W. Kliman. 2001.
Shakespeare's King Lear. Ed. Robert H. Ray. 1986.
Shakespeare's Othello. Ed. Peter Erickson and Maurice Hunt. 2005.
Shakespeare's Romeo and Juliet. Ed. Maurice Hunt. 2000.
Shakespeare's The Taming of the Shrew. Ed. Margaret Dupuis and Grace Tiffany. 2013.
Shakespeare's The Tempest *and Other Late Romances.* Ed. Maurice Hunt. 1992.
Shelley's Frankenstein. Ed. Stephen C. Behrendt. 1990.

Shelley's Poetry. Ed. Spencer Hall. 1990.
Sir Gawain and the Green Knight. Ed. Miriam Youngerman Miller and Jane Chance. 1986.
Song of Roland. Ed. William W. Kibler and Leslie Zarker Morgan. 2006.
Spenser's Faerie Queene. Ed. David Lee Miller and Alexander Dunlop. 1994.
Stendhal's The Red and the Black. Ed. Dean de la Motte and Stirling Haig. 1999.
Sterne's Tristram Shandy. Ed. Melvyn New. 1989.
Works of Robert Louis Stevenson. Ed. Caroline McCracken-Flesher. 2013.
The Story of the Stone (Dream of the Red Chamber). Ed. Andrew Schonebaum and Tina Lu. 2012.
Stowe's Uncle Tom's Cabin. Ed. Elizabeth Ammons and Susan Belasco. 2000.
Swift's Gulliver's Travels. Ed. Edward J. Rielly. 1988.
Teresa of Ávila and the Spanish Mystics. Ed. Alison Weber. 2009.
Thoreau's Walden *and Other Works*. Ed. Richard J. Schneider. 1996.
Tolstoy's Anna Karenina. Ed. Liza Knapp and Amy Mandelker. 2003.
Vergil's Aeneid. Ed. William S. Anderson and Lorina N. Quartarone. 2002.
Voltaire's Candide. Ed. Renée Waldinger. 1987.
Whitman's Leaves of Grass. Ed. Donald D. Kummings. 1990.
Wiesel's Night. Ed. Alan Rosen. 2007.
Works of Oscar Wilde. Ed. Philip E. Smith II. 2008.
Woolf's Mrs. Dalloway. Ed. Eileen Barrett and Ruth O. Saxton. 2009.
Woolf's To the Lighthouse. Ed. Beth Rigel Daugherty and Mary Beth Pringle. 2001.
Wordsworth's Poetry. Ed. Spencer Hall, with Jonathan Ramsey. 1986.
Wright's Native Son. Ed. James A. Miller. 1997.